IRELAND AND IRISH AMERICANS, 1932–1945

The Search for Identity

JOHN DAY TULLY

Central Connecticut State University

IRISH ACADEMIC PRESS
DUBLIN • PORTLAND, OR

First published in 2010 by Irish Academic Press

2 Brookside,	920 NE 58th Avenue, Suite 300
Dundrum Road,	Portland, Oregon,
Dublin 14,	97213-3786
Ireland	USA

www.iap.ie

This edition © 2010 John Day Tully

British Library Cataloguing in Publication Data
An entry can be found on request

ISBN 978 0 7165 2976 7 (cloth)

Library of Congress Cataloging-in-Publication Data
An entry can be found on request

Printed in Great Britain by the MPG Books Group, Bodmin and King's Lynn

For Nancy

mo ghrá go daingean thú, go deo

Contents

List of Illustrations

Acknowledgements

I owe so much to so many, and these brief words can only relate how deeply I realize that fact. I will start with the faculty members whose patient dedication and inspirational examples allowed me to get started. Stan Blejwas at Central Connecticut State University passed away suddenly some years ago, and I regret I never really thanked him for all of his help while I was his masters student. He also gave me my first opportunity to be in front of a college classroom, an experience that confirmed my desire to teach. At Ohio State University, Carole Fink and Peter Hahn were excellent teachers and mentors, challenging and supporting me. Kevin Boyle graciously stepped in near the end of my stay in Columbus to be on my committee and to offer invaluable job search advice. Finally, this book would not have been possible had Michael J. Hogan not taken me on as a student. He took several chances on me, from the classroom to helping start the Harvey Goldberg Program for Excellence in Teaching. I told him then that I would not disappoint him; I hope this book does not. I am proud to now call Carol, Kevin, Peter and Mike friends, and I hope one day my work will reach their levels of accomplishment.

Many people have seen me through the high and low points of starting and finishing this book. My fellow graduate students in the OSU Department of History provided many hours of constructive criticism, intellectual stimulation and rewarding conversations. We shared study groups, made each other dinner, and were there for parties, weddings, children and rides to the airport. My life would be much poorer without Matt Masur, Jenn Walton, Brad Austin, Brian Etheridge and Matt Davis. As I took the project with me back to CCSU, I have been enriched by my professional and personal relationships with colleagues in the Department of History, especially Briann Greenfield, Mark Jones, Kate McGrath, Glenn Sunshine and Robert Wolff.

I received generous financial support from a variety of sources. I would like to thank Dean Susan Pease of the CCSU School of Arts and Sciences for research reassigned time, Dean's Research Initiative funds and various travel grants. I also received funding from an AAUP

University Research grant. At OSU I received a Graduate School Summer Research Award and a Philip Poirer Award that allowed me to take my first research trip to Dublin. I wish also to thank Professor Liam Kennedy and Catherine Carey at the Clinton Institute for American Studies at University College Dublin for all of their help while I was there as a Visiting Fellow.

Taking the risk of inadvertent omission, I need to thank some of the many other people who have helped along the way. Professor Dermot Keogh of University College Cork graciously came to one of my conference presentations and took time afterwards to share some coffee and thoughts. Brian Sommers made the map of the Treaty ports. Edel de Paor provided the translation used in the dedication. Librarians at OSU and CCSU patiently filled every inter-library loan request with a smile. Archivists helped me find a number of sources important to the story that I would have missed without their guidance. Lisa Hyde, my editor at Irish Academic Press, saw potential in this study when it was only partly done. Her encouragement, patience and skill have been a blessing. Troy Davis has been a steady supporter of this project almost from the start. His insights into the wider American–Irish relationship have been crucial to my own understanding of the dynamics of the time period I examined.

I put several people through the pain of reading this before I completed it, and the book is much improved thanks to their patience and diligence. Kate Thedwall, Matt Masur, Jenn Walton, Brad Austin, Troy Davis, Kevin Boyle and Matt Warshauer all spent many hours helping me find and fix small grammatical errors and larger conceptual problems. The responsibility for any deficiencies left after their fine work is mine alone. One final word on Matt Warshauer; he has gone above and beyond the call of duty to help on this project and to assist me in getting my academic career started. I owe him an enormous debt.

Words can at best be only faint echoes of my love for my family. My parents sacrificed their whole lives for me; I cannot repay that. My wife Nancy's family has become my own, and I wish her parents were with us to see this book in print, if only to serve as some consolation for the fact that I took her so far away from home to get it started. Our daughter Erin has seen vacations come and go without me, all without complaint. She is the joy of our lives, and we work every day to be the parents she deserves.

Most important, Nancy teaches me every day what it means to be loved. With her, the journey finds its meaning. This, and everything else, is for her.

Introduction

Support for Irish neutrality is a core republican value. It has never been more relevant than at this time of great volatility in international relations. (Gerry Adams, 28 May 2004)[1]

Somewhere in the Bronx, only twenty minutes or so from the cemetery, Maeve found a small bar-and-grill ... that, lacking only draught Guinness and a peat fire, might have been a pub in rural Ireland. Or lacking dialogue by John Millington Synge, the set of a rural Irish play ...
      You could not redeem Billy's life, redeem your own relentless affection for him, without saying at some point, 'There was that girl.'
      'The Irish girl.' ...
      'That was a sad thing, wasn't it? That was a blow to him.'
      'A girl he met right after the war. Right after he came home. Out on Long Island.' (Alice McDermott, *Charming Billy*)[2]

Ireland and Irish America shared a struggle for political identity during the twentieth century that echoes in current Irish politics and Irish-American culture. After gaining independence from Britain in 1921 and enduring a civil war, Irish leaders were eager to establish a national identity that secured Ireland's place in the world and promoted internal unity. In the 1930s and 1940s, faced with the growing European crisis and eventual war, Irish leaders used neutrality to forge a distinctly Irish identity. In doing so, however, they had to balance that neutrality against competing desires to see the Allies win the war and to prevent a British backlash against Irish policy. Ireland's decision to walk a careful neutral line in these early years had a decided influence on the nation's politics and identity for years to come. That Gerry Adams, a former leader in the Irish Republican Army, a group whose goal was to eliminate the British presence in Northern Ireland through violence, embraced neutrality is a clear illustration of just how well the identity mission succeeded more than sixty years later. Neutrality, as Adams stated, 'is a core republican value'. Historians have also recognized this belief and its connection to Irish identity.[3]

The desire to forge an identity was not solely an issue for the Irish in Ireland. In the twentieth century Irish Americans faced a similar identity crisis as they struggled to find their place in American society. Like many immigrant groups, Irish Americans tried to forge an identity that recognized their ethnic and national past but allowed for assimilation into an American society that put up first racial and then religious roadblocks to their integration. Alice McDermott, like many other Irish-American novelists, explores this complicated nature of Irish-American identity in her writings. Such artists have given expression to the Irish-American dilemma of feeling forced to choose between an ethnic community that insulated them from mainstream society and the dominant culture that allowed them to rise up the economic ladder, but did not offer real assimilation.

This book explores how the Irish and Irish Americans negotiated their new identities and how each struggle played itself out, especially before and during the Second World War. More specifically, it examines how and why Irish leaders turned to Irish America for support in creating, especially through a policy of neutrality, a political identity for Ireland. For Irish Americans in particular, this book attempts an accounting of what Nathan Glazer and Daniel Patrick Moynihan called the 'persisting facts of ethnicity'. For Ireland, it explores how Irish leader Éamon de Valera, as well as his followers and his later Irish Republican Army (IRA) opponents, could all agree on neutrality as the best means to establish an identity for Ireland on the world stage.

Several arguments run through the book. The first is that Ireland's neutrality during World War Two, and indeed all of its efforts in the 1930s to set the stage for that neutrality, was as much about identity as it was about negotiating external conflicts. De Valera possessed a distinct concept of Irish identity, and he gauged what policies, given centuries of British domination, would best allow the new state to establish an international identity that would allow it to become a full member of the community of nations. De Valera and other Irish political leaders had to navigate those policies against the stark reality of the physical, economic and political gravitational pull of its more powerful neighbour, against whom Ireland had struggled for hundreds of years. Eventually, those policies had to be formulated within the confines of a world war that at times looked as if it might consume and destroy Great Britain. Finally, Irish policy makers also had to steer their way through the intricacies of a British–American security arrangement and not find themselves squeezed out of their practical independence in the process.

These obstacles lead to the book's second point: Irish leaders had to turn to public and traditional diplomacy in the United States in order to secure national objectives. Part of the success of this effort rested in the fact that Irish Americans constituted a large percentage of the American population, had a history of looking to Ireland even as they negotiated the process of becoming ' real' Americans, and that in the 1930s they continued to feel isolated from mainstream America. Éamon de Valera, recognizing the limits of Ireland's power to deal with pressure from the United States and Great Britain, made a concerted effort to enlist Irish Americans as agents of Irish diplomacy. While other ethnic groups were and often continue to be the targets of public diplomacy efforts by mother countries, the particular isolation that Irish America felt from the dominant culture, as well as the history of Irish interaction with the British that Irish America fostered within its own culture, made Irish Americans a special case. Many Irish Americans felt that they were culturally and religiously set apart from the main currents of American society, and while this was not unique to Irish Americans compared to other American ethnic minorities, the particular circumstances of their communal understanding of what caused that 'exile' made them prime targets of the Irish government's public diplomacy efforts.

As a result, Irish-American opinion played an important role in diplomatic strategy, and this is the book's third main argument. Policy makers on all sides – Irish, British and American – believed that Irish-American opinion was influential in its own right and that it played an inordinate role in overall American public opinion, and this had to be taken into account when shaping policy. For the Irish, appeals to Irish Americans became the most important diplomatic strategy of the period. For the British, concerns about how actions against Ireland might affect American support coloured all deliberations on Irish policy. For the Americans, ironically, it was a false understanding of the power of Irish America that led the wartime American minister to Dublin, David Gray, to discredit Ireland's actions during the war in an attempt to forestall Irish-American political agitation that might undermine British–American cooperation after the war.

The fourth argument is that, contrary to popular opinion but acknowledged more widely by specialists, Irish neutrality was not traditional neutrality in any sense. It was incredibly beneficial in and of itself to the Allies, especially the British, and in practice Irish leaders went out of their way to aid the Allied war effort. The canards about Nazi spies running about Dublin radioing back to Germany the location of Allied movements owe their existence in part to the misrepresentation of Irish neutrality that came from Gray and the British leader, Winston Churchill. The consequences of those misrepresentations and falsehoods were magnified in the postwar years because the Irish leaders, as part of their identity search, kept their support for the Allies secret.

This book is designed as an introduction for students and those interested in the interactions between Ireland and Irish Americans in the 1930s and 1940s. It is not an exhaustive chronicle of every diplomatic manoeuvre of the time, rather it offers fresh evidence and a new analysis of recent arguments about Irish neutrality that have appeared in the scholarly literature. It is also the first extended work to argue that Irish neutrality can only be fully understood from the perspective of an Irish identity project that depended heavily on the role of and the outreach to Irish America by Irish, British and American policy makers. For those interested in Irish-American history, it expands the understanding of the role that foreign affairs plays in the formation of ethnic identity and explores the tensions of Irish America as revealed through an exploration of its culture. For those interested in Irish history, it offers a new analysis of the nature of Irish neutrality and the public diplomacy efforts of Irish leaders. Finally, for those interested broadly in the history of the Second World War, it provides a glimpse into an important aspect of the British–American security relationship. These focal points intersect with the existing research in important ways.

A NOTE ON THE LITERATURE

Much of the early work on Irish immigrants of the nineteenth century reflected the wider historical debates over assimilation that dominated immigration and ethnic history for many years. Oscar Handlin, for example, argued that replacing 'dysfunctional Irish culture' with American mores offered the best hope for Irish-American success in the United States. Thomas Brown argued forcefully that Irish Americans' work on behalf of Irish nationalism at the end of the nineteenth century was their ticket into the American mainstream. By maintaining their ethnic identity and working for Irish independence, Brown argued, Irish Americans were able to show their respect for American values. Kerby Miller has shown the degree to which early Irish immigrants saw themselves as 'exiles', not immigrants, and how this perception formed their identity. Hasia Diner and Noel Ignatiev have highlighted the importance of gender when examining Irish America and how Irish Americans navigated the race issue in their process of creating their identity in America.[4]

The most promising recent approach to examining ethnic history and identity involves the concept of 'invention'. In 1992, Kathleen Conzen and several other prominent ethnic and immigration historians called for a wider perspective on the nature of ethnic identity and on how ethnic groups reinvent themselves over time. Such reinvention is always accomplished within a negotiation between the immigrant group and 'the dominant ethnoculture, in this case the Anglo American'. Timothy Meagher's work most clearly adopts this historical view of ethnicity, especially Irish-American identity. Meagher focuses on the generational shifts of ethnic communities who 'continually reinvent themselves through new definitions of identity'.[5] While Meagher and almost all historians of Irish America have focused primarily on the period before 1920 or after 1968, this book examines the invention and negotiation of Irish-American identity in the 1930s and 1940s as it formed in relation to the political and international efforts of Ireland to create its own identity.

As the twentieth century unfolded, Irish Americans, both because of their skin colour and knowledge of English, had a greater ability than did other ethnic and racial groups to 'choose' their public identity. This was not possible when they first came to the United States, when they had to define their identity against the powerful stereotypes of race and religion. This ability to invent a 'symbolic ethnicity', as Mary Waters describes it, makes the choices and expressions of that identity even more important in understanding the development of the Irish-American community.[6] Of course, the Irish experience was not the same in Boston as it was in Chicago or in the very Irish city of Butte, Montana. However, because of the powerful forces from the dominant culture that confronted all Irish Americans, and the effort by Irish leaders to reach all Irish Americans, regardless of their station or experience, the arguments that follow do not hinge on calibrating for regional differences.

Some of the most interesting newest work on ethnic identity and assimilation turns on this ability of European ethnic groups to construct an identity that placed them in the 'white' category among racial classifications.[7] There are two main questions that historians and sociologists grapple with in these works: to what extent did immigrant ethnic groups become American by becoming *white* Americans, and, for those in the dominant culture, to what extent was 'whiteness' a requirement of being fully American? Scholars explore these issues by examining how European ethnic groups like the Irish adapted to a social, economic and political norm in the United States that placed whites at the top of every power structure. For most Irish newcomers after the Great Famine of the 1840s, the 'racial' label imposed on them by the dominant culture centred on their Catholicism. This intermediate categorization – white, yet not quite fully white – fuelled Irish Americans' sense of alienation that played such an important role in their struggles for identity.[8]

While Irish Americans were inventing themselves anew, the newly independent Ireland was doing the same. Patrick O'Mahony and Gerard Delanty have defined national identity as 'the cultural outcome of a discourse of a nation'.[9] Throughout much of the studied time period, the desire and ability of de Valera to craft and implement a wider vision of an Ireland that was neutral, Gaelic, Catholic and rural *was* the discourse of Ireland. After he realized that effective collective security through the League of Nations was not possible, de Valera turned to neutrality as the method to safeguard Ireland and to create an Irish identity at home and in the world.

The central importance of World War Two, or the 'Emergency' as it was known in Ireland, as it relates to Irish diplomatic and identity goals, is hard to overstate. Terence Brown has called the war 'the beginning of a watershed in Irish life'. Until the late 1930s the rural aspect of de Valera's vision of Irish identity was very much a reflection of the actual life of most Irish. During and after the war, however, Brown argues that all the official and unofficial evidence 'agree in their discovery of an almost universally demoralized rural scene'.[10] This transformation of the Irish view of rural life, which had for so long been the integral element of Irish cultural experience, explains the rising importance that neutrality began to take on as an aspect of Irish identity. As the older economic and cultural structures began to decay, neutrality in many ways became a new badge of Irish identity.

Irish politics, as evidenced by Gerry Adams's statement above, is still very concerned about neutrality as an important element of what it means to be an Irish state in the world. It is therefore crucial to understand the origins and strategy of the first implementation of that policy and how it continues to shape Irish understanding. Writing in 1999, Sean Farrell Moran argued that 'the issue of identity remains at the forefront of Irish politics and culture'.[11] Neutrality remains an important part of that identity, and it has influenced Irish debates about NATO and the European Union through the early twenty-first century.

ORGANIZATION

This book is divided into five chapters. The first chapter examines the patterns of Irish-American immigration, the history of Irish-American involvement in Irish nationalist groups prior to the outbreak of World War Two, and the efforts by the post-Famine generation and their children to define their identity in their new home. It is against this backdrop that the events of 1932–45 unfolded and can best be explained. The argument about the receptivity of Irish America to later public diplomacy efforts by Irish leaders during the war is mostly explored in this chapter.

The second chapter examines the context of the relationship between the American and Irish governments from 1932, the year de Valera took office as President of the Executive Council (a post equivalent to Prime Minister) and Franklin Roosevelt was elected president, until the outbreak of the European war in September 1939. During this time de Valera was eager to press any advantage to end the partition of Ireland that began with the Anglo-Irish Treaty of 1921, even as he struggled both to achieve a greater degree of practical independence for Ireland and to maintain links to the British Commonwealth. Irish Americans, struggling like the rest of the nation with the ravages of the Great Depression, also began to question their new-found status in American society. The argument about the nature of Irish neutrality being a part of a wider search for identity is an important aspect of this chapter.

Chapters 3 and 4 examine the evolution and nature of Irish neutrality, Irish public diplomacy efforts and the concern for American public opinion by policy makers in all three countries. Chapter 3 examines the tense years from 1939 to 1941 when the British fought the war but the Irish and the Americans did not. David Gray, the new American minister to Ireland, pressured Ireland to allow the British to use Irish naval bases, known as the Treaty ports. Gray first tried to cajole de Valera into entering the war, and, after repeated failures, organized a concerted effort to discredit him and to distort the nature of Irish neutrality both to the American government and to the American people. Gray's efforts were aimed at forestalling any possible postwar Irish-American political power. For de Valera, neutrality at this time was the most, if not the only, practical option, but also the one that would most likely assist in having his dream of an independent and sovereign Irish identity come true.

Chapter 4 examines the American–Irish–British relationship from Pearl Harbor until the end of the war. Official tensions among the American, Irish, and British governments came to a head during this period. De Valera struggled to maintain neutrality in the face of a series of challenges by Gray. Despite waning British interest in Irish help after the Battle of Britain, Gray continued to press the Irish government to join the war. Much of Gray's motivation, however, was not his desire to bring about a shift in Irish policy, but his concerns about domestic American politics and postwar international developments. Specifically, Gray worried that Irish Americans might develop a postwar plan to split the British–American alliance in order to push the British out of Northern Ireland.

After the war, American policy makers were at first eager to punish Ireland for its wartime neutrality, in part because of the slanted reports about it during the war. Growing concerns about the Cold War and a knowledge that Ireland would be a firm supporter of western democracy soon led them to change their postwar policy towards Ireland; this is the subject of chapter 5. Specifically, it looks at the postwar efforts by David Gray to continue to influence American public opinion about Irish wartime actions and the consequences of Irish neutrality for the postwar American–Irish relationship.

NOTES

1. 'Positive Neutrality Should Form Basis of International Relations Policy', press release, 28 May 2004, Sinn Féin, available at http://www.politics.ie/modules.php?name=News& file=print &sid =5279.
2. Alice McDermott, *Charming Billy* (New York: Dell, 1998), 1, 5.
3. Brian Girvin and Geoffrey Roberts, 'The Forgotten Volunteers of World War II', *History Ireland* 6, no. 1 (1998): 46.
4. Oscar Handlin, *Boston's Immigrants, 1790–1880: A Study in Acculturation* (Cambridge, Mass.: Harvard University Press, 1959); Thomas Brown, *Irish-American Nationalism, 1870–1890* (Philadelphia: J.B. Lippincott, 1966); Kerby Miller, *Emigrants and Exiles: Ireland and the Irish Exodus to North America* (New York: Oxford University Press, 1985); Hasia Diner, *Erin's Daughters in America: Irish Immigrant Women in the Nineteenth Century* (Baltimore, Md.: Johns Hopkins University Press, 1983); Noel Ignatiev, *How the Irish Became White* (New York: Routledge, 1995). A short but thorough review of the literature on Irish America can be found in Charles Fanning, 'Introduction', in *New Perspectives on the Irish Diaspora*, ed. Charles Fanning (Carbondale, Ill.: Southern Illinois University Press, 2000) , 1–10.
5. Kathleen Conzen and others, 'The Invention of Ethnicity', *Journal of American Ethnic History* 12 (1992): 3–41; Timothy Meagher, *Inventing Irish America: Generation, Class, and Ethnic Identity in a New England City, 1880–1928* (Notre Dame, Ind.: University of Notre Dame Press, 2001), 8.
6. Mary C. Waters, *Ethnic Options: Choosing Identities in America* (Berkeley: University of California Press, 1990), 147–55.
7. For a good review of developments in assimilation studies, see Russell A. Kazal, 'Revisiting Assimilation: The Rise, Fall, and Reappraisal of a Concept in American Ethnic History', *American Historical Review* 100, no. 2 (April 1995): 437–71.
8. David R. Roediger, *How Race Survived US History: From Settlement and Slavery to the Obama Phenomenon* (New York: Verso, 2008), 142–7. For an excellent analysis of what he defines as this 'inbetweenness', see Roediger, *Working Toward Whiteness – How America's Immigrants Became White: The Strange Journey from Ellis Island to the Suburbs* (New York:

Basic Books, 2005), especially 57–130.

9. Patrick O'Mahony and Gerard Delanty, *Rethinking Irish History: Nationalism, Identity and Ideology* (New York: St Martin's Press, 1998), 2. For a review of the major themes of Irish historiography and revisionism, see pp. 9–11.

10. Terence Brown, *Ireland: A Social and Cultural History, 1922 to the Present* (Ithaca, N.Y.: Cornell University Press, 1985), 139, 141.

11. Sean Farrell Moran, 'History and Meaning and the Images of Irish Iconography', in Lawrence McBride, ed., *Images, Icons and the Irish Nationalist Imagination, 1870–1925* (Dublin: Four Courts Press, 1999), 174.

1

Exiles, Identity and a New Nation

–But do you know what a nation means? says John Wyse.
–Yes, says Bloom.
–What is it? says John Wyse.
–A nation? says Bloom. A nation is the same people living in the
same place.
–By God, then, says Ned, laughing, if that's so I'm a nation for I'm
living in the same place for the last five years.
So of course everyone had the laugh at Bloom and says he, trying
to muck out of it:
–Or also living in different places. (James Joyce, *Ulysses*)[1]

In the name of God and of the dead generations from which she
receives her old tradition of nationhood, Ireland, through us,
summons her children to her flag and strikes for her freedom.
Having organised and trained her manhood ... having patiently
perfected her discipline, having resolutely waited for the right
moment to reveal itself, she now seizes that moment, and,
supported by her exiled children in America ... she strikes in full
confidence of victory. (Proclamation of the Republic of Ireland,
1916)[2]

On the surface, the 'Irish' in Irish-American is fast fading ...
Unquestionably, however, an Irish identity persists. (Nathan
Glazer and Daniel Patrick Moynihan, 1963)[3]

The Irish, both in Ireland and the United States, constantly negotiated,
moulded and created their identities as they struggled to find their
role in the ever more complicated world of the early twentieth century.
The millions of Irish men and women who came to the United States
between the Great Famine of the 1840s and the eve of World War Two
brought with them collective memories of injustice, oppression and

efforts to assert independence. They passed those memories on to their sons and daughters, who faced other issues of identity as they forged their own way in America. At the same time, the Irish in Ireland crafted a resurgent Irish identity, fought for and won independence, quarrelled among themselves and ultimately asserted their national identity on the world stage.

Both groups laboured against pre-existing notions of the Irish and of Ireland that others held. The American Irish had to deal with the stereotype of the drunken, irresponsible, lazy Irishman that had existed since before the great influx of emigrants during the Great Famine.[4] The anti-Catholic elements of this stereotype reached their zenith in the American Know-Nothing party of the 1850s, and it remained a powerful stumbling block well into the twentieth century. Against this negative background, Irish Americans attempted to forge their identity. The Irish government and the Irish people faced different yet related challenges after winning independence from Great Britain in 1921. The government was acutely aware of the importance of establishing a strong international identity for the new nation and was cognizant of how that process required challenging the contemporary perceptions of Ireland. Desmond Fitzgerald, the first Minister of External Affairs of the Irish Free State, told the Dáil Éireann (the Irish Parliament) in 1924 that 'We are a new country and an unknown quantity in the world. Ireland is not only an unknown quantity in a neutral form, but in a negative form.'[5] Almost all of the new state's diplomacy centred on establishing that identity and its importance for independence. The Irish Free State targeted its efforts at both the domestic audience and the international scene, because, on the heels of the Irish Civil War, it was just as important to legitimize the state to its own citizens as it was to legitimize itself in the eyes of the world. Finally, both groups, the Irish at home and across the Atlantic, looked to each other for support and guidance.

This chapter examines these themes as they played out in both Ireland and the United States from the time of the arrival of the great mass of Irish in the United States during the Great Famine until the elections of Franklin Roosevelt and Éamon de Valera in 1932. The Irish who came to the United States during this time faced a wide variety of obstacles, but they soon found ways to position themselves in local government, the Catholic Church, labour unions and other places of influence. On the surface, especially on the eve of the Great Depression, Irish Americans had effectively shed the outward signs of an ethnic minority that faced structural hurdles to full assimilation into American society. Assimilation, however, was not synonymous with identity. That Irish identity persisted well beyond the mythical 1920 mark delineated by so many histories of Irish Americans.[6] At the same time, the Irish who stayed in Ireland reinvented their identity, as a people and as a new nation.

Identity and nationalism were intertwined for the Irish and for Irish Americans. This book's working definition of 'identity' stems from each group's self-perception and the wider cultural, social, religious and political factors that set the boundaries of each group's ability to define itself. 'Identity', therefore, is defined as the individual's or the group's sense of 'peoplehood', to borrow a phrase from Milton Gordon.[7] This includes not only the set of characteristics and traits that each group ascribed to themselves, but also, for Irish Americans, their negotiations with the wider culture about what it meant to be an Irish American, indeed, what it meant to be an American. Irish-American identity, especially, incorporated the group's relationship to Ireland. As Kerby Miller puts it, 'Ethnic identity is the result of the dynamic conjunctions of social structures and relationships and cultural patterns in the old country and the new.'[8] The working definition of 'nationalism' relies heavily on Benedict Anderson's definition of a nation as an 'imagined political community'.[9] 'Nationalism', in the context of this book, is defined as the effort to create and then support a politically independent and culturally Gaelic Irish state.

IRISH IMMIGRATION

The first concentrated influx of Irish into the United States came in the period from the end of the Revolutionary War to 1845, when approximately one million Irish made the journey. The most cited study claims that in 1790 there were 306,000 Americans who were born either in Ireland or were of Irish descent, out of an overall population of slightly less than four million. The majority of these Irish were Presbyterians from Ulster, who had first begun to arrive in the colonies in 1680 and who made up almost two-thirds of Irish immigration between 1783 and 1815.[10] By 1830, however, Catholic emigrants outnumbered Irish Presbyterians. By 1840 Irish Protestants made up only about 10 per cent of Irish emigration to the US, and that percentage remained fairly constant through 1900.[11]

The Great Famine of 1845–9 marks the pivot point for analysis of Irish emigration to the United States. Irish men and women went to the United States in limited numbers before this date, but it was the massive Famine and post-Famine emigration that marks the arrival of the

predominantly rural and unskilled Irish Catholics who eventually identified themselves as Irish Americans. Their arrival in large numbers
strengthened the already evolving self-identity of Irish Protestants in
America as 'Scotch-Irish' in their effort to differentiate themselves
from the Catholic masses then entering the country. Overall, almost
five million Irish men and women left Ireland for the United States
between 1800 and 1920.[12]

The Great Famine and its aftermath brought almost 1.7 million Irish
to the United States in the 1840s and 1850s. The British authorities,
who ruled Ireland, encouraged this population transfer as a way to ease
the crisis. An increasing population was putting a strain on the available
economic resources, and Ireland was ill-prepared to deal with such a
catastrophe because a large portion of its people relied almost exclusively on the potato for survival. By the end of the Famine in 1850,
almost two million Irish were gone: half died of starvation or disease;
the other half emigrated, mostly to the United States.[13] They brought
with them memories of suffering, loss, hopelessness and a sense of
betrayal by the British.

As the central defining element in nineteenth-century Irish history,
the Famine has long been a topic historians hotly debate. The first wave
of nationalist histories placed the onus for the catastrophe squarely on the
British. Irish and Irish-American popular memory, however, took it a step
further, viewing the lack of a British response to the suffering as the direct
result of a British genocidal policy and the logical continuation of centuries of British neglect and misrule in Ireland. Such a policy resulted in
what was essentially seen as forced migration. Richard Williams has
described the involuntary nature of Famine emigration: 'Economic
forces generated conditions that confronted many people from the
lower social group in Ireland with the prospect of starving to death.'
As such, many Irish moving to the United States considered themselves
exiles from tyranny and oppression.[14]

Economic hardship in Ireland triggered a continuous wave of emigration to America between 1855 and 1920, when another three million
Irish landed in the United States. Why did the Irish continue to leave
Ireland after the Famine? As historian David Emmons has eloquently
noted, 'In sum, there were no jobs, no inheritances, no dowries, no
access to the land, no promise – or even faint hope – of a secure
future.'[15] After the Famine, men in Ireland had to face the dismal
prospect of finding employment outside of the family farm if they were
not lucky enough to be the eldest son, who alone inherited the land.
The later emigrant groups were younger, poorer, had fewer skills, yet

were more literate than those who went to the United States before the Famine. When asked upon arrival, almost four out of five claimed to be unskilled and from a rural background. The population of people born in Ireland and living in the United States reached its peak in 1890, at just over 1.8 million. By 1900 almost five million first- or second-generation Irish lived in the United States, a number greater than the population of Ireland at the time. In 1920 approximately 20 per cent of the US population was either born in Ireland or of Irish descent.[16]

While the economic prospects were dim for men in nineteenth-century Ireland, they were worse for women. Women and men arrived in approximately equal numbers before 1900, but at that point women emigrants began to outnumber men.[17] Women in Ireland not only had to deal with economic hardship, but had to do so within the confines of a male-dominated society, one that was much more restrictive than that found in the United States. Once in the United States, however, Irish women were able to take advantage of educational opportunities not afforded them in Ireland. As Hasia Diner describes it, 'Irish girls continued to flock to the American classrooms because of what those classrooms promised for their futures.' In America they were able to prepare for careers and find employment that was not available in Ireland.[18]

HARDSHIPS IN AMERICA

The new arrivals of the 1840s found that a series of difficult challenges awaited them. While many Irish were already in the United States, the earlier emigrants had more skills and shared a religious heritage with the dominant Protestant American culture. The new Catholic immigrants, coming mostly from the west and south of Ireland, faced a set of obstacles that included ostracism, an anti-Catholic bias, and the development of social and economic stereotypes that sometimes labelled them as an unassimilable race.

The term 'Irish American' came to be closely identified with Catholics. The Protestants who predominated Irish immigration until about 1830 began to identify themselves as 'Scotch-Irish' by the time of the Famine emigration. These self-described Scotch-Irish were the descendents of Presbyterians from Scotland, who had begun to settle in Ireland from the time of the Cromwellian land settlement in the seventeenth century. They used the term to differentiate themselves from the primarily Catholic masses that entered the United States after 1845.[19]

Kerby Miller, however, has recently challenged this predominant view of the emergence of the term. He claims that it owed its appearance 'as much to social, cultural, and political tensions *within* the Ulster American Presbyterian community itself'. Miller's argument is that when Federalists (the political followers of Alexander Hamilton) applied the term 'wild Irish' – which signified the more radical Catholic elements in Ireland – to the Irish-American Republican supporters of Thomas Jefferson, the group responded by finding ways to purge its ranks of any radical elements. The origin of the term 'Scotch-Irish', then, was more a means to assert the British and Protestant nature of the group, long before the great influx of Irish Catholics. Over the course of the nineteenth century the term would expand to include all non-Catholic Irish or their descendants.[20]

This effort by earlier Irish immigrants to disassociate themselves from the influx of Irish Catholics arriving in the 1840s and thereafter is a part of the wider society's reluctance to accept this new group. Anglo-Americans viewed the poor, predominantly rural, Catholic and traumatized newcomers with varying degrees of suspicion and hostility. An 'Irish personality' or 'Irish traits' moniker soon became the dominant culture's standard description of the American Irish; they were lazy drunkards, prone to violence. The destitution, crime rates, alcoholism and other antisocial behavioural traits in the areas where the American Irish settled reinforced this view and led many to believe that it was not just a matter of economic status, but that the Irish Catholics had 'permanent racial endowments' which prevented them from ever assimilating into American society.[21]

This ethnic stereotype became the predominant depiction of the Irish in song and stage throughout the remainder of the 1800s. In Joseph Curran's vivid description:

> At his best, 'Paddy' was a happy-go-lucky buffoon, shiftless and tipsy. At his worst, he was a simian-featured barbarian: 'childish, emotionally unstable, ignorant, indolent, superstitious, primitive or semi-civilized, dirty, vengeful and violent.' His 'stage Irish' costume consisted of ragged tail coat and battered truncated conical hat, knee breeches, coarse stockings, and buckled shoes. Almost invariably, he was armed with a shillelagh [an Irish cudgel], smoked a clay pipe, and was extremely voluble. His hair was often red, as fiery as his temper.[22]

Irish-American Catholics and their descendents, therefore, were forced to negotiate their identity through this negative stereotype. It predated their arrival and struck a dissonant chord with the dominant Protestant culture, apart from any economic rivalry that occurred among those in the unskilled labour pool. Irish Americans attempted part of that rene-gotiation by appropriating the stereotype and altering some of its core features. As 'Paddy' morphed into a working-class figure near the end of the 1800s, many Irish Americans began to cheer the subtle digs that the 'stage Irishman' was able to give to the wider Anglo-American culture and those Irish who aspired to move from the 'shanty' Irish neigh-bourhood into the 'lace curtain' crowd.[23]

These were not enough, however, to overcome the prejudice and stereotype that had taken such a strong hold by the late 1800s and early 1900s. One element that Irish Catholics would not, and could not, change was their Catholicism. Anglo-Saxon Protestants considered the United States to be a Protestant country, founded on Protestant values. Their anti-Catholicism, then, was not just based on mere religious dif-ferences, but on their belief that Catholicism and the power of the Pope threatened the very foundation of American values and democracy. Francis Carroll succinctly summarized this view: 'Briefly, many Americans viewed Catholicism as an anti-christian [sic] conspiracy which threatened political, religious, intellectual and educational free-dom.' An influx of superstitious and dogmatic Catholics, especially from Ireland, seen as the militant opponent of Anglo-Saxon Protestant rule who looked to Rome for guidance, would bring ruin on America.[24] A second major strain of anti-Irish American feeling grew out of the emerging Anglo-Saxon racism that began to take shape in the late 1800s. In a worldview that placed Anglo-Saxons as the pre-eminent civilizing force in the world and relegated others to lower rungs on a racial ladder, the Irish, with their resistance to the tutelage of years of Anglo-Saxon rule, seemed hopeless. This view was 'popular in academic, political, and journalistic circles'. So even as more 'new' immigrants came to the United States and as Irish Americans moved into the middle class, they were still negotiating and creating an iden-tity with the baggage of a decidedly antagonistic legacy.[25] The rise of the temperance movement, the attempt to abolish the use of alcohol, also placed Irish Americans in a defensive position with respect to white middle-class reformers. Social drinking had always been an important part of Irish culture, even in the homeland. There was a vigorous temperance movement in Ireland, led by Father Theobald Mathew, designed to curtail the extensive social drinking of Irish men. But the efforts by American reformers can only be understood within the wider context of what they perceived as a threat posed by immigrants. In the United States, temperance 'soon became indistinguishable from the general nativist critique of Irish immigration'.[26] In sum, anti Catholicism, racial stereotypes and a strong temperance movement combined to exclude and marginalize Irish Americans from the dominant Anglo-Protestant culture.

IRISH AMERICANS AND NINETEENTH-CENTURY IRISH NATIONALISM

In Ireland during the 1800s, as religious allegiance became the defining characteristic of the political and cultural world, Catholicism became a central element in the Irish nationalist movement. Both political and cultural nationalists came to regard Catholicism as the true mark of the Irish people. Drawing on this development, Daniel O'Connell created the Catholic Association in 1823. It eventually became a mass movement after O'Connell instituted the 'Catholic rent', allowing Catholics to join the organization for only a penny a month. Riding this popular wave of mass politics, O'Connell stood for and won election to Westminster in 1828. He refused to take an oath that described Catholicism as 'superstitious', and, fearing an Irish uprising, Parliament removed the last of the official restrictions on Catholics the next year. This reinforced O'Connell's reputation with the Irish people, but more important, it reinforced the importance of Catholicism as, in the words of historian Kevin Whelan, 'the principal repository of a distinctive Irish nationhood'.[27] The Famine generation of Irish that came to the United States brought this sense of Catholic identity and experience of the power of political action with them. When O'Connell's Repeal movement – an effort to repeal the 1801 Act of Union and re-establish a separate Irish Parliament – failed, emigrants also brought with them a profound disillusionment about the efficacy of constitutional nationalism.[28]

In 1848, at the height of the Famine, the Young Irelanders – a group of Irish nationalists who called for a renewed Irish culture designed to bridge the gap between Protestants and Catholics – led a short-lived and unsuccessful rebellion in Ireland. Yet their legacy was not a renewed effort to bring the Irish together, but rather a reinvigorated support for 'physical-force nationalism', which called for direct military action against British rule, something O'Connell had tried to constrain. As the Young Ireland leaders emigrated to the United States, they carried that militant philosophy with them. John Mitchell, one of the 1848 leaders, upon landing in the United States in 1853 said:

> I mean to make use of the freedom guaranteed to me as a citizen or inchoate citizen of America to help and stimulate the movement of ... Irish independence. I mean to claim for the revolutionary

refugees here … that America shall be to them the very stamping
ground prayed for by Archimedes whereon they may plant a lever
that shall move the world.[29]

The first organized expression of Irish nationalism by Irish
Americans came in 1858 when John O'Mahoney and Michael Doheny
founded the Fenian Brotherhood. It was associated with the Irish
Republican Brotherhood (IRB), founded in Ireland that same year. Both
organizations hoped to mobilize American money and support for physical-force nationalist efforts to overthrow British rule in Ireland. The
Fenians, who were mostly US civil war veterans, numbered approximately 250,000 by 1865. Hoping to take advantage of British-American
tensions, they staged several ill-planned and unsuccessful raids into
Canada. Those failures, and a failure of an uprising in Ireland in 1867,
led to the quick demise of the Fenian Brotherhood by 1870.[30]

There also existed within the Fenian Brotherhood a factionalism
that plagued the organization and led Jerome Collins in 1867 to found
the Clan na Gael (Band of the Irish). The Clan thought that the open
membership of the Fenians allowed for greater numbers but that it also
brought them to the attention of the authorities. The Clan was a secret,
oath-bound organization, willing to trade a large membership for the
advantages of a covert underground organization. Soon it had created
revolutionary cells across the country, known as 'camps', with membership by invitation only. In 1877 the IRB and the Clan developed a
revolutionary directory to coordinate actions. By the end of the 1870s
the Clan was the single most influential Irish nationalist organization
in the United States, with a membership estimated at about ten thousand. Many of the rank and file appear to have been working-class
Irish, but the leadership was drawn from politics, the labour movement
and journalism. For example, Terence Powderly, leader of the Knights
of Labor and former mayor of Scranton, Pennsylvania, was the 'senior
guardian' of Camp 470.[31]

What motivated these early Irish-American nationalists? Thomas N.
Brown developed the classic theory on this question. In *Irish-American
Nationalism, 1870–1890* (1966) he wrote that Irish-American nationalism at the time was a product of 'the realities of loneliness and alienation,
and of poverty and prejudice'.[32] Brown argued that Irish Americans,
faced with economic hardship and prejudice in the United States,
looked to Irish independence as the means to legitimize themselves. If
Ireland were free, then maybe Americans would accept the Irish among
them. For Brown, 'the hard life of the immigrant' formed the basis of
Irish-American nationalism. He assumes that these immigrants strove

towards assimilation into the American middle class, and that being from a free Ireland, an equal country in some sense, might make other Americans treat them more as equals.[33]

There are, however, more persuasive answers that go to the heart of why Irish Americans continued their quest for identity into the twentieth century. First, Brown diminished the influence of a wide segment of the Irish-American community that was more concerned with working-class values than an ascension into the middle class. Many were happy to live out their lives in their own neighbourhoods. Those who gave time and money to Irish nationalist causes did not have economic motivation at the core of their activism. David Emmons argues persuasively that, at least for the majority of Irish Americans of all classes, their desire to see a free Ireland stemmed from the fact that they were 'historically conditioned to wish it'.[34] Those born in Ireland but living in the United States saw themselves as exiles, with a natural desire to right the wrong that had forced them to leave. In turn, they passed that identity down to their sons and daughters. As a speaker at an 1870s St Patrick's Day rally in Worcester, Massachusetts phrased it:

> Though I have never breathed the invigorating air of the land of happiness … from my infancy my father has instilled in my mind and impressed it so deep in my heart, that for his sake and in detestation of the wrongs inflicted by the hand of tyranny, it shall never be erased from my memory.[35]

Kerby Miller argues that a 'crisis of identity', only partly explained by the rejection Irish Americans felt from Protestant America, helped fuel Irish-American nationalism. Irish Americans shared a deeper level of alienation from the dominant culture that played itself out through a resurgent ethnocentric Catholicism as well as through Irish nationalism. That alienation stemmed from a combination of experiences, both in Ireland and the United States, and led the American Irish to consider themselves exiles. The horrors of the Famine and the English responsibility for it became the defining memory within Irish families for the rest of the century. Emigrants, then, 'landed in America already predisposed … to perceive emigration as forced exile and to respond to unpleasant situations abroad with resentments and desires easily translated into nationalist expressions and activities.' At some level, Irish-American interest in Irish affairs was irrational and emotional, but it was quite real, and it grew out of their sense of exile from Ireland and their non-acceptance in America.[36]

Irish-American nationalism in the later part of the nineteenth century exhibited several diverse streams, echoing the diversity of Irish nationalism across the Atlantic. Some physical-force nationalist groups, especially Clan na Gael, then led by the ex-Fenian John Devoy, called for the violent overthrow of British rule. Jeremiah O'Donovan Rossa led the United Irishmen, another physical-force Irish-American nationalist group. Conservative Irish-American nationalists, characterized by their espousal of constitutional nationalism and calls for middle-class respectability for Irish Americans, looked to John O'Reilly, the editor of the Boston *Pilot*, for leadership. Patrick Ford published the *Irish World*, which allowed him a platform to push for Irish-American working-class issues as well as for Irish land reform concerns. Ford believed that 'the cause of the poor in Donegal is the cause of the factory slave in Fall River'. The *Irish World* was the most popular Irish-American newspaper of the time, reaching a circulation of almost 120,000 by 1900.[37]

John Devoy, who attempted to bridge some of the gaps among the groups by his proposal of what became known as the New Departure, was the dominant Irish-American nationalist figure from his arrival in the United States in 1871 until his death in 1928. He was born in County Kildare in 1842, and after his imprisonment for recruiting for the Irish Republican Brotherhood, sailed to the United States and settled in New York. For a time he was the foreign editor of the New York *Herald*, and he published the *Gaelic-American* from 1903 until his death. He was an ardent supporter of physical-force nationalism and the chief fundraiser of the 1916 Easter Rising.[38]

Devoy's 1879 New Departure plan was an attempt to meld together the various strands of Irish and Irish-American nationalism. By bringing together ardent, physical-force republicans, those in favour of constitutional nationalism and those interested in land reform, Devoy hoped to create a scenario that would create the basis for a revolution in Ireland. His objective was to mobilize and radicalize the Irish peasant class around land reform, which would, when the British failed to accede to the demands, lay the grounds for a widespread revolution. Such a combination, funded and eventually armed by Irish Americans, would be a formidable force. To accomplish the goal, Devoy worked with Patrick Ford, Charles Stewart Parnell, a member of the Irish Parliamentary Party and Parliament, and Michael Davitt, another ex-Fenian who, like Devoy, had also served time in prison.[39]

The Land War, the political and social unrest that enveloped Ireland from 1879 to 1882, grew out of the New Departure alliance. Davitt returned to Ireland in 1879 and founded the Land League. Building on widespread discontent over the land-owning system throughout Ireland (2,000 people owned 70 per cent of the land and over three million tenants were renters), the Land League pushed for reform through a series of rent strikes, sporadic violence and the innovation of the boycott. Parnell served as President of the League and arrived in the United States in early 1880 to drum up American support. He raised over $300,000 during his visit and organized the American branch of the Land League. In a February 1880 address to a joint session of Congress, Parnell declared that American public opinion should be on the side of Irish nationalists and should push the US government to confront the British because 'the laws of freedom are not observed' in Ireland.[40]

It is not surprising that a coalition consisting of proponents of such widely divergent strategies and ultimate goals, faced with a combination of determined outright opposition and a policy of limited appeasement by the British government, would be short-lived. In 1881 Devoy, who was already under fire from other hard-core republicans for working with the constitutionalists, had declared that Home Rule would not be a satisfactory resolution of the Land War. By mid-1882 Davitt began calling for the abolition of private property, leading to condemnations from Parnell and Devoy. Parnell's arrest and his subsequent agreement to call off the Land War in exchange for his release and an expansion of land legislation, relegated radical nationalists such as Davitt and Ford to the fringes of the Irish and Irish-American nationalist movement. The New Departure was gone.[41] Its demise stemmed in part from the type of Irish-American in-fighting lamented in this excerpt from an 1880 letter to Devoy: 'It is the same sad, sad, old story. Divisions, ill-wills, lack of common courtesy to one another, and a failure, therefore, to present a front of unity to the world.'[42]

TURN-OF-THE-CENTURY IDENTITY AND NATIONALISM

Sorting out their own identity became a more complicated process for Irish Americans in the early 1900s. They were, as Timothy Meagher has vividly described them, 'enmeshed in a process of transition'. They were numerous; in 1910 more than 4.5 million people in the United States were born in Ireland or had at least one Irish-born parent.[43] They had made inroads into politics, labour movements and the hierarchy of the Catholic Church. They loudly proclaimed their patriotism. They founded the American-Irish Historical Society and commissioned books that listed Irish-American accomplishments, almost as if in an effort to prove that they had made it in America.[44] And it was true; many had moved up the economic ladder of assimilation.

But through it all, many still felt that *acceptance* was out of reach. This Irish-American struggle for acceptance and identity played itself out as the United States also underwent a period of growth and development. Industrial and urban growth changed the cultural and economic landscape. A flood of new immigrants, mostly non-Protestant and many non-English speaking, made second- and third-generation Irish Americans seem less foreign and less dangerous by comparison, in the dominant culture's view. The first two decades of the twentieth century also presaged the United States as a major presence in world affairs and witnessed a closer relationship with Great Britain, largely as a result of their alliance during World War I. One result was a renewed Irish-American nationalism that had lain dormant for almost twenty years.

So while many Irish Americans found ways to advance economically, their own cultural identity as exiles and the antagonism of the dominant culture often made them long for the security if not the poverty of the older Irish neighbourhoods. George McManus satirized the Irish-American ambivalence on joining the mainstream as well as the class conflicts within the Irish-American community in his comic strip, 'Bringing Up Father'. The strip began in 1913 and for forty years chronicled the adventures of an Irish-American couple, Maggie and Jiggs. Jiggs was constantly in trouble with his wife Maggie for his friendships with former working-class pals. Maggie was forever trying to join the Anglo elite and get invitations 'to the opera from the Van Snoots or some other feckless members of Manhattan's aristocracy'. They even had a no-good son-in-law named Lord Worthnotten. The strip was so popular, MGM and W.R. Hearst's Cosmopolitan Pictures made it into a movie, *Bringing Up Father*, in 1928.[45]

The McManus comic strip is indicative of a widely held perception among Irish Americans in the early 1900s: their full acceptance into the American mainstream was out of reach. It was their Catholicism, Thomas Rowland argues, that was 'undoubtedly the greatest impediment to Irish-America's assimilation'.[46] They had grown tired of efforts to hide or diminish their Catholic identity, a strategy that had not succeeded. Only by embracing their Catholicism and combining it with an overtly self-conscious American patriotism did they feel confident of gaining a secure place in America. Archbishop John Ireland of St Paul, Minnesota, declared that 'America demands that all who live on her soil and are protected by her flag be Americans.'[47] Irish Americans, always teetering between a desire to 'join the ins' or 'lead the outs', decided that the price of true inclusion and assimilation, the abandon-ment of their religion, was too great to pay. In many ways, even though many of their families had been in the United States for more than fifty years, they had more in common with the newer immigrants than with most Anglo-Americans. The new strategy, one that developed more fully through World War Two, was to become the leader of a broad-based Catholic ethnic movement. Timothy Meagher argues that Irish Americans wanted to create 'a militantly Catholic, patriotically American pan-ethnic, American Catholic people, with themselves as leaders of this new group, arbiters of this new identity'.[48] As part of this effort, the Knights of Columbus added a 4th Degree of membership (a high honour) in 1900, designed exclusively as a reward for those who met elevated standards of patriotism.

This class consciousness and antagonism, as well as the co-option of 'Paddy' by Irish Americans, can be seen clearly in the career of Edward Harrigan. Harrigan wrote a series of musical comedies in the 1870s and 1880s that highlighted the 'Mulligan Guard', an Irish-American social club. Dan Mulligan, the central character of the stories, was hard-drinking and impulsive, but he was also well-meaning, loyal and honest. As more Irish Americans joined the middle classes by the turn of the century, however, their criticisms of any negative Irish stereotype became louder and more frequent. The Ancient Order of Hibernians (AOH) stepped up its critique of Irish stereotypes in the popular culture, as did Irish-American politicians. By the eve of World War One, the 'stage Irishman' was no more. Irish-American songwriters would eventu-ally turn to parodies of Harrigan. George M. Cohan wrote ' H-A-R-R-I-G-A-N', along with 'Yankee Doodle Boy' and 'You're a Grand Old Flag', a signal that Irish Americans felt there was only room for fully patriotic Irish Americans on the wider American stage and in American songs.[49]

Tending to the public representations of Irish Americans in films fell in part to the renewed Ancient Order of Hibernians. The AOH, with a membership in excess of 180,000 by 1910 and now joined by the fairly influential ranks of Irish-American politicians, worked to combat the remaining Irish-American stereotypes in the media. A variety of early films in the nickelodeon era perpetuated the image of the drunken, vio-lent and lazy Paddy. Only after 1910, with concerted efforts by the AOH, Irish-American politicians, the Catholic hierarchy and a subset of Progressive reformers, did film depictions of Irish Americans begin to move beyond the stereotype. What is significant, however, is that the surface changes occurred only *after* these efforts. The underlying anti-Irish and anti-Catholic views remained.[50]

Why did Irish Americans take such offence at the negative depictions of themselves after the turn of the century, especially when for so long they were content to tolerate and satirize the stereotype? John Ibson observes that the shift 'did not signal the "Americanization" of the Irish. The matter merely became less amusing as the Irish moved in greater numbers out of physical slums while remaining in a psychological ghetto.'[51] In effect, the process of assimilation allowed the Irish to move up the economic ladder, but their failure to acquire full accept-ance made the sting of the stereotype that much harder to accept.

On the eve of World War One, Irish America could look proudly on many accomplishments. Indeed, many Irish Americans felt a need to look for them everywhere, as far back as possible, to make exaggerated claims about their importance, and to proclaim them loudly. Driven by a basic insecurity about their status in American society, faced with obstacles and never feeling entirely at home in an Anglo and Protestant America, Irish Americans had a desperate desire to look 'American'. Doing so might prove their worth and thus their 'Americanism'. They sought this in many ways, but stopped short of giving up their Catholicism and Catholic identity. John Ibson is correct when he writes that 'Irish-Americans sought success to prove their worth before Protestants.'[52]

As Irish Americans struggled to define themselves at the start of the twentieth century, their Irish cousins laboured to create a new sense of Irishness as well. Many at home, frustrated with ineffective political initiatives to create an Irish state, hoped a cultural rebirth would create the necessary conditions for a political liberation. These cultural devel-opments centred on sports and language, forming the basis of a new nationalism, the cultural nationalism that came to dominate Irish revo-lutionary thought in the twenty years prior to 1916.

In one of the best examples of this approach, Michael Cusack, disturbed by the role of English sports in Ireland, founded the Gaelic Athletic Association (GAA) in 1884. Soon after, Irish nationalists took control of the GAA and ousted Cusack from a leadership position. Gaelic football and hurling became the basis of the GAA's efforts to create a new Irish identity. With the worldwide growth of spectator sports in the early years of the twentieth century, GAA events began to draw huge crowds. At the same time, the Irish Republican Brotherhood transformed the GAA into a distinctly nationalist, although not revo-lutionary, organization by excluding anyone who played or watched 'imported games'.[53]

Additionally, Irish Americans and the Irish also became concerned about the survival of the Irish language during the late 1800s and early 1900s. Douglas Hyde, who later served as President of Ireland during World War Two, was the first president of the Gaelic League, founded in 1893. A few years earlier he had become motivated to push this effort after visiting New York's Gaelic Societies and observing their efforts to promote Irish. The Gaelic League consciously attempted to remain apolitical, enabling it to draw support from across the political and religious spectrums. As the new cultural nationalism began to gain momentum, however, Irish nationalists began to use the Gaelic League as an instrument of IRB policy. Many members of the League participated in the Easter Rising of 1916, and the British finally outlawed the League in 1919.[54]

These new nationalists found common cause with a revived nationalism among Irish Americans. In 1903 John Devoy created the *Gaelic American*, a New York-based weekly designed to publicize the activities of Clan na Gael. The Clan by this time had almost 40,000 members and, as Lawrence McCaffrey argues, the 'emotional and financial backing of many other Irish Americans'.[55] The Clan faced a difficult challenge in putting the issue of Irish independence before the American public. British–American relations were strong in the early twentieth century, boosted by American neutrality during the Boer War and Great Britain's benevolent neutrality during the Spanish-American War. The United States and Great Britain had also settled the Venezuelan border dispute of 1899 and signed the Hay-Pauncefote Treaty in 1901. Add those developments to the common Anglo-Saxon culture and the Anglophile Republican elites, and the obstacles faced by the Clan become clear. In response, the Clan attempted to influence public and official opinion by 'identifying themselves with traditional themes in American foreign policy, most notably non-alignment in the European balance of power'. Even the more conservative Ancient Order of Hibernians signed a pact in 1907 with the German–American National Alliance to work at disrupting any growing British–American partnership.[56]

WORLD WAR ONE AND THE EASTER RISING

Political developments in Great Britain in the years before the First World War reinforced the growing power of the new nationalism and its cultural manifestations.[57] After the 1910 elections the ruling Liberal Party needed the support of the Irish MPs to stay in power. The price of that support was the introduction of a home rule bill, designed to give Ireland control over most of its domestic affairs. Other home rule

bills had failed when the House of Lords vetoed them, leading to growing Irish disillusion with constitutional nationalism. Recent reforms,
however, had curtailed the absolute veto power of the Lords, and the
House of Commons had merely to approve a bill three times for it to
become law.

Home Rule galvanized both diehard Unionists in Ulster, eager to
remain a part of Great Britain, and the new Irish nationalists, intent on
seeing Home Rule pass. Unionists, anxious about the impending passage
of Home Rule legislation, organized several existing militias into the
Ulster Volunteer Force (UVF) in 1913. It soon had over 90,000 members
and had smuggled in over 25,000 rifles. The UVF hoped the threat of
civil war would lead to the rejection of Home Rule, or at least to a
modification that would exclude Protestant Ulster. Irish nationalists
responded later that year by forming the Dublin-based Irish
Volunteers. On the surface the Volunteers were designed to defend
Home Rule, but the IRB had a strong presence in its leadership. John
Devoy and the Clan na Gael created an Irish Volunteer Fund to support the new militia, prompting Sir Cecil Spring-Rice, the British
ambassador to Washington, to write to London that should fighting
break out in Ireland 'men and guns will almost certainly be sent' from
the United States.[58]

After the start of World War One the British government attempted
to put the Home Rule debate aside for the duration of the war (as it
had done with other reforms, such as women's suffrage). The government had submitted the Amending Bill in June 1914, designed to allow
the counties in Ulster an opportunity to remove themselves from the
effects of Home Rule legislation. Once Britain was at war, the government removed the Amending Bill and passed a Suspension Act, delay-
ing the implementation of Home Rule until the end of hostilities. John
Redmond, the leader of the Irish Parliamentary Party, hoping that a
strong showing of support for the British during the war would ensure
the implementation of Home Rule at its end, called for the Irish people
to join the war effort. Most of the Irish Volunteers joined with Redmond
and formed the National Volunteers. Only about three thousand
committed nationalists remained with the Irish Volunteers, but by
1916 they numbered around fifteen thousand. By the end of the First
World War over 200,000 Irish served in the British Army.[59]

The war also influenced the Irish-American community's attitude
towards nationalism and British-American relations. A growing number
of Irish Americans began to see the war in the traditional mindset of
Irish nationalism, that 'England's difficulty is Ireland's opportunity.'

Many Irish-American nationalists began to sense a change in Irish-American opinion. One that steered away from support for Redmond's pro-war stance and reliance on eventual Home Rule and towards a more radical and immediate call for Irish independence. In February 1916 Devoy knew that Irish nationalists were planning an uprising in Ireland against British rule. Eager to arrange a strong show of Irish-American resolve, and after discussions with the Clan leadership, Devoy and over three hundred and fifty high-profile Irish Americans sent out an invitation for an Irish Race Convention to be held the next month in New York. That convention founded the Friends of Irish Freedom (FOIF), which eventually included over 250,000 members, who supported 'any movement that will tend to bring about the National Independence of Ireland'.[60]

On Easter Monday, 24 April 1916, despite pleas from the head of the Irish Volunteers to stop activities, a dedicated group of physical-force nationalists staged an uprising in Dublin. Numbering just over fifteen hundred, they took control of the General Post Office and other strategic points throughout the city. Padraic Pearse, the commander-in-chief of the rebel forces, knew that the chances of military success were slim, but he felt a blood sacrifice was needed to create the situation necessary for independence. In less than a week the British authorities had routed the rebels and arrested the main leaders, including Éamon de Valera. More than five hundred people died during the week's fighting.

Initial reaction to the Rising was similar in both Ireland and the United States. Most Irish reacted to the violence with surprise and horror. John Redmond criticized the rebels for damaging the nationalist cause and possibly upsetting the awarding of Home Rule at the end of the war. Yet the subsequent executions by the British of many of the leaders of the Rising caused a firestorm of protest on both sides of the Atlantic. One Irish American wrote to Redmond:

> The present wave of fury sweeping through Irish America origi-nated with the executions and not with the rising. The rising only called out sympathy for you, except in a small circle. The execu-tions enabled that circle to spread their ripple further than they had hoped or dreamed.

In July the US Senate passed a bill urging clemency for those leaders arrested by the British, but to no avail. The end result of the executions was the effective end of Irish-American support for constitutional nation-alism and the belated realization by British officials that Irish-American opinion was an important component of British-American relations.[61]

Such occurrences were complicated further by American entry into the war in April 1917, presenting Irish Americans with a fresh challenge. They naturally felt compelled to prove their loyalty if they were to have any influence over public or official opinion, but the pro-German stances previously held by the more radical nationalists meant an uphill fight to gain credibility. Irish-American leaders took a two-track approach to the problem: persuade other Americans of their loyalty and patriotism; and work to have Irish independence become a war aim that was included in the final peace settlement. Daniel Cohalan, a leader of the Clan na Gael and of the FOIF, as well as a justice on the New York Supreme Court, organized a meeting on 8 April of 4,000 Irish Americans in Carnegie Hall that urged President Woodrow Wilson to 'take such action as will secure the independence of Ireland'. Wilson readily recognized that an Irish settlement would promote British-American cooperation. On 12 April he wrote to Secretary of State Robert Lansing that the British should be informed, unofficially, that 'substantial self-government' for Ireland would add 'a very great element of satisfaction and enthusiasm ... to the co-operation now about to be organized' between the United States and Great Britain.[62]

For the Irish, the end of the war allowed for a renewed effort to secure Irish independence. Éamon de Valera, spared execution after the Rising, probably because he was born in the United States, led a renewed Sinn Féin (roughly translated as 'ourselves' or 'ourselves alone') party to a resounding victory in the December 1918 elections. Rather than take their seats at Westminster, the Sinn Féin MPs convened in Dublin on 21 January 1919 to establish the first Dáil Éireann (Irish Parliament) and unanimously elected de Valera as the Dáil's president. They reaffirmed the 1916 Declaration of the Irish Republic, began the process of forming a government, and appealed to the world for representation at the Paris Peace Conference.[63] The two tracks of Irish efforts to secure independence, constitutional nationalism and physical-force nationalism, soon collided. On the same day members of the Irish Volunteers, now being referred to as the Irish Republican Army, ambushed British soldiers and officers of the Royal Irish Constabulary, killing two of them. A long time in the making, the Anglo-Irish War had begun.

Although this action complicated support for Irish independence, the US Congress worked throughout 1919 to include an Irish delegation at the Paris Peace Conference. Over Wilson's objections, both houses passed resolutions during the spring and summer in support of Irish independence and calling on the Conference to meet with the Irish representatives. On 28 March 1919 a group of Democratic office holders wrote to Wilson expressing concern that his unwillingness to bring Irish issues to the table would hurt them in the next election. Wilson was unmoved. Eventually, those opposed to the Versailles Treaty used the extensive logistical support of a variety of Irish-American organizations to help defeat the treaty's passage in the Senate.[64]

De Valera was in the United States during much of the Anglo-Irish War, and his stay exacerbated a split among Irish-American activists and cemented his own hard-line republican stance. His official purpose during his eighteen-month stay (June 1919–December 1920) was to seek the American government's support for the new Irish government and to raise funds. Both of these depended, as did so much of the Irish nationalists' efforts, on the support of Irish Americans. The ideological split within Irish America that complicated de Valera's efforts centred on whether Irish-American organizations were too concerned with American political considerations and were thereby insufficiently supporting efforts to create an Irish republic. This was the charge that aspiring leader Joseph McGarrity of Philadelphia hurled at John Devoy and Judge Cohalan of the FOIF. When de Valera went ahead with his bond drive effort against the advice of Devoy and Cohalan, his tour of the United States was accompanied by active efforts by each side to undermine the efforts of the other. It all burst into the wider public sphere after de Valera mentioned in an interview that Ireland could assume a relationship with Great Britain similar to Cuba's relationship with the United States under the Platt Amendment. De Valera's critics quickly countered that the Platt Amendment after the Spanish-American War effectively reduced Cuba to little more than an American property. Arguing that such a goal was a mockery of Irish nationalism, critics questioned de Valera's ability to lead Ireland. His time in the United States taught de Valera that in order to be effective his public diplomacy had to be wider in scope, moving beyond just the 'professional' Irish-American activists to influence the whole of Irish America. His future guiding principle of working with Irish America is summed up in a February 1920 letter back to Ireland:

> Fundamentally, Irish Americans differ from us in this – they being Americans first would sacrifice Irish interests if need be to American interests – we, Irish first, would do the reverse. It is therefore a question of finding the lines along which our interests are parallel.[65]

De Valera's concern with American and Irish-American opinion was always a critical part of his political calculations. By late 1921, after a British–Irish truce and recognizing that the British seemed willing to end the hostilities in Ireland, de Valera anticipated a split in the Irish government about Ireland's future relationship with Great Britain. Because the Government of Ireland Act in 1920 had already effectively divided the island into two political entities by allowing Ulster to form its own parliament (and gave the British government the political cover to agree to a truce), the negotiations to establish an independent Ireland in the south centred on what status that state would have with Great Britain.[66] As it became clear that there would be profound differences over issues of allegiance to the British crown and whether Ireland would remain in the Commonwealth, and recognizing the need for American and Irish-American support, de Valera wrote to the Dáil's representative in Washington about the need to keep the issue before the American public.[67] In December, with the British representatives threatening a renewal of the war, both sides signed the Anglo-Irish Treaty, giving the 'Irish Free State' independence, but only with the constitutional status of a self-governing dominion within the British Commonwealth.[68]

IRISH AMERICANS, IRELAND AND THE UNITED STATES: 1921–32

Most Irish Americans viewed the creation of the Irish Free State as the fulfilment of the long-held nationalist desire for a free and independent Ireland, thus they were confused and disengaged as diehard Republicans in Ireland started the Irish Civil War.[69] In fact, even though many Irish would have preferred complete independence from Britain, more than 80 per cent of the new nation supported the Treaty. Éamon de Valera, who resigned from the Dáil when the Treaty passed because he felt it did not go far enough in advancing real independence for the whole island, helped lead the anti-Treaty forces. Violence broke out in June 1922 when the provisional government's army attacked the Irregulars, the anti-Treaty Irish Republican Army members. More than eight hundred people had died in the war by May 1923, when the IRA command ordered its troops to dump their arms, signalling the end of the conflict. The pro- and anti-Treaty split would be the main element in Irish political life for the remainder of the century.

After the civil war issues of national identity formed the core concern of Irish foreign policy in the 1920s, especially the importance of disassociating Ireland from Britain. Early Irish foreign policy focused on the contention that it would be much more difficult for Britain to interfere in Irish affairs if the international community embraced the Irish Free State as a fully independent nation. Irish policy makers had the difficulty of playing this strategy out as a member of the British Commonwealth.[70] For example, Dominion status within the Commonwealth meant that the Irish Free State could have trade representatives, but not official diplomats, in foreign countries. Still, in the next ten years Ireland made considerable gains in expanding the range of its diplomatic activity. The government became the first Dominion to appoint its own minister plenipotentiary when Timothy Smiddy became Irish minister to the United States in 1924. While a significant development in the Irish government's effort to bolster its image on the international scene and within the United States, the appointment was also designed to show the Irish people – only one year removed from a civil war – that the government was able to assert itself on the international scene. One of Smiddy's main charges in the United States was to work to unify Irish Americans after the fractures of the de Valera visit.[71]

The effort by the Irish government to elevate Smiddy's status began earlier, and its target was not only public opinion in Ireland, but also public opinion in the United States. In 1923 the Dáil secretary wrote that appointing a minister would have the effect of countering propaganda from de Valera and possibly cut off the flow of funds from Irish America to the Irregulars. In the appeals to London to allow such an appointment, the Irish government played the Irish-American card that loomed over all Anglo-Irish discussions for the next twenty years. Writing to the British Colonial Secretary, the Irish government noted that 'nothing could be more effective in promoting amongst Irish people in America cordial relations with the Nations of the Commonwealth than the presence of an Irish Minister Plenipotentiary in the United States'.[72]

Ireland's membership and participation in the League of Nations during the 1920s was another effort to secure for the new state a legitimate international foundation as a bulwark against Britain. Irish leaders stressed the importance of joining the League as a symbol of the Free State's independence and, as a practical matter, as an outlet to appeal for international help should Great Britain seek to reassert political or economic control over Ireland. As a part of this effort, it became important for the Irish government to have the League recognize the Anglo-Irish Treaty as an *international* treaty between two sovereign states. The League did so in 1924, over heavy initial British opposition. Subsequent Irish governments continued to pursue active agendas within the League, focusing on the role of small states in the world. The League recognized those efforts in electing Ireland to the League Council in 1930.[73]

Irish Americans also played an important part of the new nation's foreign policy and defence considerations. The diaspora, with Irish Americans as the primary component, was one of the most significant factors in Irish foreign policy during the nation's first decade. Ironically, Irish-American leaders opposed Ireland's entry into the League of Nations. This opposition grew from the intense opposition to the League during the treaty fight in the United States after the Paris Peace Conference.[74]

Irish leaders in the 1920s also factored in Irish Americans in defence planning. Recognizing the important strategic location of Ireland in relation to Great Britain, planners knew that it would be a challenge for Ireland to remain neutral in any war involving its more powerful neighbour. Not only might British forces want to occupy Ireland to strengthen what Irish planners described as the 'Aerial and Submarine key to England', but that Britain's enemies might want to do the same. While knowing that Irish forces would be insufficient to mount any concerted or even limited effort to infringe on Irish sovereignty, planners noted that propaganda aimed at the Irish diaspora was the most important weapon in the Irish arsenal. Before even the option of an Irish air force, the Council of Defence on Irish Defence Policy listed as its primary policy option 'Propaganda and Diplomacy. The Irish in America and elsewhere make these particularly powerful weapons for such a small State ... The adroit use of these weapons will help to prevent either England or any other Nation from encroaching on our rights or liberties.'[75]

While the Irish government throughout the 1920s and into the 1930s turned to Irish America for validation and support in its effort to forge a national identity, Irish Americans continued to wrestle with similar concepts of identity and power. True, Irish Americans *were* making more money, getting better jobs, living in better conditions and achieving much of the stereotypical trappings of the American Dream, but they still did not feel accepted. The rise of Catholic institutions – schools, colleges, hospitals, social clubs, etc. – were part of the larger pan-ethnic Catholic leadership role that Irish Americans sought to acquire. They are also evidence that even as Irish Americans were climbing the economic ladder on the outside, they continued to feel that no matter how high they reached they would never be able to climb into the 'real' American home. The 'extensive organizational network' that they built as a counter to the barriers erected by the dominant American culture 'functioned to separate their lives, at the primary level, from those of Anglo Protestants'.[76]

CONCLUSION

Historian John Patrick Buckley has written that by 1921 Irish Americans were 'largely indistinguishable from their fellow Americans'.[77] Likewise, Kerby Miller has argued that in the early years of the twentieth century Irish Americans remained in figurative exile, 'remarkably estranged from the dominant culture of their adopted country', but that by 1923 'the long, dark winter of Irish exile in America was over'.[78] These and other arguments that equate a decline in Irish-American nationalism and the rise in the Irish-American standard of living with the end of Irish-American identity miss the mark. Throughout the 1930s and 1940s Irish Americans continued to develop their sense of place in American society. When the international situation thrust Ireland into a crisis, Irish Americans responded by again looking across the Atlantic to help discover their identity as both Irish and American. That could not have happened if their internal acceptance of complete assimilation had been complete. Irish leaders, with Éamon de Valera in the lead, would similarly use the international situation as an opportunity to shape an Irish identity, with an eye towards Irish America's potential to help.

NOTES

1. James Joyce, *Ulysses* (Paris: Shakespeare & Co., 1922), 317.
2. Arthur Mitchell and Pádraig Ó Snodaigh, eds, *Irish Political Documents, 1916–1949* (Dublin: Irish Academic Press, 1985), 17.
3. Nathan Glazer and Daniel Patrick Moynihan, *Beyond the Melting Pot: The Negroes, Puerto Ricans, Jews, Italians, and Irish of New York City* (Cambridge, Mass.: Harvard University Press, 1963), 250.
4. Throughout this book the term 'American Irish' refers to the first generation of Irish immigrants. 'Irish American' generally refers to second and subsequent generations of those who trace their ancestry back to Ireland. 'Ireland' and 'Irish' are associated with either the whole of Ireland prior to 1921, the Irish Free State to 1937, or Ireland (*Éire* in Irish) thereafter.
5. *Dáil Debates*, 9 July 1924, col. 800. All Dáil debates are available at http:www//historical-debates.oireachtas.ie/.
6. For example, see Patrick J. Blessing, 'Irish Emigration to the United States, 1800–1920: An Overview', in *The Irish in America: Emigration, Assimilation and Impact*, ed. P.J. Drudy (Cambridge: Cambridge University Press, 1985), 11–37; Joseph Edward Cuddy, *Irish-America and National Isolationism, 1914–1920* (New York: Arno Press, 1976); and Timothy J. Meagher, ed., *From Paddy to Studs: Irish-American Communities in the Turn of the Century Era, 1880 to 1920* (Westport, Conn.: Greenwood Press, 1986). The 1920 date is often chosen as a convenient demarcation because of several influential events so close to each other in time: the end of the First World War, Irish independence, partition, American immigration restrictions, etc.

7. Milton M. Gordon, *Assimilation in American Life: The Role of Race, Religion, and National Origins* (New York: Oxford University Press, 1964).
8. Kerby A. Miller, *Ireland and Irish America: Culture, Class, and Transatlantic Migration* (Dublin: Field Day, 2008), 248.
9. Benedict Anderson, *Imagined Communities: Reflections on the Origin and Spread of Nationalism*, rev. edn (New York: Verso, 1991), 5–6.
10. Blessing, 'Irish Emigration', 12–13.
11. Ibid., 13–15; Kevin Kenny, *The American Irish: A History* (New York: Longman, 2000), 45–6.
12. Blessing, 'Irish Emigration', 11.
13. Ibid., 17; David M. Emmons, *The Butte Irish: Class and Ethnicity in an American Mining Town, 1875–1925* (Urbana: University of Illinois Press, 1990), 1–3; Kenny, *American Irish*, 89–91.
14. Richard Williams, *Hierarchical Structures and Social Value: The Creation of Black and Irish Identities in the United States* (New York: Cambridge University Press, 1990), 133. For a review of Famine historiography, see James S. Donnelly, Jr, *The Great Irish Potato Famine* (Charleston, S.C.: History Press, 2008). The classic work explaining the self-identity of nineteenth-century Irish Americans as 'exiles' is Kerby A. Miller, *Emigrants and Exiles: Ireland and the Irish Exodus to North America* (New York: Oxford University Press, 1985).
15. Emmons, *Butte Irish*, 3; Kenny, *American Irish*, 130–8.
16. Francis M. Carroll, *American Opinion and the Irish Question: 1910–1923* (New York: St Martin's Press, 1978), 3.
17. Blessing, 'Irish Emigration', 16, 19; Lawrence McCaffrey, 'Forging Forward and Looking Back', in *The New York Irish*, ed. Ronald H. Bayor and Timothy J. Meagher (Baltimore, Md.: Johns Hopkins University Press, 1996), 217.
18. Hasia Diner, *Erin's Daughters in America: Irish Immigrant Women in the Nineteenth Century* (Baltimore, Md.: Johns Hopkins University Press, 1983), 141, 70–5; Marjorie R. Fallows, *Irish Americans: Identity and Assimilation* (Englewood Cliffs, N.J.: Prentice-Hall, 1979), 27–30, 101. Janet A. Nolan provides an excellent review of the experience of Irish women in *Ourselves Alone: Women's Emigration from Ireland, 1885–1920* (Lexington: University Press of Kentucky, 1989).
19. Thomas Brown, *Irish-American Nationalism: 1870–1890* (Philadelphia: J.B. Lippincott, 1966), 35; Noel Ignatiev, *How the Irish Became White* (New York: Routledge, 1995), 39.
20. Kerby Miller, '"Scotch-Irish" Myths and "Irish" Identities in Eighteenth- and Nineteenth-Century America', in *New Perspectives on the Irish Diaspora*, ed. Charles Fanning (Carbondale, Ill.: Southern Illinois University Press, 2000), 76–80. The 'Republican' Party of Jefferson is not the same current Republican Party in the United States.
21. Fallows, *Irish Americans*, 26. The sociologist Richard Williams makes a similar argument, but he bases his conclusion on the assumption that Anglo-Americans based their negative perception of Irish Americans solely on economic grounds. That might be true for those Anglo-Americans in the lower economic levels, but it fails to explain the wider acceptance of the stereotype. See Williams, *Hierarchical Structures and Social Value*, 142–7.
22. Joseph M. Curran, *Hibernian Green on the Silver Screen: The Irish and American Movies* (New York: Greenwood Press, 1989), 5.
23. See William H.A. Williams, *'Twas Only an Irishman's Dream: The Image of Ireland and the Irish in American Popular Song Lyrics, 1800–1920* (Urbana: University of Illinois Press, 1996), especially 237–45. The Irish use of satire to counter stereotypes can be traced back to the 1820s; see Charles Fanning, *The Irish Voice in America: 250 Years of Irish-American Fiction*, 2nd edn (Lexington: University Press of Kentucky, 2000), 6–38.
24. Carroll, *American Opinion and the Irish Question*, 11.
25. McCaffrey, 'Forging Forward and Looking Back', 226.
26. Kenny, *American Irish*, 78.
27. Kevin Whelan, *The Tree of Liberty: Radicalism, Catholicism and the Construction of Irish Identity, 1760–1830* (Notre Dame, Ind.: University of Notre Dame Press, 1996), 55.
28. Ibid., 99–130; Glazer and Moynihan, *Beyond the Melting Pot*, 225; L.A. O'Donnell, *Irish Voice and Organized Labor in America: A Biographical Study* (Westport, Conn.: Greenwood Press, 1997), 202.
29. Quoted in Alan J. Ward, *Ireland and Anglo-American Relations, 1899–1921* (Toronto: University of Toronto Press, 1969), 7–8.

30. Kenny, *American Irish*, 128; McCaffrey, 'Forging Forward and Looking Back', 223. The term 'Fenian' referred to ancient warriors of Ireland as described in the Celtic myth of Fionna.
31. Brown, *Irish-American Nationalism*, 65–70.
32. Ibid., 23.
33. Ibid., 41.
34. Emmons, *Butte Irish*, 294.
35. George W. Potter, *To the Golden Door: The Story of the Irish in Ireland and America* (Westport, Conn.: Greenwood Press, 1973), 511.
36. Miller, *Emigrants and Exiles*, 550, see also 345–555; Sean Farrell Moran, 'Images, Icons and the Practice of Irish History', in *Images, Icons and the Irish Nationalist Imagination*, ed. Lawrence W. McBride (Dublin: Four Courts Press, 1999), 173. Moran deals with Irish nationalists, but his observations could easily be applied to Irish Americans as well.
37. Bayor and Meagher, 'Introduction', in *New York Irish*, 4; Miller, *Emigrants and Exiles*, 441–3. Ford quotation in Kenny, *American Irish*, 175.
38. For the most recent study of Devoy, see Terry Golway, *Irish Rebel: John Devoy and America's Fight for Ireland's Freedom* (New York: St Martin's Griffin, 1999).
39. Most historians argue that Devoy's interest in land reform and social issues was cosmetic and that his main goal was always the creation of an Irish republic. For example, see the most recent synthesis of Irish America, Kenny, *American Irish*, 175–80. Terry Golway, however, argues that Devoy 'was leading Irish-American nationalism into the wider world of social protest and progressive reform'. See Golway, *Irish Rebel*, 104, 103–13.
40. Quoted in Seán Cronin, *Washington's Irish Policy, 1916–1986: Independence, Partition, Neutrality* (Dublin: Anvil Books, 1987), 15.
41. Brown, *Irish-American Nationalism*, 85–130.
42. Alexander Sullivan to John Devoy, 13 October 1880, in William O'Brien and Desmond Ryan, eds, *Devoy's Post Bag, 1871–1928*, vol. 1, *1871–1880* (Dublin: C.J. Fallon, 1948), 556.
43. Meagher, 'Introduction', in *From Paddy to Studs*, 10; Alan J. Ward, 'America and the Irish Problem, 1899–1921', *Irish Historical Studies* 16, no. 61 (1968): 64.
44. Dennis Clark, *Erin's Heirs: Irish Bonds of Community* (Lexington: University Press of Kentucky, 1991), 2; William D. Griffin, *The Irish Americans* (New York: Hugh Lauter Levin Associates, 1998), 138–42; Ward, *Ireland and Anglo-American Relations*, 4.
45. Curran, *Hibernian Green*, 35; Thomas Rowland, 'Irish-American Catholics and the Quest of Respectability in the Coming of the Great War', *Journal of American Ethnic History* 15 (winter 1996): 8.
46. Rowland, 'Irish-American Catholics', 8.
47. Ibid., 9.
48. Timothy J. Meagher, *Inventing Irish America: Generation, Class, and Ethnic Identity in a New England City, 1880–1928* (Notre Dame: University of Notre Dame Press, 2001), 4. This sense of the importance of a Catholic identity cut across all regional Irish-American concentrations. See Meagher, 'Conclusion', in *From Paddy to Studs*, 181–8.
49. Curran, *Hibernian Green*, 10–13.
50. Ibid., 16–19; Ward, *Ireland and Anglo-American Relations*, 27.
51. John Duffy Ibson, *Will the World Break Your Heart?: Dimensions and Consequences of Irish-American Assimilation* (New York: Garland, 1990), 41.
52. Ibson, *Will the World?*, 43.
53. For an account of the influence of sports on Irish nationalism, see Mike Cronin, *Sport and Nationalism in Ireland: Gaelic Games, Soccer and Irish Identity since 1884* (Dublin: Four Courts Press, 1999).
54. For a discussion of the wider influence of the Gaelic League on cultural nationalism, see John Hutchinson, *The Dynamics of Cultural Nationalism: The Gaelic Revival and the Creation of the Irish Nation State* (Boston, Mass.: Allen & Unwin, 1987).
55. McCaffrey, 'Forging Forward and Looking Back', 224. On the founding of the *Gaelic American* and the Clan's effort to portray the British as trying to trick the United States into a military alliance, see Golway, *Irish Rebel*, 173–96.
56. Joseph P. O'Grady, *How the Irish Became Americans* (New York: Twayne, 1973); Ward, 'America and the Irish Problem', and Ward, *Ireland and Anglo-American Relations*.
57. This brief summary section relies heavily on R.F. Foster, *Modern Ireland 1600–1972*

(London: Allen Lane, 1988); Dermot Keogh, *Twentieth-Century Ireland: Nation and State* (New York: St Martin's Press, 1995); Declan Kiberd, *Inventing Ireland: The Literature of the Modern Nation* (Cambridge, Mass.: Harvard University Press, 1996); McBride, *Images and Icons*; and Charles Townshend, *Ireland: The Twentieth Century* (New York: Oxford University Press, 1998).

58. Quoted in Stephen Hartley, *The Irish Question as a Problem in British Foreign Policy, 1914–18* (New York: St Martin's Press, 1987), 11.

59. Foster, *Modern Ireland*, 471.

60. Michael Doorley, *Irish-American Diaspora Nationalism: The Friends of Irish Freedom, 1916–1935* (Portland, Oreg.: Four Courts Press, 2005), 38; Carroll, *American Opinion and the Irish Question*, 51–2; Golway, *Irish Rebel*, 215–20.

61. For quote, Carroll, *American Opinion and the Irish Question*, 65; see also 55–80. See also Cronin, *Washington's Irish Policy*, 18–20; Hartley, *The Irish Question as a Problem*, 195; Miller, *Emigrants and Exiles*, 541–5; Timothy Sarbaugh, 'British War Policies in Ireland, 1914–1948: The California Irish-American Reaction', *San Jose Studies* 9, no. 1 (1983): 112; and Ward, 'America and the Irish Problem', 24.

62. Quoted in Thomas J. Noer, 'The American Government and the Irish Question During World War I', *South Atlantic Quarterly* 72, no. 1 (1973): 95, 98.

63. *Dáil Debates*, 21 January 1919, col. 20.

64. Cronin, *Washington's Irish Policy*, 22–3; O'Grady, *How the Irish Became Americans*, 128–30; Ward, 'America and the Irish Problem', 84–7.

65. 'De Valera to Arthur Griffith', 17 February 1920, National Archives of Ireland, Dáil Éireann files, 2/245 (hereafter as NAI/DE with file numbers). For the implications of de Valera's tour on his views of Irish America, see Troy D. Davis, 'Éamon de Valéra's Political Education: The American Tour of 1919–20', *New Hibernia Review/Irish Éireanach Nua* 10, no. 1 (spring 2006): 65–78.

66. Writing in 1929, Winston Churchill argued that the passage of the Government of Ireland Act made 'the position of Ulster unassailable … The Act of 1920 ended for ever that phase of the Irish Problem'. Winston Churchill, *The Aftermath* (New York: Charles Scribner's Sons, 1929), 299–300.

67. 'Éamon de Valera to Harry Boland (Washington)', Dublin, 29 November 1921, in Royal Irish Academy and Department of Foreign Affairs, *Documents on Irish Foreign Policy*, vol. 1, *1919–1922*, ed. Ronan Fanning and others (Dublin: Royal Irish Academy, 1998), 318–19 (hereafter as *DIFP*, vol. number and document number).

68. 'Final Text of the Articles of Agreement for a Treaty between Great Britain and Ireland as Signed, London, 6 December 1921', NAI/DE/2/304/1.

69. 'T.A. Smiddy to George Gavan Duffy', 28 April 1922, *DIFP*, vol. 1, doc. 270; 'Lester to Cosgrave', 10 May 1923, *DIFP*, vol. 2, doc. 80.

70. As an example of the concern over international image, Irish diplomats routinely carried the Irish flag to international sporting events out of fear that organizers would use the Union Jack as the symbol of Irish athletes. Such was the case in Belgium in 1926. See Gerard Keown, 'Taking the World Stage: Creating an Irish Foreign Policy in the 1920s', in *Irish Foreign Policy, 1919–66: From Independence to Internationalism*, ed. Michael Kennedy and Joseph Morrison Skelly (Dublin: Four Courts Press, 2000), 38.

71. Troy D. Davis, 'Diplomacy as Propaganda: The Appointment of T.A. Smiddy as Irish Free State Minister to the United States', *Eire-Ireland* 31, nos. 3–4 (1996): 117; Cronin, *Washington's Irish Policy*, 47; Keown, 'Taking the World Stage', and 'Duffy to Smiddy', 10 March 1922, *DIFP*, vol. 1, doc. 250.

72. 'O'Hegarty to MacNeill', 19 October 1923, National Archives of Ireland, Department of the Taoiseach, S1983A (hereafter as NAI/DT with file number). 'Healy to Thomas', 3 March 1924, NAI/DT/S1983.

73. 'Secret and Confidential Memorandum', 10 February 1923, *DIFP*, vol. 2, doc. 35; D. W. Harkness, *The Restless Dominion: The Irish Free State and the British Commonwealth of Nations, 1921–31* (New York: New York University Press, 1970); Michael Kennedy, *Ireland and the League of Nations, 1919–1946: International Relations, Diplomacy, and Politics* (Dublin: Irish Academic Press, 1996); Keown, 'Taking the World Stage.'

74. Keown, 'Taking the World Stage', 33–4. For Irish American opposition to Ireland's entry into

the League, see 'Smiddy to FitzGerald', Washington, 20 April 1923, *DIFP*, vol. 2, doc. 67. The definitive work on Irish actions within the Commonwealth during the 1920s is Harkness's *Restless Dominion*.

75. 'Memorandum by the Council of Defence on Irish Defence Policy (Secret)', 22 July 1925, NAI/DT/S4541. For more on Smiddy's efforts to cultivate Irish American and the wider American press, see 'Smiddy to FitzGerald', 5 May 1924, *DFIP*, vol 2, no. 212.
76. Fallows, *Identity and Assimilation*, 80.
77. John Patrick Buckley, *The New York Irish: Their View of American Foreign Policy, 1914–1921* (New York: Arno Press, 1976), 389–90.
78. Miller, *Emigrants and Exiles*, 493, 555.

2

Searching for Identities: 1932–1939

Let it be made clear that we yield no willing assent to any form or symbol that is out of keeping with Ireland's right as a sovereign nation. Let us remove these forms one by one, so that this State that we control may be a Republic in fact. (Éamon de Valera, 1933)[1]

True, some of our people still hold high places in the various phases of our city, state and national life, but what about the hundreds of thousands who are never heard from, who are the backbone of our race? (Daniel Danaher, American Federation of Irish Societies, 1938)[2]

The Irish and Irish-American efforts to create identity during the 1930s shared a set of characteristics, and each played out within the context of the other. De Valera's programme of the 1930s envisioned an Ireland that could gain the respect and acceptance on the world stage worthy of a truly sovereign nation. He sought to dismantle both the symbolic and real impediments to that by creating a neutral, economically viable, Catholic Gaelic state and enlisted Irish-American support in that effort. Similarly, Irish Americans, while proud of their advancement to higher positions within American society, never felt that their accomplishments equated to acceptance. Many Irish Americans felt left out of the American dream, and their culture reflected that sense of displacement.

In Ireland, Éamon de Valera embodied a similar search for identity and a place in the world for the Irish. He spent much of the 1930s trying to give birth to a renewed and truly independent Catholic rural nation, and he continually turned to Irish America for support in that effort. In the United States, Irish Americans attempted to establish their place in American culture, and in Ireland De Valera and the Irish attempted to forge independent economic and diplomatic strategies. Both were looking for acceptance.

IRISH AMERICANS IN THE 1920S AND 1930S

Most histories of Irish America mark 1920 or 1921 as the point at which extensive Irish-American participation in the Irish nationalist movement ceased, a product of the creation of the Irish Free State and Irish-American lack of understanding, and hence concern, over the issues that triggered the Irish Civil War. A typical example comes from the conclusion to *How the Irish Became Americans* by Joseph O'Grady: 'By the 1930s and 1940s, Irishmen were absorbed into American life, pursuing their careers as Americans and not as Irish-Americans.'[3] While it may be true that the level of Irish-American participation in Irish national affairs dropped considerably, Irish-American organizations such as the Clan na Gael continued to be an important part of Irish-American identity for many people. This standard interpretation misses the mark, however, when it implies that this development meant that Irish Americans had assimilated into American society to such a degree by the early 1920s that they had lost their sense of 'Irishness'.

Charles Fanning more accurately describes Irish America in the 1920s and 1930s as an 'ambivalent culture in transition', a transition that continued well through World War Two.[4] In fact, in the 1920s and 1930s many Irish Americans began to explore other dimensions of their Irish identities, and they continued to cultivate that identity, primarily as a result of their lack of full integration into American society. The marginalization process was especially true for lower-class and working-class Irish Americans. The economic effects of the Great Depression during the 1930s reinforced their fringe status within American society and helped to renew the latent anti-Catholicism in the dominant culture, which had helped to fuel the immigration restrictions of the previous decade.

Historian Timothy Meagher opens his investigation of Irish-Americans' 'quest to define their identity' in 1880–1920 with a discussion of Patrick Lonigan's reflections about the changing nature of Irish-American neighbourhoods at the start of James Farrell's fictional *Studs Lonigan* trilogy. Farrell wrote the trilogy in the 1930s, but Meagher focuses on the opening, set in 1916, when Patrick, Studs' father, remembers his immigrant parents and impoverished childhood. Now, by 1916, Patrick Lonigan declares himself 'comfortable and content', 'a good Catholic and a good American', yet not quite at home with himself or society. Meagher argues that there were 'thousands, perhaps millions' of Irish Americans like Lonigan in 1916, and that Farrell's observations of Irish America reflect a 1930s reality.[5] In fact the Irish-American search for identity and acceptance into mainstream

American society did not resolve itself in 1920; it continued throughout most of the twentieth century. Reflecting on his own childhood
growing up Irish and Catholic in 1950s America, Gary Wills recalled
that 'we grew up different ... there were places we went and others did
not ... and also places we never went and others could'. Irish
Americans were 'stranded in America, out of place'.[6]

The severe dislocation of the Great Depression saddled Irish
Americans struggling to gain firmer social ground with an added burden
in their effort to be a part of the American mainstream. In addition to
the continuing anti-Catholic prejudices, they now had to deal with the
fallout from an economic downturn that affected all classes, regions
and ethnic groups. The economic challenge delayed Irish America's
journey to acceptance and assimilation.

In 1929 the *Irish World* editorialized about the basic insecurity of
the Irish in America: 'We see all around us, the people of other races
forging ahead.'[7] This insecurity would lead to conflicts between Irish
Americans and other ethnic groups, especially Jews, struggling to maintain their economic and social position in a desperate economic envi-
ronment.[8] Irish Americans felt that 1930s America did not truly accept
them, in part owing to the anti-immigrant political developments of
the 1920s, the renewed Ku Klux Klan and the anti-Catholic backlash
from Al Smith's 1928 presidential campaign, among other developments that highlighted for Irish Americans their outsider status.
Historian Kevin Kenny correctly assesses that Irish-American support
for Father Charles Coughlin, the anti-Semitic 'radio priest', reflected a
basic insecurity and anti-Semitism on the part of middle-class and
working-class Irish Americans who were 'not fully assimilated into the
American mainstream despite several generations in this country'.[9]

One of the best ways to examine the state of Irish America in the
1930s is to examine how Irish Americans portrayed themselves and
their situation. The continuing success of George McManus's popular
comic strip, 'Bringing Up Father', highlighted tensions within the Irish-
American community about their level of acceptance into the wider
culture. Its popularity made McManus the highest paid cartoonist of
his time.[10] In the 1930s the strip's main characters, Maggie and Jiggs,
began a series of reminiscences about the social relationships of their old
Irish-American neighbourhood, relationships that were unattainable
given their current situation. A strip from 1933 (figure 2.1) is one of
many in a continuing series about Irish-American reminiscences. The
second strip (figure 2.2) is a 1936 piece satirizing the social unease felt
by many middle-class Irish Americans and their longing for the ethnic

2.1 McManus's 'Bringing Up Father' from 1933, © King Features[11]

community's urban past. The popularity of the strip during the 1930s and 1940s, especially among Irish Americans, testifies to its ability to tap into an important element of the Irish-American experience.

These selections showcase McManus's recurring theme of the tension between success and alienation. His characters often reminisce about the social life of the ' old neighborhood', replete with the darker

2.2 'Bringing Up Father', 1936, © King Features[12]

elements of criminals and drunks. In spite of a lack of material wealth, the characters seem happier and more connected. When, as seen in the second strip, McManus portrays Jiggs's material success, it is always tempered by a lack of spiritual fulfilment. Jiggs would much rather go back to the pleasures of his old friends.

In literature, John O'Hara's characters in *BUtterfield 8* offer the fullest expression of the experience of many Irish Americans in the 1930s; they reflect the particular strands of alienation evident in the self-identity of so many. O'Hara was born in 1905 to a prosperous Irish Catholic family in Pottsville, Pennsylvania. His father was a doctor, yet in spite of his family's standing, O'Hara never felt accepted by the local Protestant elites. He left Pottsville in 1928, but it became the setting (Gibbsville) for most of his best fiction.[13] In *BUtterfield 8*, James Malloy tells his girlfriend: 'I want to tell you something about myself that will help to explain a lot of things about me ... First of all, I am a Mick.' Malloy says that even the Irish were 'non-assimilable'; he maintains the outward appearances of acceptance and argues that he is 'pretty God damn American, and therefore my brothers and sisters are, and yet we're not Americans'.[14] It is clear that O'Hara's Irish Catholic background served as the backdrop to his fiction and his insights into Irish-American life in the early part of the twentieth century. He modelled his characters after himself, his family and his friends. The struggles of gaining wider acceptance into American society take the foreground in his work. O'Hara himself described his schoolmates as 'the Studs Lonigans of our place and time', evoking the eponymous creation of James T. Farrell.[15]

Farrell is the other most important literary interpreter of the Irish-American experience in the 1930s. After growing up as the son of an Irish-born teamster in a tough Irish neighbourhood on Chicago's South Side, Farrell used his fiction to examine the economic, cultural and spiritual impoverishment that he experienced living in Irish America in the 1930s.[16] In the *Studs Lonigan* trilogy, Farrell creates the story of Studs Lonigan, an Irish Catholic kid from Chicago's South Side who struggles to find his way in the world, ultimately dying a tragic death in his family's home. Farrell later wrote that one of the most important goals he had for the work was 'to reveal the concrete effects of spiritual poverty'.[17] He wanted to capture the sense that even as Irish Americans were moving up the economic ladder, they never truly became a part of the mainstream, in part because of their Catholicism. The novel starts in 1916 with Studs graduating from the eighth grade of St Patrick's school. He barely goes to high school, finishing only two years, and spends his days roaming the streets of Chicago. He later works for his father's painting business, but as that slowly begins to unravel, so too does Studs. At one point, a couple of friends have this exchange: '"Andy, are the Irish hundred-per-cent Americans?" "No, because they believe in the Pope."' He dreams of a boyhood crush,

Lucy, and carries her as a lifelong fantasy that will make him a true man, carrying him out of the despair and uncertainty of the South Side. After his family finally moves from the neighbourhood, Studs feels lost. He goes back, only to find that the old gang are gone, dead or in prison. On a trip back from one friend's funeral, Studs sits alone on the train:

> It was funny that he should be riding home now from the funeral of Shrimp Haggerty, and so many things should have been changed from what they used to be, and from what he had expected them to become. But since his kid days, there had been many years, all piled on top of one another, and now, each year, each month, each week, each day, every hour, every minute and every second even, carried him further and further away from them, just as if he was on a moving express train which was shooting him forever away from some place where he very much wanted to be, and all the while carrying him nearer and nearer ... to his own death.[18]

Near the end of the trilogy, and with a sense of being lost in the world that is similar to that which McManus captured in his mid-1930s cartoons, Patrick Lonigan, as his son Studs is at home dying, drives around the old neighbourhood longing for the certainty and security that came with the familiar. Faced with economic ruin as the Depression deepened, Patrick saw 'another closed bank ... more men on the corners. Kids. More idle men'.[19]

Farrell was remarkably conscious of the dual identity of the Irish American in the 1930s and utilized his writing to bring out that underlying uncertainty and searching. Writing in 1932 to Ezra Pound, who had just read the galleys of *Young Lonigan*, the first part of the trilogy, Farrell commented: 'As to the Irishness of it. I generally feel that I'm an Irishman rather than an American.' Later, in 1962, Farrell wrote: ' I am a second-generation Irish-American. The effects and scars of immigration are upon my life. The past was dragging through my boyhood and adolescence.' Charles Fanning's assessment of Farrell's portrayal of Irish Americans in the 1930s is correct: 'In their struggles, silences, and unshared epiphanies, their alienation and loneliness and endurance, Farrell's Irish continue to express essential realities of American immigrant and ethnic experience.'[20]

John Ford, the legendary second-generation Irish-American film director, made his first two sound movies explicitly about Ireland in the 1930s: *The Informer* and *The Plough and the Stars*. Ford, perhaps more than any other filmmaker, helped to convey and reflect the wider culture's prewar views of Ireland, and by extension, Irish America. The son of Irish immigrants and fluent in Irish, Ford brought his Irish Catholic upbringing and outlook to his movies. *The Informer*, his adaptation of Liam O'Flaherty's novel about an Irish Republican Army informer, follows a dark pattern of shame, remorse and forgiveness, while stressing the overriding values of solidarity within Ford's 'militant nationalist' views. *The Plough and the Stars*, Ford's depiction of Sean O'Casey's play about a widow whose husband dies in the Easter Rising, portrays Irish nationalism in a sympathetic and romantic light. In effect, Ford portrayed the longing of Irish Americans to be a true part of the American dream.[21]

The fictional representations Irish Americans made of their 1930s alienation finds confirmation in historical works examining the period. In her study of St Sabina's and other Catholic parishes in Chicago, ones very much like the real and fictional parishes of Farrell, Eileen McMahon shows how much the church proved to be a vehicle for Irish-American identity throughout the first half of the twentieth century. Faced with rising economic status but 'second-class citizenship' in a predominantly Anglo-Protestant community, Irish Americans clung to their church as a way to maintain 'an integral part of their identity'. This sense of exclusion from the mainstream led to feelings of 'defensiveness' on the part of the parishioners, much like that of Lonigan.[22]

This interplay between self-identity and the perceptions of others was a defining characteristic of Irish American culture during the 1930s. It provided a fertile ground for Irish policy makers to find assistance during Ireland's identity project, as a similar dynamic played itself out in how Ireland attempted to create an Irish identity for itself during the same period. While the vast majority of Irish Americans were not active participants in Irish affairs, the Irish government continued to look for their support and found many willing to help.

BRITISH–IRISH RELATIONS AND IRISH AMERICANS IN THE 1930S

By the late 1920s de Valera realized that his movement could have no real influence in Ireland without returning to electoral politics. Released from jail in 1924 following the Irish Civil War, de Valera sought to persuade members of his Sinn Féin party that they had to take part in the Dáil. This would require accepting the distasteful oath of allegiance to the British throne needed in order to take their seats. The eventual party split on this issue pushed de Valera and his followers to establish a new party, Fianna Fáil (Soldiers of Destiny), in April 1926. De Valera tried

to get Joseph McGarrity and other physical-force Irish-American nationalists to support the new party by arguing that 'unless those who stand
for the Republican cause can get a majority of the elected representatives
of the people on their side, there can be no success for force'.[23] In the
June 1927 elections Fianna Fáil won forty-four seats and announced
that the deputies would claim their seats in the Dáil without taking the
oath. In August de Valera and the other members of his party took the
oath (with 'mental reservations' and declaring in Irish that signing
the oath was not actually taking the oath) in an effort to be part of the
Dáil debates about forming a new coalition government. That effort
failed, but the party was now the predominant opposition party in the
parliament.[24]

De Valera and Fianna Fáil had as their overriding goal in the 1930s
the creation of a state entirely independent of Great Britain: politically,
militarily, culturally and economically. This mission centred on policies
designed to create an internal and external Irish identity that reflected
de Valera's vision of a self-contained, rural, Gaelic, Catholic state. De
Valera outlined his vision for Ireland in the February 1932 Fianna Fáil
election manifesto. He sought above all to remove the oath that bound
members of the Dáil to declare allegiance to the British crown, to reunite
the island and to keep the land annuity payments that the Irish government had been sending to Great Britain. In addition, he sought tariff pro-
tection for Irish agriculture and industry as well as the expansion of Irish
as a national language. The overall goal was to create a sustainable
national identity at home and abroad.[25]

De Valera realized that British–Irish relations were pivotal aspects of
his programme, and so when his party took power in 1932 he maintained the External Affairs portfolio for himself. His vision of a
renewed Irish identity rested on his hopes for an undivided Ireland that
could stand separately from Great Britain in all fields, from economics
to language. He knew, however, that the geographic proximity of the
two states and the long list of historical interconnections would make
that difficult. He was already receiving advice to take a hard-line
approach in order to isolate Great Britain internationally by using the
power of the Irish living abroad. Officials in the US State Department
were concerned that de Valera's election would mean a renewed tension between Ireland and Great Britain and a 'renewal of anti-British
agitation by Irish elements in the United States'.[26]

One of the first tasks facing de Valera was determining how to deal
with his old cohort, those who did not follow him into constitutional
politics by joining Fianna Fáil, but, rather, remained committed to the

physical-force nationalism espoused by the Irish Republican Army (IRA) and its Irish-American allies and financiers. De Valera met with the IRA leader Sean MacBride several times in 1932 and 1933 in an effort to win him over to Fianna Fáil's newly found faith in constitutional politics. In an effort to convince Irish-American activists, chief among them the Clan na Gael leader Joseph McGarrity, de Valera sent the Irish Vice-Premier Sean T. O'Kelly to the United States. De Valera made clear the importance of persuading Irish America to join in his efforts: 'If our friends over there could be got to bring pressure on the IRA to throw their weight behind the Government, tremendous progress could be made.'[27]

McGarrity and the IRA remained unconvinced. McGarrity, writing to de Valera, argued that the IRA and Fianna Fáil could benefit from a working agreement that would allow the IRA to 'do the things that you will not care to do', presumably carry out bombing missions.[28] De Valera responded back angrily:

> Is this need and desire for unity to be used as a means of trying to blackmail us into adopting a policy which we know could only lead our people to disaster? ... What is the use of talking any more with people who are too stupid or too pig-headed to see this ... We have undertaken a responsibility to the people at present living, to the future, and to the dead. We will not allow any group or any individuals to prevent us from carrying it out.[29]

De Valera then refocused his efforts on British–Irish relations, specifically the oath of allegiance. British objections to the removal of the oath revolved around two concerns. The first was what the removal meant for the place of Ireland within the Commonwealth. The second, and more important concern, was what the oath's removal from the Irish Constitution portended for the future of the entire Anglo-Irish Treaty of 1921.[30] De Valera countered that the Irish Constitution was a purely domestic matter and that the British government had imposed the oath on the Irish government, which only accepted it under the threat of war. In the Dáil, de Valera argued that if Commonwealth nations had equal status under the law, then the fact that the British Parliament could enact legislation dissolving the oath for MPs at Westminster meant that the Dáil should have the same right to do so for its members.[31] For de Valera, the removal of the oath, which was an integral element of his election platform, represented the first step in creating a truly independent Ireland. The Dáil passed the Constitution (Removal of Oath) Act on 19 May 1932.[32]

De Valera's attempt to create a new Irish identity also included a religious component. As such, he was glad to build on the planning begun under the previous government to host the 31st International Eucharistic Congress in June 1932. De Valera was a deeply religious man, but the Irish hierarchy had united against him during the Irish Civil War. De Valera saw the Congress as a perfect vehicle to shore up his relations with the nation's bishops, showcase Ireland's independence to the world and reaffirm his view that the nation's Catholic faith was an integral element of its identity. Representatives from around the world converged in Dublin, and the event culminated with a Mass attended by more than one million people. The entire event was a 'manifestation of Catholic nationalism'.[33]

De Valera saw the Economic War, precipitated by his refusal to pay the land annuities, as another step to realizing his wider vision of Ireland's identity. These payments stemmed from various British Land Acts that were designed to finance Irish farmers' purchases of land on which they had been tenants previously. De Valera based his position on the fact that the previous government of William Cosgrave had never submitted the 1926 agreement, which called for the payments, to the Dáil. Although realizing that the economic dislocation from British retaliation would harm Ireland's industrial sector, de Valera was willing to make the sacrifice because it would be 'made up by the foundation here of the sort of economic life that every Irishman who thought nationally in the past hoped for and prayed for and, so far as he was able in his own time, worked for'.[34] De Valera hoped that economic strife with Great Britain would help to bring about the pastoral vision of Irish identity so near to his heart.

Negotiations between Ireland and Great Britain over the disputed land annuity payments continued during the spring and early summer of 1932. They collapsed, however, on 1 July when de Valera withheld £1.5 million due to the British, who soon retaliated by imposing a 20 per cent duty on most Irish imports. Part of the British negotiating strategy was to make the economic suffering so tough on the Irish that de Valera would lose the next election. British policy makers held out for that goal while at the same time voicing concern that too tough a stance would put them at odds with other members of the Commonwealth.[35] The British were also concerned about the lasting effects of an economic war with Ireland on its relations with the United States. Members of the Foreign Office and business leaders who had dealings in both Ireland and the United States raised their concerns with the government's Irish Situation Committee, which had been organized that March. In August the British Lord Chancellor wrote: 'the present situation cannot be allowed to go on forever'.[36]

Despite these warnings, British Prime Minister James Macdonald was hesitant to pursue further negotiations with de Valera. MacDonald headed a coalition government that had to work with a vocal Conservative press and Conservative politicians who argued that nego-tiation with or concessions to de Valera would simply lead to a long list of additional Irish demands. He also felt the chilling effect of Winston Churchill, who was waiting in the wings hoping to form a Conservative government, and insisted: 'English people are better pleased that the Duties are weighing on the Irish ... and they will be very sulky if any-thing happens to take these duties off, and woe unto the man by whom it happens.'[37] The Anglo-Irish Economic War had begun, and it would continue until 1938.

De Valera, in his bid to create an independent Irish identity, took on another battle with the British in 1932. Irish republicans had always resented the symbolism of the British crown's dominion of Ireland, especially as it was represented by the office of the Governor-General, who was appointed by the King. De Valera, through John Dulanty, the Irish High Commissioner in London, requested in September that King George V remove James McNeill as Governor-General. By the end of November, McNeill was gone and de Valera had the King appoint one of Dev's old supporters to the office. As was planned by de Valera, the new Governor-General did not take up residence in the official Viceregal Lodge and did not attend social functions. De Valera effec-tively eliminated this public symbol of the British monarch's role in Irish affairs.[38]

It was not long after Fianna Fáil's second government took office, after the general election of January 1933, that de Valera started to enlist the support of Irish Americans in his vision to remake Ireland. Drawing on references to Lincoln's saving the Union, de Valera made his case that the partition of Ireland was 'imposed by force' and is 'main-tained by subsidies' solely to satisfy British imperial policy. He derided the notion that partition was necessary to prevent the religious persecution of a minority as 'an invention without any basis in the facts'. What the British in fact had done, according to de Valera, was to create a reli-gious minority by forcing Northern Catholics to live in an artificial state where they became the persecuted. He ended by appealing for the help of our 'generous and loyal' friends.[39]

De Valera outlined his continuing assault on the Treaty and the sym-bolic and substantive signs of British power over Ireland in an important

April 1933 speech commemorating the fallen leaders of the 1916 Rising. After opening remarks in Irish that hailed the military defeat in 1916 as the spark that ignited modern republicanism among the majority of the Irish people, de Valera spelled out what would become his policies for the next six years:

> Let it be made clear that we yield no willing assent to any form or symbol that is out of keeping with Ireland's right as a sovereign nation. Let us remove these forms one by one, so that this State that we control may be a Republic in fact and that, when the time comes, the proclaiming of the Republic may involve no more than a ceremony, the formal confirmation of a status already attained.[40]

The intense efforts made by de Valera to remove all vestiges of British rule from Irish life embroiled the US Department of State during the credentials presentation of the newly appointed minister to Ireland, William McDowell, in March 1934. McDowell presented his credentials directly to de Valera and not to the Governor-General, as had been the custom. Even though the British had cleared the procedure beforehand, when Irish Vice-Premier Seán T. O'Kelly used the occasion to announce that 'every day something is being done to oust the British from control of our county', the de Valera regime assured listeners that the Irish, British and American press would highlight the ceremony and the remark.[41]

While working now as the leader of the Irish government to define Irish independence and identity against the legacies of British rule, de Valera also had to negotiate challenges from his former Irish and American allies who did not abandon physical-force nationalism. After the split with de Valera, the IRA and its American supporters faced a crucial turning point. Internal struggles over the strategy to achieve a united Irish Republic began to revolve around precisely what social policy the organization would call for in the as yet unrealized new state. Many IRA leaders, including James Graltan, who lived in the United States from 1909 until 1932, called for a Republican Congress that would be an 'organizing centre for anti-Imperialist activity'. This short-lived movement split the IRA when the governing Army Council forbade members to be a part of the Congress. While only a few members left, the split left the IRA operating from a weakened position for the rest of the decade, even before de Valera began his full-scale assault on his old comrades.[42]

After the split, Joseph McGarrity in Philadelphia drafted a plan for the future of IRA activities. Hoping to lift the spirits of IRA members,

McGarrity argued that future IRA activities should focus on ending partition, eliminating from the group's agenda the fight over the legitimacy of the Irish government in Dublin. McGarrity wanted to carry the fight to the North and to England. The goal would be the 'demoralization of the enemy', in an attempt to make the cost of keeping partition too high for the British government and public. The opening phase of the campaign should be public, McGarrity argued, in order to influence public opinion in the United States and Great Britain before any bombing took place. He wanted to once again 'make the name of Ireland a household word in America'.[43] The small and ineffective bombing campaign threatened to derail de Valera's diplomacy when it finally started in 1939.

While the IRA was planning violence, the Irish and British governments began to explore ways to end, or at least tamp down, the Economic War. The main impetus came from the British, because it had become clear to them that the economic pressure had failed to drive de Valera from power and moreover that the British economy was suffering as much or worse than the Irish economy. In addition, the growing international instability stemming from Hitler's rise in Germany led many policy makers to rethink the value of maintaining such an adversarial relationship with Ireland. Two British officials and the Irish representative to London initiated the conversations: Neville Chamberlain, then Chancellor of the Exchequer; Sir Warren Fisher, the Permanent Secretary of the Treasury; and the Irish government's High Commissioner in London, John Dulanty. Chamberlain was concerned with the depressed coal and shipbuilding districts; Fisher had long been troubled about the state of British–Irish relations, realizing that the Irish had 'in the past been desperately wronged'; Dulanty felt that the Economic War was a mistake and had been looking to end it 'from its inception'.[44]

After meeting with Irish representatives who stopped in London in October 1934 en route to Germany to negotiate the transfer of Irish cattle for German coal and iron, Dulanty hoped a similar arrangement could be made between Ireland and Great Britain. He sounded out Fisher about having Great Britain increase the quota of Irish cattle to the fullest amount possible, with the Irish then diverting coal orders from Germany or Poland to South Wales in an equal amount. Negotiations proceeded very quickly and the widely praised Coal–Cattle Pact announcement came on 3 January 1935. The pact, however, did not result in further movement to a political settlement, nor did it address many of the wider economic issues.[45]

The next important movement in British–Irish relations came after Malcolm MacDonald joined the British Cabinet in November 1935 as Secretary of State for the Dominions. His job was to find a way to improve Britain's relations with Ireland as the British government was becoming increasingly concerned with settling matters before relations with Nazi Germany became critical. After several clandestine meetings with de Valera, MacDonald produced a report for the Irish Situation Committee that concluded that there was an opportunity for a break-through in relations, that the British public would not look kindly on a missed chance at resolution, and that the state of British–Irish relations was 'unsatisfactory in itself, and inevitably tends to weaken the moral authority of the British Commonwealth of Nations in world affairs'.[46] Discussing Britain's position with regard to Germany over its breaches of the Locarno Pact (that dealt with German demilitarized zones), he argued more explicitly that 'without ridicule or damage' British policy could not be 'less realistic and generous in our treatment of a Dominion Government than in our treatment of a Foreign Government'.[47] MacDonald convinced the majority of the Cabinet, including the soon-to-be prime minister Neville Chamberlain, that British policy should accommodate Irish demands as much as possible, as long as Ireland remained in the Commonwealth.

Part of the Cabinet's reasoning for working with de Valera was the sense that while his rhetoric might make it difficult to sell any agreement to the British public, any deal struck with him would more than likely bring with it the acceptance of all but the most radical Irish republicans. In order to shore up his own credentials and to diminish any attacks, either political or military, from the right, de Valera proclaimed the IRA an 'unlawful association' on 18 June 1936.[48] The order solidified in British eyes de Valera's ability to have Irish republicans adhere to any agreement. De Valera's political opponents in the Dáil, although not in favour of physical-force tactics, charged him with a complete reversal of his position. De Valera countered that the repeal of the obligation to take an oath to the crown, previously required in order to take a seat in the Dáil, removed the last obstacle to any person's full participation in the government. There was, therefore, no more need for groups such as the IRA.[49]

Yet the IRA was hardly willing to walk away quietly or to disband. While much of the IRA's ruling Army Council urged a time of restraint and regrouping, the Quartermaster-General Richard Russell believed only a renewed campaign could save the organization and end partition. The Irish government's outlawing of the IRA forced the group to turn even more to its supporters in Irish America, chief among them Joseph McGarrity. Russell went to the United States in July 1936, met with McGarrity, and together the two reached a 'complete understanding' on a bombing campaign in Britain, with McGarrity pledging Irish-American money and support. Upon Russell's return to Ireland, the Army Council court-martialled and suspended him. He continued his planning, however, and returned to the United States in 1937, visiting Clan na Gael groups in Pittsburgh, Cleveland, Chicago, San Francisco, Boston, New York City and the largely Irish-American Butte, Montana. In November 1937 he wrote to McGarrity that only a few of the groups wanted to postpone the bombing campaign until a vote of the IRA's Army Council.[50] At the Council's meeting in April 1938, Russell supporters took over a majority of the Council, eliminating a logistical barrier to the campaign planned for the next year.

In the meantime, de Valera took advantage of the crisis precipitated by King Edward VIII's abdication in December 1936 to advance Irish efforts at securing a more independent Ireland. De Valera moved to exploit the situation to remove the role of the monarch in any Irish internal affairs, but to retain its role in certain matters of foreign relations. The unusual transfer of power of the throne meant all of the Dominions had to pass legislation to regularize their relations with their new head of state, but on 10 December de Valera merely told the British Dominions Office the title of the two bills he planned to introduce, not what the bills would do. He was very concerned about the timing of the legislation and the abdication out of fear that the British Parliament's legislation concerning the transfer of royal power be construed as that body legislating for Ireland. The first bill de Valera introduced, the Constitution (Amendment No. 27) Bill, removed all references in the Irish constitution to the King and the Governor-General. In effect, the executive authority of the state no longer flowed from the authority of the British crown, but resided in the power of the Executive Council. With Fianna Fáil's majority in the Dáil, the bill passed easily. De Valera thought it was the best he could do 'at this stage'.[51]

Once the constitution no longer contained references to the British crown, de Valera had to deal with the potentially difficult issue of diplomatic activity. All diplomats in Ireland held official status because of their accreditation by the King. Likewise, Irish diplomats in other countries carried credentials from the King. To lack any legal association with the British crown placed all of the state's diplomatic activity into legal limbo. De Valera always had the option of simply declaring Ireland a republic, but he did not want to declare a twenty-six county republic (detached from Northern Ireland) and felt that declaring an all-Ireland thirty-two county republic while the British were in the midst of a constitutional crisis would only invite more difficult problems down the road. His solution was to rush through the External Relations Act that he had been working on for some time. This Act stated that as long as Ireland remained in the Commonwealth, the British monarch would, 'when advised by the Executive Council to do, be authorized to work on behalf of the state for the appointment of representatives and the conclusion of international agreements'.[52]

Irish-American leaders from the American Association for the Recognition of the Irish Republic (AARIR) faulted de Valera for not taking fuller advantage of the abdication crisis by establishing a republic and severing all ties with the British crown and Commonwealth. De Valera had founded the AARIR in December 1920 visit to the United States as a result of his split with Irish-American leaders over the priorities of Irish-American organizations. Now, AARIR leaders were criticizing de Valera for voluntarily aligning with the British by allowing the British crown to continue its involvement in Ireland's foreign affairs. Many AARIR leaders questioned whether the organization could continue to support Fianna Fáil, complaining that 'this was the first time in history that there had been free acknowledgment of the sovereignty of a British King'. The secretary of the Irish Legation in Washington, Robert Brennan, argued back that the Act gave the King no control of Ireland's foreign policy, that the Act could always be amended with a simple vote of the Dáil, and that eliminating the King completely could lead to renewed economic reprisals from Britain. Most important, and what he reported to Dublin as being the most persuasive argument, he told Irish Americans that only Fianna Fáil 'could march any further on the road to freedom'. Breaking with Fianna Fáil would mean that the AARIR would no longer have any ability to be a part of that march.[53]

DE VALERA'S CONSTITUTION

The next step in de Valera's identity project was the 1937 Irish Constitution. *Bunreacht na hÉireann*, literally 'Ireland's Basic Law', fundamentally changed the Irish nation's self-identity as an independent state. Structurally, the constitution made important changes in the government's operating procedures. First, the official name of the state changed from Saorstát Éireann, or Irish Free State, to 'Éire, or in the English language, Ireland' (Article 4). The new office of the President assumed the duties of the head of state, although without any real power. The Taoiseach (pronounced tee-shock), literally 'Chief', was entrusted with the powers of 'head of Government, or Prime Minister', replacing the President of the Executive Council (Article 13). The constitution did not, though, declare Ireland to be a republic.[54]

The most significant aspects of the new constitution related to the nature of the Irish state. The preamble cited the 'Most Holy Trinity' as the basis of all temporal authority and acknowledged the nation's 'obligations to our Divine Lord, Jesus Christ'. Article 1 stated the basis of the constitution, reiterating de Valera's most valued political philosophies:

> The Irish nation hereby affirms its inalienable, indefeasible, and sovereign right to choose its own form of Government, to determine its relations with other nations, and to develop its life, political, economic and cultural, in accordance with its own genius and traditions.

Article 2 declared that the national territory of the state was 'the whole island of Ireland', but Article 3 acknowledged the political reality that the laws and actions of the state were limited to the twenty-six counties in the South.[55] The constitution enshrined Irish and English respectively as the first and second official languages. Even though de Valera drafted the constitution in English, the Irish translation stood as the official version.

Articles 40–44 dealt with 'Fundamental Rights' and 'directive principles of social policy'. De Valera's goal in these articles was to protect those elements of Irish society and values that he felt might be most at risk and to define the essential nature of the Irish nation. These sections committed the state to 'guard with special care the institution of Marriage' and to 'endeavour to ensure that mothers shall not be obliged by economic necessity to engage in labour to the neglect of their duties in the home'. De Valera highlighted the 'special position' of the Catholic Church in Article 44. Other sections recognize other Christian denominations, including the Church of Ireland, Presbyterians, Methodists and Jewish congregations, but it was clear that Ireland was going to be a Catholic nation. During debates in the Dáil prior to the submission of the constitution for a national vote, de Valera argued that in a democratic state, the people's 'whole philosophy of life is going to affect the state's politics and that that reality should be recognized'.[56] De Valera was unconcerned that tying the state so closely to Catholicism might serve as an obstacle to national unity, either within Ireland or with a possible reunification with Northern Ireland. He took comfort in the support of the outgoing leader of the Presbyterians in Ireland, who welcomed the Christian tone of the constitution and was 'impressed by the unbiased fairness' that Protestants received in Ireland.[57]

The Irish government viewed the constitution as a watershed event in the British–Irish relationship and in respect to Ireland's place in the world. Joseph Walshe, the Secretary of the Department of External Affairs, instructed Irish diplomats to describe the constitution as marking a 'completely new stage in our relations with GB'. He urged that the British be made to understand that the Irish government's voluntarily acceptance of a limited role for the British monarch in Irish affairs was so significant that the British 'would be wise ... [to] let things be'. Citing the fact that de Valera had recently allowed for the possibility of Britain coming to Ireland's aid if Ireland were attacked, Walshe concluded that recent British grumblings about the cost of doing so seem

> grotesque before the acceptance by the strongest Irish Leader of our times of such a principle. Do get them to see light on this point. Why will they be blind where we are concerned and so farseeing when they are dealing with purely foreign peoples.

Coming back to the issue of the United States, as these debates almost always did, Walshe argued: 'from the propaganda point of view alone agreement with us on this vital issue (with all the implications in America and the Commonwealth) would be worth millions'.[58]

In a 15 June speech to the United States, de Valera called the constitution the 'spiritual and cultural embodiment of the Irish people'.[59] He summed up his view of the constitution on the eve of the referendum on its acceptance:

> It is a renewed declaration of national independence and its enactment will mark the attainment of one definite objective in the national struggle. It consolidates the ground that has been gained and forms a secure basis from which we can move forward towards the recovery of the national sovereignty over our ports and the reunion of the whole national territory into one State.[60]

As he wanted, the Treaty ports still controlled by Great Britain soon became the main topic of British–Irish discussions.

THE TREATY PORTS

The Anglo-Irish Treaty of 1921 contained an annex that allowed Great Britain to maintain control of the harbour defences and facilities at three Irish ports: Berehaven, Cobh and Lough Swilly.[61] During the negotiations, the Irish delegation did not raise serious objections to the provisions, assuming that the British would not be willing to move on the issue. De Valera even included the British right to the harbour defences in 'Document No. 2', his proposed alternative to the Anglo-Irish Treaty.[62] But by the middle to late 1930s the ports served as an obstacle to de Valera's efforts to forge a clear Irish identity on the international scene and were an impediment to the ability to be neutral in any future European war.

2.3 The Treaty Ports

It was fortunate for de Valera that by 1937, just as he was eager to take back the ports in order to achieve full sovereignty over the whole territory, if not the island, of Ireland, a series of developments in Great Britain and the Commonwealth made the British government willing to turn them over. At the Imperial Conference in June 1937 the Commonwealth nations discussed the continuing Economic War and reached a consensus that the sooner it was resolved the better it would be for the Commonwealth's image in the world. South Africa's representative summarized the delegates' positions by saying that 'what the British Government does now as regards Ireland is, in my opinion, most important for the future of the Commonwealth'.[63] Later, Neville Chamberlain argued that even a partially satisfactory agreement would be preferable to the 'insecurity of the present situation'.[64] With mounting challenges from Germany, the British government also wanted to be sure that Ireland would at least not be an active impediment during a war. This was a response to de Valera's 1936 statement that Ireland 'would be almost certainly hostile as long as her independence was interfered with' by the British presence in the ports.[65]

De Valera's position developed in part as a result of a May 1936 Irish Department of Defence policy paper outlining 'the military alternatives' available to the government should a European war break out and Britain become involved. The premise of the report was that the under-staffed and under-equipped Irish military was incapable of deterring any aggressor for any period of time. The three main factors the military considered important were the strategic location of Ireland, its lack of potential defensive capability, and the existing political status. The geographic position of Ireland forced any Irish policy to be based on the likely reaction to it by Britain. The Irish generals realized that, in the end, the British effectively controlled what actions the Irish could pursue: 'geographical factors must be taken as the fundamental influence of Saorstat defence policy'. As long as the British maintained control over the ports, the report concluded, Irish neutrality would be close to impossible to maintain.[66]

Several reports by the British military on the status of the ports and their utility in the event of a war influenced the views of Chamberlain and others in the British government. The reports outlined the poor maintenance of the ports between 1921 and 1938. Although they were reserved for the use of the British Navy, the British Army bore the financial and operational burden of maintaining and securing them. As a result, the ports did not receive any substantial renovations during the period.[67] In addition, the reports stressed that during a war the ports would have no benefit to the British if Ireland was not either an active ally or a friendly neutral. The best chance for either of these alternatives was if Ireland continued its status as a member of the Commonwealth. An Ireland outside of the Commonwealth would be more likely to oppose British interests, and access to the ports under that scenario would involve first subduing the whole of Ireland. The reports also listed the ports as being of only secondary value if Great Britain was at war with Germany.[68] An additional report in January 1938 re-emphasized that attempting to use the ports with a hostile Irish government in power would be a 'formidable military commitment and might, even so, be impossible'.[69]

After getting the British military to accept turning over the ports to the Irish government, Dominions Secretary Malcolm MacDonald met with de Valera in September 1937. MacDonald hoped to get de Valera to agree to accept the transfer of the ports under the condition that the British would maintain the right to use them in case of war. De Valera flatly refused. Not only did he fail to give on that point, he pushed matters further by stressing that the ending of partition was 'absolutely necessary for the good relations we both desired' and that the land annuity payments would never be renewed. He did open up one avenue for a solution: finding a way to equate Ireland's increased commitment on defence with the amount of the disputed annuity payments.[70]

To press his points on the ports, de Valera used a three-pronged strategy. He first played, as usual, the Irish-American card by pointing to the benefit of a British–Irish settlement on British–American relations. His argument was that the financial benefits of annuity payments or of occupying the ports against the will of most of the Irish population could not possibly outweigh a 'real unqualified friendship' between Great Britain and the United States. He then played the IRA card by emphasizing that certain 'irresponsible' elements of Irish society would probably attack the ports during a war if Britain continued to maintain them. Finally, he argued that Ireland with the ports would never be used as a base of attack against Britain, a position he had held since 1920. MacDonald was not convinced, but both sides were eager enough for a settlement that they agreed to enter into formal ministerial negotiations in January 1938.[71]

THE SETTLEMENT

The British–Irish negotiations of January–April 1938 dealt with the Economic War, partition and the ports. The British negotiators were most eager to come to some satisfactory agreement on overall defence, even if that meant an unconditional return of the ports. Chamberlain, especially, wanted to resolve the outstanding issues with Ireland in order to be in a better position to face the mounting challenges from Germany. Sir Warren Fisher, the Permanent Secretary of the Treasury, highlighted British concerns in an internal memo the day after the talks began. He urged the negotiators to avoid debating from a purely legal standpoint, writing that the issue was 'primarily a *psychological* problem'. Granting the Irish the 'incontestable ground' that historically England had been the aggressor in the relationship, Fisher urged Chamberlain not to take a 'haggling, huckstering attitude'. The overall concern should be: 'If a showdown is forced by Germany, do we want to face both East and West?' In that spirit, and after hearing de Valera reiterate again his position that he would not allow the ports to be used against Great Britain, Chamberlain opened the second day's talks with an offer to take 'as sympathetic a view as possible on the ports'.[72]

From the start of the final negotiations in January 1938 until the signing of the final agreement that April, de Valera sought to bring Irish Americans and the United States into play during the talks. In his notes going into the conference he wrote about the importance of appealing to the Irish diaspora as one of the only viable, if still unlikely, means to end partition. One of de Valera's first moves was to meet with the US Minister to Ireland, John Cudahy, who had arrived in Ireland in August 1937. Cudahy was born into a prominent Irish-American family in the meat-packing business in Wisconsin. He was an uncle by marriage to FDR's Secretary of Interior, Harold Ickes, and before his appointment to Dublin had served as Ambassador to Poland.[73] Very quickly after his appointment, Cudahy and de Valera established a close working relationship. After their first meeting, Cudahy sent the State Department a gushing evaluation of de Valera's intelligence and demeanour.[74] After leaving Ireland, Cudahy wrote that de Valera was 'the greatest leader in all of Irish history, a man of singular force and outstanding high intelligence, but above all of uncompromising conviction'.[75]

When de Valera and Cudahy met on 21 January 1938, four days after the start of the British–Irish negotiations, the Taoiseach convinced Cudahy that partition was the major sticking point. De Valera again used the analogy of the American Civil War to draw out the dangers of a divided nation. Cudahy then wrote to Roosevelt that if the United States could help resolve this dispute it would mean 'the approval by a great share of American public opinion of closer American–British relations', something close to FDR's heart. Cudahy urged that the president call in the British Ambassador in Washington to stress the importance of movement on the issue of partition.[76]

Just a few days later, de Valera dispatched his friend Frank Gallagher to Washington with a personal letter to Roosevelt asking for him to intervene with the British. De Valera wrote that partition was the main issue, noting that the British, 'if they really have the will, can bring about a United Ireland in a very short time'. Noting the important backdrop of international events, de Valera attempted to tie the British–Irish negotiations into the wider international security debate while also playing the Irish-American card again: 'Reconciliation would affect every country where the two races dwell together, knitting their national strength and presenting to the world a great block of democratic peoples interested in the preservation of Peace.'[77]

De Valera's efforts to have the United States get involved with the partition question stemmed from his realization that there was not much likelihood that the British would acquiesce in his demands. By appealing to the United States, however, de Valera was able to give himself an outside shot at some movement. President Roosevelt decided to intervene with the British, but only unofficially. Roosevelt's official response to de Valera came on 22 February. Drafted by Cordell Hull, the letter agreed with de Valera's position that an end to partition would be a benefit 'from every point of view', but FDR maintained that there was simply no benefit to discussing the matter with the British through official channels. He did, however, agree to send Chamberlain a personal message via the newly appointed Ambassador to Britain, Joseph Kennedy, that he hoped the partition issue could be resolved. Kennedy's discussions with the British came at a crucial point in the negotiations, as the British had already decided to return the ports without condition, but the problem of Northern Ireland was still outstanding. Kennedy told the Irish High Commissioner in London on 15 March that he had communicated FDR's views to Chamberlain that a British–Irish settlement 'was a matter of importance in regard to the question of Anglo–American relations'. Chamberlain had at first pressed for an agreement to hand the ports back to the British government in the event of war, but dropped that request when de Valera refused. The annuity payment problems and the Economic War were already resolved with the agreement by de Valera for a one-time payment of £10 million and both sides agreeing to drop the duties on the other's goods. The remaining points, however, partition and Ireland granting special trade rights to Northern Ireland, threatened to derail any final agreement.[78] MacDonald later wrote that FDR's participation had little effect. Harold Ickes' diary entries for July 1938, however, convey a sense that FDR felt he had played a significant role, if not on the partition issue, at least by getting the parties to continue the negotiations. Gallagher supports this claim: he credits Roosevelt for 'a resumption of negotiations when they had broken down'.[79]

Chamberlain was frustrated in his attempts to have James Craig, the Prime Minister of Northern Ireland, agree to drop his financial demands. On 8 April, the day after Kennedy met with the British Foreign Secretary and stressed the importance to British–American relations of a speedy British–Irish settlement, Chamberlain wrote a personal appeal to Craig:

> [It is time] to implement what you said to me ... namely that you meant to help and not to hinder. In my anxieties over the international situation it has become almost essential for me to show some evidence that the policy of peace by negotiation can be successful ... [A]n Anglo-Irish agreement ... would add greatly to the impression made upon the world.

He added that he would conclude the agreement in one week, 'one way or another'.[80] Craig dropped his demands, de Valera agreed to postpone any discussion of partition and reiterated his long public stand that Ireland would never be a base for a foreign power to attack Britain, and the parties signed the Anglo-Irish Agreement of 1938 on 25 April. At a luncheon following the signing, Chamberlain returned to de Valera the field glasses that a British officer had taken from him upon his arrest after the Easter Rising in 1916.[81]

In the House of Commons, Chamberlain urged members to realize that the main strength of the agreement was Britain's achieving 'those intangible, imponderable, but nevertheless invaluable fruits which have on various occasions in the past rewarded a liberal and unselfish act of generosity by a great and powerful country towards a State weaker and poorer than itself'.[82] The agreement, however, also brought several discreet advantages to Britain. It allowed Chamberlain a victory in his efforts to argue that appeasement was the best policy to prevent the outbreak of war in Europe. In addition, the British security service, MI5, and the Irish Army's intelligence agency, G2, began to set up the communication channels that would allow for the significant cooperation they would have during World War Two.[83]

Not everyone supported the Agreement. Winston Churchill made a vitriolic speech in Parliament against it, concentrating on the folly of giving away the ports. Ten years later in his memoirs he wrote that 'a more feckless act can hardly be imagined' and that the entire episode was 'lamentable and amazing'.[84] The Tory newspaper the *Daily Telegraph and Morning Post* challenged Churchill and provided a more accurate assessment:

> Mr Churchill impressively marshalled a number of dire possibilities which cannot be lightly dismissed. The answer to them is that the *Defeat* of the present agreement would not avert those possibilities, but would help to realise them. The acceptance of the agreement offers at least the chance of banishing them forever. It is an act, not only of faith, but of prudence.[85]

Also of major importance is the Agreement's influence on British–American relations. In his conclusion to the debate in the House of Commons, MacDonald pointed to the positive influence of the agreement on British–American relations. Discussing the fact that in the United States 'Irishmen take a great part in foreign affairs and politics', MacDonald concluded that the Agreement 'has resulted in improving the friendly relations which exist between the United States and this country'.[86] MacDonald was correct; the response in the United States was overwhelmingly supportive. The *New York Times* editorialized that 'none of the larger agreements which the British Government has made or seeks to make in the effort for European appeasement will give greater satisfaction to English-speaking people everywhere'. Roosevelt commented that the new pact would go 'a long way' towards removing the hostility between Ireland and Britain.[87]

In his address introducing the Agreement to the Dáil, de Valera focused on issues of national identity involved in the transfer of the ports, stressed again that he had no desire to see Ireland used as a base against Britain, and pre-empted any possible future rumours that there was a secret deal to hand over the ports during a war. The most important element of the Agreement involved 'Irish sovereignty', in that for the first time the Irish government had complete control of all the territory of the island that was not part of Northern Ireland. De Valera also reiterated his pledge that he first made 'as long ago as 1920, when, on behalf of the State of that time – of the Republic – I made a request to the Government of the United States for formal recognition', that Ireland would not be used as a base of operations against Britain. Concerned about any future attempts to claim that there was a secret deal, de Valera made sure he would go on record stating:

> There has been no bargain. There are no conditions. There is no secret understanding, but there is a belief, I am certain – a belief

which I have tried, over 20 years, to get into the minds of British Governments and of the British people, in so far as I could – that it is far better for Britain, far more advantageous for Britain, to have a free Ireland by its side than an Ireland that would be unfriendly because of liberties which Britain denied.[88]

He concluded that partition remained as the only impediment to completely harmonious relations between Ireland and Britain.

On 11 July 1938, when Ireland took possession of the ports, de Valera decided not to embarrass the British by having any national celebrations. He was concerned that because the Irish government did not yet have the six counties of the north, any large celebration might make it 'too difficult for the British to give them back'. Irish unity was very much on de Valera's mind on that day. The Taoiseach remarked after the ceremony at Cobh that he prayed God would help the Irish achieve the 'final success' of 'restoring the unity of our country and bringing the whole of this island again into the possession of the Irish people'.[89]

IRISH AMERICANS AND THE IRA

Notwithstanding de Valera's remarkable diplomatic success, not all elements of Irish society appreciated or supported his efforts. At the same time that de Valera was in London negotiating an end to the Economic War and the return of the ports, the IRA was planning a bombing campaign, with McGarrity's heavy involvement.[90] The campaign began in early 1939 with the publication of a formal ultimatum to the British government. The IRA, acting as the self-described 'Government of the Irish Republic', demanded the withdrawal of all British forces from Ireland. The campaign, as one historian has noted, 'did not amount to much', but there was a large explosion in Coventry in August 1939 that killed five and wounded another seventy.[91] The campaign met with such severe public criticism in Ireland that the Dáil passed the Offences against the State Act in June 1939. De Valera was particularly upset because the bombings were undermining his long-stated and recently effective stance that Ireland would never be a base of attack against Britain. Using much of the same tactics that de Valera criticized while out of power, the Act enabled the government to hold people without trial and to use military tribunals to handle political crimes.[92]

The IRA campaign dealt a blow to de Valera's plans, because by the summer and fall of 1938 he had begun to put partition at the forefront of British–Irish and Irish–American relations. He began a press campaign in the United States in August, giving a series of interviews to

American newspapers calling for Irish-American support. 'The present Partition of Ireland is a dangerous anachronism which must be ended', de Valera noted in October, which kept alive the 'ancient antagonisms' between the British and the 'overwhelming majority of the Irish race'. Later that month he announced at a Fianna Fáil meeting that he was going to ask two Irish-American newspapers, the New York *Irish World* and the San Francisco *Leader*, to concentrate on the continuing injustice of partition.[93] Early in 1939, with an invitation in hand from FDR to attend the New York World's Fair, de Valera decided to use his visit that May as a rallying cry to raise the partition issue directly with Irish Americans and with American public opinion. De Valera had planned to visit Washington, New York, Boston and twenty-one other cities, speaking to Chambers of Commerce, the Council on Foreign Relations, Irish Societies and at a variety of civic events. Public meetings were planned for Madison Square Garden and Chicago Stadium. Cudahy, however, urged him to avoid raising any anti-British feeling in the United States, because 'it would be resented by the people in our country and would react to the detriment of the Irish cause'.[95]

As tensions in Europe continued to rise, a crisis erupted when Great Britain announced plans on 26 April 1939 to introduce conscription, causing de Valera to cancel his May trip to the United States. Northern Ireland's Prime Minister James Craig immediately called for the draft to be extended to Northern Ireland. There ensued a major dispute between the Irish and British governments over the issue, with de Valera writing to Chamberlain in April that the implementation of conscription in the 'Six counties', considered part of Ireland by the Irish Constitution, would be regarded as 'an act of war'. The next month, Chamberlain got Craig to relent by writing: 'if you really want to help us, don't press for conscription'. Craig's wife later noted about the incident that 'American opinion, as ever, had to be considered.'[95] British Home Secretary Samuel Hoare and Defence Minister Thomas Inskip wrote that 'the American reaction to the contention that Great Britain is exercising a tyrannical coercion over Irishmen is a greater danger than the reaction in Eire itself'.[96] Once again, Irish ties to Irish Americans and their influence on British–Irish relations were clear.

CONCLUSION

The 1930s were a time of searching and uncertainty for the Irish in America and for Éamon de Valera, as leader of the Irish in Ireland. Both were looking for ways to reclaim or create identities that validated their status either in America or the world. Irish Americans had never felt completely integrated into the American mainstream, but the Depression put their socioeconomic gains into doubt at the same time that the dislocations associated with many joining the middle class merely exacerbated their tensions. Their insecurities are evident in the artistic representations they leave behind. For de Valera, and the growing majority of Irish who supported him at the polls, however, the 1930s were a period of confident and active steps to create a new identity. That identity, de Valera believed, was only to be achieved by breaking away from all things British. In spite of all the gains in the process, paid for in part by the economic dislocations of the Economic War, 1939 still saw a partitioned Ireland.

The Second World War soon pulled the Irish on both sides of the Atlantic together again. De Valera struggled to keep Ireland's new-found identity intact by remaining neutral, as the United States was, and Irish Americans rushed to his support.

NOTES

1. 'The Republican Goal', 23 April 1933, in Éamon De Valera, *Speeches and Statements by Eamon De Valera, 1917–1973*, ed. Maurice Moynihan (New York: St Martin's Press, 1980), 237.
2. *Irish World*, 3 September 1938.
3. Joseph P. O'Grady, *How the Irish Became Americans* (New York: Twayne, 1973), 158.
4. Charles Fanning, *The Irish Voice in America: 250 Years of Irish-American Fiction*, 2nd edn (Lexington: University Press of Kentucky, 2000), 239.
5. Timothy J. Meagher, *From Paddy to Studs: Irish-American Communities in the Turn of the Century Era, 1880 to 1920* (Westport, Conn.: Greenwood Press, 1986), 1–25; and Timothy J. Meagher, *The Columbia Guide to Irish American History* (New York: Columbia University Press, 2005), 146.
6. Garry Wills, *Bare Ruined Choirs: Doubt, Prophecy, and Radical Religion*, 1st edn (Garden City, N.Y.: Doubleday, 1972), 15, 18.
7. *Irish World*, 4 February 1929.
8. See Ronald H. Bayor, *Neighbors in Conflict: The Irish, Germans, Jews, and Italians of New York City, 1929–1941* (Baltimore, Md.: Johns Hopkins University Press, 1978). Writing in September 1932, the Irish Consul General in New York wrote to Dublin that Irish Americans in New York had a 'growing resentment' against the 'increasing penetration of Jews and Italians into Tammany Hall', in Royal Irish Academy and Department of Foreign Affairs, *Documents on Irish Foreign Policy*, vol. 4, *1932–1936*, ed. Ronan Fanning and others (Dublin: Royal Irish Academy, 2004), 124 (hereafter given as *DIFP*, vol. number and document number).
9. Kevin Kenny, *The American Irish: A History* (New York: Longman, 2000), 208. See also William D. Griffin, *The Irish Americans* (New York: Hugh Lauter Levin Associates, 1998), 165–90.
10, Moira Davison Reynolds, *Comic Strip Artists in American Newspapers: 1945–1980* (Jefferson, N.C.: McFarland & Co., 2003), 20.
11. George McManus, *Jiggs is Back* (Berkeley, Calf.: Celtic Book Co., 1986), 54 (27 August 1933).

12. Ibid., 16 (2 February 1936).
13. John O'Hara, *BUtterfield 8* (New York: Harcourt, Brace & Co., 1935). See also Frank MacShane, *The Life of John O'Hara*, 1st edn (New York: Dutton, 1980), and Geoffrey Wolff, *The Art of Burning Bridges: A Life of John O'Hara* (New York: Alfred A. Knopf, 2003), 3–79.
14. O'Hara, *BUtterfield 8*, 66–7.
15. Wolff, *Burning Bridges*, 34.
16. See Edgar Branch, *James T. Farrell* (New York: Twayne, 1971).
17. James T. Farrell, *The League of Frightened Philistines and Other Papers* (New York: Vanguard Press, 1945), 86. See also Edgar Branch, *Studs Lonigan's Neighborhood and the Making of James T. Farrell* (Newton, Mass.: Arts End Books, 1996).
18. James T. Farrell, *Studs Lonigan: A Trilogy Comprising Young Lonigan, the Young Manhood of Studs Lonigan, and Judgment Day* (Urbana: University of Illinois Press, 1993), 238, 495.
19. Farrell, *Studs Lonigan Trilogy*, 828.
20. Quoted in Fanning, *Irish Voice*, 257; James Farrell, 'The World I Grew Up In', *Commonweal* 83 (25 February 1966): 606; Fanning, *Irish Voice*, 291.
21. Joseph M. Curran, *Hibernian Green on the Silver Screen: The Irish and American Movies* (New York: Greenwood Press, 1989), 73–9.
22. Eileen M. McMahon, *What Parish Are You From?: A Chicago Irish Community and Race Relations* (Lexington: University Press of Kentucky, 1995), 187.
23. 'De Valera to McGarrity', 30 April 1927, National Library of Ireland, MS17,441/McGarrity Papers (hereafter given as NLI/file number/file name).
24. Frank Pakenham Longford and Thomas P. O'Neill, *Éamon De Valera* (London: Arrow Books, 1974), 253–8; Dermot Keogh, *Twentieth-Century Ireland: Nation and State* (New York: St Martin's Press, 1995), 39–49.
25. 'Election Manifesto', 9 February 1932 and 'Aims of Fianna Fáil in Office', 17 March 1932, in *Speeches and Statements*, 188–91. On the Ulster question and the 1932 election, see John Bowman, *De Valera and the Ulster Question, 1917–1973* (New York: Oxford Univeristy Press, 1982), 109–16. The land annuities were the sums paid by Irish farmers for becoming the owners of land on which they had previously been tenants. It was collected by the Irish government and paid to Great Britain under the 1926 Ultimate Financial Settlement: '1. The Government of the Irish Free State undertake to pay to the British Government at agreed intervals the full amount of the annuities accruing due from time to time under the Irish Land Acts 1891–1909', 'Financial Settlement between Free State and British Government', in *Irish Political Documents, 1916–1949*, ed. Mitchell Arthur Mitchell and Pádraig Ó Snodaigh (Dublin: Irish Academic Press, 1985), 173.
26. 'MacEntee to De Valera', 18 March 1932, UCD, MacEntee Papers, P67/94. See also 'MacWhite to Walshe', 24 March 1932, *DIFP*, vol. 4, doc. 23.
27. Joseph McGarrity, *The McGarrity Papers: Revelations of the Irish Revolutionary Movement in Ireland and America, 1900–1940*, ed. Sean Cronin (Tralee: Anvil Books, 1972), 155–6.
28. McGarrity, *McGarrity Papers*, 156.
29. 'De Valera to McGarrity', 31 January 1934, NLI/MS 17,441/McGarrity Papers.
30. 'Despatch from the British Secretary of State for Dominion Affairs to the Minister for External Affairs', 23 March 1932, in Mitchell and Ó Snodaigh, *Irish Political Documents*, 196. See also the discussion in Paul Canning, *British Policy Towards Ireland, 1921–1941* (New York: Oxford University Press, 1985), 121–75.
31. *Dáil Debates*, 27 April 1932, col. 571. All Dáil debates are available at http:www//historical-debates.oireachtas.ie/. De Valera was referring to the 1931 Statute of Westminster; see Nicholas Mansergh, ed., *Documents and Speeches on British Commonwealth Affairs, 1931–1952* (Oxford: Oxford University Press, 1953), vol. 2, 1–6. Dulanty also told the British government that the oath was not a 'mandatory' aspect of the Treaty: 'Dulanty to British Secretary of State for Dominon Affairs', 22 March 1932, National Archives of Ireland, Department of the Taoiseach, 9361A (hereafter NAI/DT/file number).
32. *Dáil Debates*, 19 May 1932, col. 2141. The bill later stalled in the Seanad, but eventually became law on 3 May 1933.
33. Keogh, *Nation and State*, 70. De Valera's welcome speech to the Papal Legate is in de Valera, *Speeches and Statements*, 217–19.
34. *Dáil Debates*, 18 July 1932, col. 1322.
35. David George Boyce, *The Irish Question and British Politics, 1868–1996*, 2nd edn (New York: Macmillan, 1996), 85–9; Canning, *British Policy Towards Ireland*, 130–52; T. Ryle Dwyer, *De Valera: The Man & the Myths* (Dublin: Poolbeg, 1991), 166–9.

36. 'Sankey to MacDonald', 10 August 1932, quoted in Canning, *British Policy Towards Ireland*, 140.
37. 'Churchill to Edward Marsh', 17 September 1932, in Winston Churchill, *Winston S. Churchill: Companion*, vol. 5, *1922–1939*, ed. Martin Gilbert (Boston: Houghton Mifflin, 1978), 474.
38. 'Executive Council Minutes', 22 and 24 November 1932, NAI/DT/S8532, NAI/DT/S8540A. See also Longford and O'Neill, *De Valera*, 280–4.
39. 'Taoiseach Broadcast on Lincoln's Birthday', 12 February 1933, NAI/DT/S11023.
40. 'The Republican Goal', 23 April 1933, *Speeches and Statements*, 236–7.
41. 'Envoy Clarifies Dublin Incident', *New York Times*, 29 March 1934; 'New US Minister in Dublin', *The Times*, 28 March 1934.
42. Tim Pat Coogan, *The IRA: A History*, 4th edn (London: HarperCollins, 1995), 48–69; Cronin, *McGarrity Papers*, 158–61. See also 'The Republican Congress Manifesto', published 5 May 1934, in Mitchell and Ó Snodaigh, *Irish Political Documents*, 208–10.
43. Cronin, *McGarrity Papers*, 162.
44. Canning, *British Policy Towards Ireland*, 154–7.
45. See DIFP, vol 4, $240 ff. For a full treatment of the effects of the Coal–Cattle pact, see ibid., 160–4. See also Keogh, *Nation and State*, 87–90.
46. Quoted in Longford and O'Neill, *De Valera*, 304–5.
47. Quoted in Canning, *British Policy Towards Ireland*, 167.
48. Constitution (Declaration of Unlawful Association) Order, 1936. All Irish legislation is available at http://www.irishstatutebook.ie/.
49. *Dáil Debates*, 23 June 1936, cols. 108–19.
50. 'Russell to McGarrity', 5 November 1937, in Cronin, *McGarrity Papers*, 164.
51. Longford and O'Neill, *De Valera*, 190. For de Valera's rationale for the External Relations Act, see 'Notes by the Department of External Affairs', 11 December 1936, UCD, De Valera Papers, P150/2345; *Dáil Debates*, 11 December 1936, cols. 1341–85.
52. Executive Authority (External Relations) Act, 1936.
53. 'Brennan to de Valera', 21 December 1936, UCD, De Valera Papers, P150/2285.
54. Bunreacht na hÉireann. Constitution of Ireland. The new constitution passed in a national referendum in July 1937 and took effect that December.
55. The Nineteenth Amendment to the Constitution Act in 1998 amended Articles 2 and 3 in accordance with the 1998 Good Friday Agreement. The full text of the current Constitution is available at http://www.taoiseach.gov.ie/.
56. *Dáil Debates*, 4 June 1937, col. 1890.
57. *Irish Press*, 8 June 1937.
58. 'Walshe to Dulanty', 21 May 1937, *DIFP*, vol. 5, doc. 60.
59. *Irish Press*, 16 June 1937.
60. Quoted in Longford and O'Neill, *De Valera*, 300.
61. 'Final Text of the Articles of Agreement for a Treaty between Great Britain and Ireland as Signed', 6 December 1921, *DIFP*, vol. 1, doc. 214.
62. 'Proposed Treaty of Association between Ireland and the British Commonwealth', NAI/DE/4/5/14.
63. Quoted in Deirdre McMahon, *Republicans and Imperialists: Anglo–Irish Relations in the 1930s* (New Haven, Conn.: Yale University Press, 1984), 220.
64. Quoted in Boyce, *Irish Question*, 88.
65. 'Interview Given by the Taoiseach to Mr Truelove of the "Daily Telegraph"', 22 February 1936, NAI/DT/S10701A.
66. 'Fundamental Factors Influencing Irish Defense Policy', May 1936, Irish Military Archives, Cathal Brugha Barracks, Dublin, G2/0075, p. 40 (hereafter all manuscript collections from the Irish Military Archives will be given as IMA/file number).
67. Canning, *British Policy Towards Ireland*, 178–88.
68. 'Report of the Joint Planning Subcommittee of the Committee of Imperial Defence', 23 July 1936 and 'Memo by Chiefs of Staff, COS 405', 30 July 1936; see Canning, *British Policy Towards Ireland*, 186–8.
69. Quoted in Joseph T. Carroll, *Ireland in the War Years, 1939–1945* (San Francisco, Calif.: International Scholars Publications, 1998), 26.
70. Longford and O'Neill, *De Valera*, 309.
71. 'Press Statement', February 1920, *Speeches and Statements*, 32–4; Canning, *British Policy Towards Ireland*, 191–2.

72. De Valera, 'Various Rough Notes', 17–19 January 1938, *DIFP*, vol. 5, doc. 121; 'Minutes of the Conference', 18 January 1938, *DIFP*, vol. 5, doc. 124.

73. See also 'Confidential Report: O'Brien to Walshe', 2 June 1937, *DIFP*, vol. 5, doc. 61; Seán Cronin, *Washington's Irish Policy, 1916–1986: Independence, Partition, Neutrality* (Dublin: Anvil Books, 1987), 54; McMahon, *Republicans and Imperialists*, 221.

74. 'First Interview with Mr Eamon de Valera', 24 August 1937, National Archives of the United States, Record Group 84 (Foreign Service Post Files), Dublin Legation Classified Records, DF 800.1 (hereafter NAUS/RG84/file number).

75. *DIFP*, vol. 5, no. 121. John Cudahy, *The Armies March: A Personal Report* (New York: Charles Scribner's Sons, 1941), 17.

76. 'Cudahy to Washington', 24 January 1938, NAUS/RG84/DLCR, 24 January 1938; 'Cudahy to President', 22 January 1938, Franklin D. Roosevelt Library, President's Secretary Files, PSF 56 (hereafter FDR/PSF/file number).

77. 'De Valera to Roosevelt', 25 January 1938, UCD, De Valera Papers, P150/2836.

78. 'FDR to de Valera', 22 February 1938, in US Department of State, *Foreign Relations of the United States: Diplomatic Papers, 1938*, vol. 2, *The British Commonwealth, Europe, Near East and Africa* (Washington, D.C.: US Government Printing Office, 1955), 271 (hereafter *Foreign Relations of the United States* citations will be *FRUS*, year, vol. number: page); 'Dulanty to Walshe', 15 March 1938, UCD, De Valera Papers, P150/2171. The £10 million amounted to roughly two years' worth of revenue the British were collecting by imposing duties. See *Dáil Debates*, 27 April 1938, cols. 42–3.

79. NLI/MS 18,375/Gallagher Papers; Bowman, *De Valera and the Ulster Question*, 168–9.

80. 'Chamberlain to Craig', 8 April 1938, in Canning, *British Policy Towards Ireland*, 218–19.

81. 'Agreements between the Government of Ireland and the Government of the United Kingdom', NAI/DT/S10389A; *Irish Times*, 26 April 1938.

82. *Commons Debates*, 5 May 1938, col. 1074. All debates in the House of Commons are available at http://www.hansard.millbanksystems.com/commons/C20.

83. Eunan O'Halpin has written extensively on the Anglo-Irish security and intelligence cooperation after 1938. See Eunan O'Halpin, *Defending Ireland: The Irish State and its Enemies since 1922* (New York: Oxford University Press, 1999); 'Irish Neutrality in the Second World War', in *European Neutrals and Non-Belligerents During the Second World War*, ed. Neville Wylie (Cambridge: Cambridge University Press, 2002), 283–303; 'Intelligence and Security in Ireland, 1922–45', *Intelligence and National Security* 5, no. 1 (1990): 50–83; *Spying on Ireland: British Intelligence and Irish Neutrality During the Second World War* (New York: Oxford University Press, 2008); and Eunan O'Halpin, ed., *MI5 and Ireland, 1939–1945: The Official History* (Dublin: Irish Academic Press, 2003).

84. *Commons Debates*, 5 May 1938, cols. 1094–105; Winston Churchill, *The Second World War*, vol. 1, *The Gathering Storm* (Boston: Houghton Mifflin, 1948), 277–8.

85. *Daily Telegraph and Morning Post*, 6 May 1938. Churchill was the only MP to oppose the 1938 Agreement; see Carroll, *Ireland in the War Years*, 79.

86. *Commons Debates*, 10 May 1938, col. 1548.

87. *New York Times*, 24 and 27 April 1938.

88. *Dáil Debates*, 27 April 1938, cols. 35–7. De Valera told Cudahy earlier that there was no bargain; see 'Dublin to State Department', 20 April 1938, NAUS/RG84, DLCR.

89. NLI/ MS 18,375/Gallagher Papers; Keogh, *Nation and State*, 107; *Irish Times*, 12 July 1938. See 'Ceremonial Order 7/1938', 7 July 1938, NAI/DT/S10701A.

90. Cronin, *McGarrity Papers*, 160–74. The Army Council had tried to delay the bombing campaign in 1937. 'IRA Army Council to Joe McGarrity', NLI/MS 35,364/2.

91. Throughout its history the IRA has maintained that its legitimacy derives from its direct link to the Republic proclaimed in 1916. 'Oglaigh Na h-Éireann (Irish Republican Army) Ultimatum to the British Government', Dublin, 12 January 1939, published in the *Wolfe Tone Weekly*, 4 February 1939, in Mitchell and Ó Snodaigh, *Irish Political Documents*, 220–1; Canning, *British Policy Towards Ireland*, 236; J. Bowyer Bell, *The Secret Army: The IRA, 1916–1979*, rev. edn (Cambridge, Mass.: MIT Press, 1983), 145–95. The British were concerned about IRA activity in April and asked the Irish for help; see 'Walshe to De Valera, Enclosing a Note from Dulanty Regarding IRA Activities in Britain', 15 April 1939, UCD, De Valera Papers, P150/2183.

92. 'Offences against the State Act, 1939'.

93. 'Interview with Walter Milgate, *Detroit News*', UCD, De Valera Papers, P150/2537. 'Taoiseach's Interview on Partition', 17 October 1938, NAI/DT/S1010701A; Dwyer, *De Valera*, 220.

94. NAI/DT/S11230; *Irish Press*, 28 April 1939; 'Cudahy to President', 6 April 1939, FDR Library, PSF 40; Bowman, *De Valera and the Ulster Question*, 192. See also, T. Ryle Dwyer, *Irish Neutrality and the USA, 1939–47* (Dublin: Rowman & Littlefield, 1977), 15.
95. 'Dulanty to Chamberlain', 26 April 1939, *DIFP*, vol. 5, doc. 305, quoted in Tim Pat Coogan, *Éamon De Valera: The Man Who Was Ireland* (New York: HarperCollins, 1995), 535.
96. Canning, *British Policy Towards Ireland*, 238.

3

Being Neutral(?): 1939–1941

But then look eastward from your heart, there bulks
A continent, close, dark, as archetypal sin,
While to the west off your own shores, the mackerel
Are fat – on the flesh of your kin. ('Neutrality'
by Louis MacNeice)[1]

The Irish Government's neutrality policy has produced a feeling of
contentment in the Country because it provides clear proof to all
shades of nationalist opinion that independence is an established
fact. (John J. Hearne, Irish High Commissioner to Canada)[2]

It is only within the last decade that our position as an independent
sovereign state has been emphasized to the world. (Éamon de
Valera, 1939)[3]

The period between the start of World War Two and American entry
into the war was the most crucial of Ireland's effort to foster its
independent political identity through its neutrality. Of the twelve
'Moments of Special Crisis' for Ireland that Joseph Walshe, the
Secretary of the Department of External Affairs, came up with at the
conclusion of the war, ten of them fell between September 1939 and
December 1941.[4] The war in the North Atlantic, the collapse of France
and the Battle of Britain all placed heavy pressures on British policy
makers and military planners, making them look west towards Ireland.
After defeat on the Continent, the supply link with the United States
became Britain's lifeline. Many British policy makers (especially
Winston Churchill) felt that if the three Irish ports relinquished by the
British in 1938 were available to British warships it would be an advantage in the fight against German U-boats. The British also worried that
a German invasion of lightly defended Ireland would provide Hitler
with a base to begin a two-pronged invasion of Britain, from Ireland
and France.

The strict public face of Irish neutrality, however, masked the numerous ways that the Irish government and people helped the Allies. In part because of this strict public stance, de Valera did not publicize, during or after the war, the support Ireland gave to Britain and the United States. The British, and later American, propaganda campaigns during the war therefore served to reinforce the mistaken public view that Ireland at best did not aid Britain or, at worst, supported Germany. In addition, the American Minister to Ireland, David Gray, led an active campaign to discredit de Valera and the Irish to Americans. With his slanted and false reports to Washington and to the American press, it is clear, as historian Dermot Keogh has concluded, that Gray 'tarnished de Valera's reputation and thus distorted the truth about Irish neutrality'.[5]

VIEWS OF NEUTRALITY

There are a number of reasons why de Valera wanted to keep Ireland out of the war, but it is a mistake to conclude that because Ireland proclaimed a very public neutrality it actually *was* neutral in any conventional or international law sense of the word. First and foremost in de Valera's worldview was his desire to avoid having his people suffer the type of potential devastation he foresaw before the war and the devastation evident in the German-conquered nations. With practically no military capabilities, Ireland would have been unable to mount even the slightest defence against Germany, or as de Valera was later concerned, against Britain. He was also aware of the historic view of Irish nationalists, that 'England's difficulty is Ireland's opportunity', and wanted to avoid any IRA action that might precipitate another civil war.

In addition to the practical matters concerned with Ireland's involvement in the war, de Valera maintained an overarching goal of securing Ireland's *sense* of sovereignty as a nation truly independent of Britain. For de Valera, it was important that the Irish and British both saw Ireland as an independent nation. For the Irish, it was part of de Valera's vision of Ireland's identity. Yet breaking away from centuries of British domination could only occur if the British also truly realized that the fairly recent Irish independence meant that while Ireland was still in the Commonwealth, it was no longer part of the British Empire. As Trevor Salmon has noted, 'More important than [the principle] of neutrality *per se* was the imperative of proving to the world and itself its independence.'[6] For de Valera, the fundamental basis of neutrality was that it firmly established Ireland as a fully independent nation, no longer tethered to the will of the British.

De Valera did assert the practical and theoretical rights of small nations to remain neutral when larger nations went to war, but this did not equate to an endorsement of neutrality as the preferred universal strategy. Neutrality became a symbol of Irish identity only after de Valera had tried and failed in the 1930s to bolster a system of collective security in which small nations such as Ireland would play a role together with larger nations in maintaining international peace. During debates in the League of Nations throughout much of the 1930s he had been pushing for collective security arrangements and the attendant responsibilities of states to commit military forces.[7] His wartime policy, therefore, was not based on theoretical support of neutrality as a concept, but on the concept of *sovereignty*. As he told a press conference in New York in 1929, while discussing the possibility of overthrowing an empire, 'What we want above all is to be able to remain neutral in case of war.'[8] For de Valera, neutrality was a symbol, consequence and guarantor of sovereignty and of Irish identity. He was not likely to give it up easily.

De Valera's high hopes for the League as a guarantor of small nations' rights evaporated by 1936. Initially, Ireland saw promise in the League, registering the Anglo-Irish Treaty with it in 1924 as a symbol of Ireland's independence. By the mid-1930s it had a seat on the Council, de Valera served as President and Irish officials took great interest in League diplomacy.[9] The Irish delegation often supported Article 16 of the League Covenant, which called for member states to commit military forces in the event of war. De Valera was even prepared to send Irish troops to Saar in 1935 to police a plebiscite by the League. But when the League voted in July 1936 to withdraw sanctions from Italy for its invasion of Ethiopia, de Valera felt that Ireland was now left alone to face any international crisis. Addressing the League, he said: 'All the small States can do, if the statesmen of the greater States fail in their duty, is resolutely to determine that they will not become the tools of any great Power, and that they will resist with whatever strength they may possess every attempt to force them into a war against their will.' Less than four years later, De Valera decided to do just that.[10]

'THE EMERGENCY' BEGINS

One practical element limited de Valera's options as the war began. While his actions to limit the influence and strength of the Irish Republican Army through a series of laws and executive orders were largely a success, he knew that much of the populace still maintained a deep affinity for the IRA's goals, if not its methods. Indeed, much of his own political support derived from those who were eager to unify the island. Any overt assistance to Britain would provide the IRA with a recruiting bonanza and increase the likelihood of their actions against both the Irish and British governments. In spite of this concern, de Valera, and through him, Fianna Fáil, held a complete lock on Irish politics, including the politics of nationalism, on the eve of the war.[11] Bolstered by the new constitution and the successful resolution of the Economic War, de Valera enjoyed widespread support among the Irish people. He was able to draw on that support as he moved the country towards a policy of neutrality.

The day after Germany's invasion of Poland, the Dáil convened to consider two pieces of legislation by de Valera: the First Amendment to the Constitution and the Emergency Powers Act. The first allowed for an extension of the 'time of war' provisions of the Constitution to any periods of armed conflict, even if Ireland were not involved. This allowed the legislature to declare: 'a *national emergency* exists affecting the vital interests of the State'.[12] It is from this provision that the term 'the Emergency' became the official Irish description of World War Two. The Emergency Powers Act provided for 'censorship, restriction, control, or partial or complete suspension of communication'and the 'control and censorship of newspapers and periodicals'. The strict censorship the Act allowed throughout the Emergency gave the Irish state the ability to maintain the fiction of absolute neutrality. Portrayed as part of an effort to mitigate the role of the IRA during a crisis, censorship also eliminated from public debate any discussion of the official and unofficial associations with Britain that belied the public face of a strict neutrality. The Irish public could not read the obituaries of fellow citizens who had enlisted in the British forces and died in battle. Of course, there was also no criticism of the censor's powers. Part of the censor's responsibility was to hide the numerous efforts of the Irish government to support Great Britain, and eventually the United States, in the war effort. This official news blanket played an integral part in the postwar misinterpretation of the nature and effect of Irish neutrality in Great Britain, the United States and around the world.[13]

The announcement of Irish neutrality in September 1939 was certainly no surprise to British policy makers. As de Valera reminded everyone at the conclusion of the Economic War, he had been advocating an Irish benevolent neutrality towards Britain as far back as 1920, when he wrote to Woodrow Wilson: 'Ireland is quite ready by treaty to ensure England's safety and legitimate security against the danger of foreign powers seeking to use Ireland as a basis of attack against her.' De Valera had been advocating neutrality for small states since the failure of the League to act against Italy in 1936. In July 1938 he told the Dáil that in addition to issues of sovereignty, his actions to end the Economic War and acquire the ports rested on the 'very strong consideration of our responsibility here for the defence of our people, seeing that if there was a European war we should not be taken unawares'. Only by removing British forces from Ireland could the government make possible its intention to be neutral in the next war.[14]

The night before war broke out, the German Minister to Ireland, Eduard Hempel, called on de Valera, who warned him that Germany must not make any contacts with the IRA over the issue of partition. Hempel's later report to Berlin, after there were rumours of such contact, made it clear that 'complete restraint continues to be advisable for us', because it would give Great Britain a 'pretext for intervening'. He also reported that the declaration of Irish neutrality 'has strengthened the Irish national self-consciousness'.[15]

Within a few days of the war's start, de Valera made it clear to the British government his desire to maintain neutrality and emphasized to British policy makers Ireland's position with regard to American public opinion. He sent Walshe to London to meet with Anthony Eden, the new Secretary of State for Dominion Affairs, to state his case. Walshe began by telling Eden that de Valera felt the war would lead 'to a new world order', and that the British government should realize how efforts to treat Ireland with more flexibility might allow Ireland, with its importance in the 'English speaking Catholic world', to play 'a friendly role in the relation between the British and American peoples'. He concluded that partition remained the fundamental issue and that movement towards the unity of Ireland would open up a new set of possible relationships between the two governments.[16]

The official notice to Britain of Ireland's methods to implement neutrality came on 12 September 1939. The British government later advised de Valera that the note was read by the Cabinet with profound feelings of disappointment. Anthony Eden, after hearing of Ireland's decision a few days later that Irish territorial waters would be off-limits to belligerents, felt that Britain had no choice but to accept the status quo, for a challenge 'might have unfortunate reactions on neutral and particularly United States opinion'. Churchill did not want to take such a laissez-faire view, in part because he never believed that Ireland, as a member of the Commonwealth, had the legal right to declare neutrality. He argued in October 1939 that legally, Ireland was 'At war but Skulking'.[17]

With the war bringing a new sense of urgency and importance to

British–Irish relations, de Valera consented a few weeks into the war to receiving Sir John Maffey as the 'British Diplomatic Representative in Ireland'.[18] Prior efforts to create permanent liaisons in Dublin and London failed over flaps about whether the office would be that of Minister, Ambassador or High Commissioner; all were arguments about what type of legal relationship existed between the Irish Free State and Great Britain. With the war on, however, that fight became less important than having direct contact in each respective capital to manage the relationship in light of Irish neutrality. In his first report back to London, Maffey made it clear that neutrality was the only viable political option in Ireland:

> The creed of Ireland today was neutrality. No Government could exist that departed from that principle. The question of the ports was at the very nerve center of public interest in the matter, and the public mood would react with intense violence to any action invalidating their integrity.

He went on to describe how de Valera would respond with force to a demand for the return of the ports, and how a voluntary transfer of the ports, however highly unlikely, would probably lead to the collapse of the government. Knowing also how much had already been accomplished in the cause of Ireland assisting the Allies 'within the limits of neutrality', Maffey observed that 'in many ways the government of Eire and the set-back over the ports has obscured the bright side of the picture'.[19]

It was Robert Brennan's job, as the Irish Minister to the United States, to manage the public relations aspect of Irish neutrality to American officials, to the American public and to Irish Americans. Brennan came to this position through a background and interest in journalism and diplomacy. He had served as Secretary to the Irish Legation in Washington from 1934 until 1938, when he became Minister. Born in Wexford in 1881, his first association with Irish nationalism came, as it did for many, through an association with the Gaelic League and its drive to preserve and extend the Irish language and traditional Irish culture. He later became the County Secretary for Sinn Féin in Wexford, managed to escape execution for his part in the Easter Rising, but spent time in six British jails. Before the war he was the General Manager of the *Irish Press*, the newspaper founded by de Valera, and after the war became the Director of Radio Éireann.[20] Brennan used his media experience extensively in cultivating a relationship with the Washington press corps and the Irish-American press, two activities he felt were as important as his official contacts with the

State Department. But Brennan's efforts to gain support for Ireland in the United States were hampered by Irish efforts to keep secret both the government's active support of the British and the many ways in which Irish neutrality itself benefited the Allies.[21]

IRISH SUPPORT FOR ALLIED EFFORTS

There are many examples of how the practice of Irish neutrality took shape in ways that supported the Allies. Allied airmen who landed or crashed in Ireland were regarded as being on 'non-operational' flights. If their planes were still air worthy, the Irish military refuelled them and released both aircraft and crew. The Irish government made arrangements for all stranded Allied airmen to return to Britain, while all German airmen who crashed and survived in Ireland, except for one, landed in prison for the duration of the war. In addition to the intelligence coordination between Ireland and Britain, the governments arranged a formal military defence liaison, but kept it secret from American officials. The Irish government also gave the Allied forces air clearance over parts of Donegal to facilitate easier travel to the North Atlantic. Perhaps of most benefit for the British war effort, the government allowed more than 200,000 Irish citizens to travel to Britain to work in the war industries. While the Irish government never took any active steps to encourage this migration, it did order that British listings of available war jobs be made available at all local Irish unemployment offices. Finally, during their meeting of 20 September 1939, de Valera and Maffey developed a plan for Irish authorities to radio Dublin in the clear with any information about German planes, ships or submarines spotted along the coast.[22] In fact, it was de Valera who personally pushed for the high level of cooperation between Irish and British security services. Historian Eunan O'Halpin concludes that de Valera was instrumental in this support for British actions and that the successful cooperation of the two agencies 'was founded on a clear direction from [de Valera,] the key figure in Irish politics'.[23]

The Irish government draughted a list of the ways in which it supported the British in 'relation to the Actual Waging of the War':

1. Information on all roads, rails, and military in Ireland
2. Broadcasting of information on German planes and subs
3. Permission to use Irish air space in designated areas
4. No protest over other fly-overs
5. Constant stream of intelligence information in reply to 'almost daily' series of questions

6. All information from coast-watching service
7. Routing of all German and Italian communications through Britain
8. Suppression of wireless and capture and internment of real or potential spies
9. Use of Shannon airports for West African service, though probably used for military purposes
10. Allowing Great Britain to have two secret wireless sets and a private line to London and Belfast
11. Complying with requests of British naval and military attaches
12. Obscuring out lighting system at request of British military
13. Allowing the setting up of apparatus which has resulted in destruction and decreased efficiency of our broadcasting system in order to prevent it being used by Germans

A hand-written note on the document lists '150,000 men to British forces; almost 60,000 workers; all our surplus production going to them'.[24]

That note overestimated the numbers involved in perhaps the most effective way Irish citizens supported the Allied war effort: through their participation in the war as soldiers and sailors in the British military. One of the most difficult statistics to tease out from the data is how many Irish citizens actually served in the British military during the war. In 1989 Trevor Salmon wrote that the 'consensus appears to be that around 40,000' Irish men served in the British forces. Using a much more thorough statistical analysis, Richard Doherty in 1999 estimated that about 78,000 Irish were in the British Armed Forces during the war, with about 58,000 of them enlisting after September 1939.[25]

Irish neutrality also aided the British by eliminating the need for the British to prop up Irish military preparedness. The paltry Irish military would not have provided any significant military assistance to the British if Ireland had abandoned neutrality. In fact, active Irish military participation in the war effort might have been more of a drain on British resources than a benefit. The British would have had to extend their air support over the island, to train and equip the Irish Army, and to replace the Irish volunteers who would probably join the Irish Army instead of the British Army. Simply preparing the Irish military for the defence of Ireland would have been a tremendous strain on British resources. There were probably fewer than 6,000 soldiers in the Irish Army in September 1939. There was no air force, only a few lightly armed former fishing vessels that served as a makeshift navy, and little to no supplies or ammunition for even the very few under arms. It was a woefully unprepared defensive arrangement. Historian Dermot Keogh has observed that 'the

3.1 David Gray and his wife Maude leaving New York for his post in Ireland. *New York Times*, 10 March 1940, Times Wide World / Redux

ill-fated Polish cavalry stood a better chance against the mechanized Nazi war machine than the Irish armed forces would have done had Hitler launched a full-scale invasion of Ireland in 1939'.[26]

The British Security Service (MI5) completed its official history of its Irish Section work in January 1946, and it was opened to researchers in 1999. The history supports the contention that bringing Ireland into the war would not have aided Britain. In his review of the history, Sir David Petrie, the director general of MI5 at the time of the report's completion, commented: 'the one factor indispensable to success was the good-will of the Eire officers'. Indeed, the first contact between the services came from an Irish initiative soon after the signing of the Anglo-Irish agreement in 1938. The report's conclusion about Irish neutrality was that, 'as things turned out, Eire neutral was of more value to the British war effort than Eire belligerent would have been'.[27]

DAVID GRAY IN DUBLIN

The American presence in Dublin changed dramatically when the American Minister John Cudahy left Ireland in January 1940 and Roosevelt replaced him with David Gray. Cudahy had been eagerly trying to get out of the Dublin assignment for some time, hoping for a more crucial position elsewhere in Europe, and was later named Ambassador to Belgium. In August 1939 Cudahy met Gray during a trip across the Atlantic. When Gray mentioned that he would enjoy Cudahy's position and Cudahy learned of Gray's relationship with

Roosevelt, Cudahy petitioned Washington for the change. Later, in several personal visits with the Roosevelts, Gray confirmed his interest in the job. He accepted the appointment, he wrote, only because he did not think FDR would run for a third term in November 1940. He did not want to open up FDR to criticism that the appointment was a case of nepotism.[28]

Gray was far from the ideal candidate for the position in Ireland. His early career was a series of failures, first in his family's newspaper business and then for a brief time as a criminal lawyer. He eventually found some success as a writer, mostly with short stories, but also as a playwright. His play *The Best People* had runs in the United States and London. He was not Roman Catholic, he was 69 years old at the time of his appointment, and he had no real interest in cultivating an understanding of Irish political culture. He brought with him no experience with Ireland, other than a few hunting trips in the 1930s. Gray's natural social inclinations and background made him more comfortable with the Anglo-Irish and Protestant ascendancy in Ireland than with de Valera, and he made it a point to avoid social engagements with members of the Irish government during his time in Dublin. His appointment to the position in Dublin, therefore, can only be seen as a function of his marriage to Eleanor Roosevelt's favourite aunt, Maude Hall. Throughout the 1930s and 1940s Eleanor wrote to Maude almost every week. Long after his term in Dublin, Gray admitted that he only received the post because of his relationship to Roosevelt: 'The appointment was obviously nepotic. The President's wife was the niece of my wife.'[29]

Gray's predilection for viewing all American–Irish relations through the prism of American politics and regarding Irish Americans as having an undue and negative influence is exemplified by his trip to Rome in March 1940, prior to taking his post in Dublin. Gray wanted to be assured that Pope Pius XII would not object to a distancing between church and state in Ireland, which Gray thought would have been a necessary precondition to the end of partition. He reported back to Roosevelt that in his discussions with the Pope he had emphasized that 'the Irish question had maintained an abnormal and almost continuous pressure on American foreign relations which the great majority of Americans resented'. He also emphasized to Irish officials prior to his appointment that Irish-American groups in the United States would continue to make it difficult for the American government to support the British as long as partition remained.[30]

At the end of 1939 and into the first months of 1940 the pending

British executions of two bombers from the renewed IRA terror campaign put an additional strain on British–Irish relations and again
brought concerns about American public opinion into the policy mix.
Peter Barnes and James Richards were sentenced to die for their roles
in a 25 August 1939 bombing that killed five people in Coventry. De
Valera appealed to the British government that the motivation for their
actions should be taken into account, and that executing them would
not act as a deterrent but would engender further violence. In January
he asked Brennan to approach the State Department and President
Roosevelt to ask them to intervene with the British, telling Brennan
that he should bring up the 'root cause of all these dangers – Partition'.
The State Department refused any official response, but did pass
on the entreaties to the president. The efforts failed, and the British
executed Barnes and Richards on 7 February 1940.[31]

Soon after, the strain in British–Irish relations resulting from the
executions, Germany's attacks on Belgium and the Netherlands
brought an end to the Phony War in May 1940 and prompted Britain
to renew its calls for the Treaty ports. The importance of the North
Atlantic supply line with the United States increased after it appeared
certain that a long fight loomed on the Continent. Coupled with the
ascendancy to Prime Minister of Winston Churchill, who vigorously
protested the British handover of the ports in 1938, the stage was set
for a much more contentious relationship between the two governments. On 10 May 1940, the day that Churchill took office and the
German Army attacked Belgium, Luxemburg and the Netherlands,
Maffey called on de Valera and argued that the new aggression by
Germany necessitated an Irish reappraisal of its neutrality. De Valera
responded that as long as partition remained in effect it would be
impossible for Ireland to join the British in the war. He did, however,
agree to arrange a series of secret meetings between the British and
Irish militaries in order to draw up a coordinated defence policy in the
event of a German invasion of Ireland.[32]

The new situation required de Valera to work both publicly and privately to maintain Irish neutrality. Two days after meeting with Maffey,
de Valera commented on the developments in Europe during a speech
in Galway. Stressing the practical benefits of neutrality, he declared that
the country had been in danger since the beginning of the war and
would continue to be so for its duration. His role, and the role of all
Irish citizens, was 'to save himself and his neighbour, and the whole
community' from the war's consequences. The emphasis on the practical nature of Irish neutrality was de Valera's attempt to ease the fears

of the Irish, as it became clear the war was moving into a more dangerous phase. Behind the scenes, de Valera was hoping that his 'benevolent
neutrality', as Walshe had described it to Eden in London a few days
earlier, would preclude any unilateral British action to end Irish neutrality. Walshe had laid out an 'impressive' list of Irish actions that
aided the British and reported that Eden 'seemed to be getting the picture as a whole for the first time'. As always, the Irish government
played the Irish-American card. He told Eden that any British interference with Irish neutrality would reduce public support for Britain in
the United States.[33]

With Churchill now firmly in control of British policy towards
Ireland, de Valera expected this tougher line. Churchill opposed the
return of the Treaty ports in 1938 and had taken a dim view of Irish
efforts to remove itself from the symbols of British control throughout
the 1930s. He had an almost visceral hatred of Irish neutrality, one that
did not extend to other European neutrals. This can in part be
explained by Ireland's geographic proximity to Great Britain, but also
to a deeper sense that Ireland was a recalcitrant former dominion sur-
viving off the efforts of the British. Now that Churchill had the ability
to control Irish policy, his first salvo involved denying the back order
of weapons the Irish government had ordered until it signed a formal
defence agreement. The second was a series of articles in the British
press, loosely coordinated by the British government, decrying Irish
neutrality. The final effort was direct talks aimed at bringing Ireland
into the war or at least having de Valera surrender the Treaty ports.[34]

Faced with growing pressure from Britain, and thinking that only
American pressure might dissuade Churchill from seizing the ports, de
Valera turned to Roosevelt. Through Gray, de Valera inquired if the
United States would make a public statement that the preservation of
the status quo in Ireland was vital to American interests. Roosevelt
responded that such a declaration would be a departure from traditional policies and would 'lead to misunderstanding and confusion in
the United States and abroad'. Roosevelt was not going to be dragged
into the fight between Churchill and de Valera, not when he probably
agreed with Churchill and especially not while he was determined to
do everything possible to aid the British in the war.[35]

Gray was eager to help Churchill behind the scenes from Dublin.
He knew that Roosevelt could not get publicly involved against the
Irish stance because of the ongoing effort to inch the American public
towards war. In May 1940 Gray wrote to the British Minister of
Information suggesting two possible rationales for justification of a

British seizure of the Treaty ports. Gray first suggested that the British could put forward the false claim that the seizure was necessary to ensure the delivery of supplies to Ireland. The second suggestion was that when the Treaty ports were relinquished to Ireland de Valera had made a secret agreement guaranteeing British use of them in case of war. De Valera had anticipated such a move when he addressed the Dáil on the return of the Treaty ports two years earlier.[36]

Even while resisting the efforts to persuade him to abandon neutrality, de Valera continued to practice a benevolent neutrality that aided the British and to prepare for joint action should Germany invade Ireland. On 23 and 24 May representatives of the British military met with Joseph Walshe and Colonel Liam Archer, the director of Irish Military Intelligence (G2), for secret meetings in London on military cooperation should Germany invade Ireland. The meetings were held under the operating assumption that British military forces would not enter Ireland until invited to do so by the Irish government, and that the invitation would only be extended after 'the Irish people fully realised that the attack had come'. Walshe acknowledged that the delay might make it more difficult to dislodge the German forces, but explained that it would be politically impossible for the Irish government to move more quickly. The participants agreed on a number of issues, including the sharing of intelligence reports, Irish preliminary defensive measures and communication protocols. Even though he would later falsely tell reporters that he knew of no ways the Irish were preparing to help the British, Gray learned of these talks in October.[37]

NEUTRALITY AND PARTITION: 1940

Prompted by inaccurate intelligence reports in May and June 1940 that warned of Germany's imminent plans for an invasion of Ireland, Neville Chamberlain approached the British War Cabinet with a proposal to open talks with de Valera, and possibly Northern Ireland leader Lord Craigavon, over neutrality, the ports and partition. Chamberlain hoped that if de Valera could be convinced that the Germans would soon overrun the country, then he would agree to abandon neutrality and invite in British troops. The negotiations almost never occurred because de Valera rejected the invitation to London because it could be seen as compromising Irish neutrality, and as a result the British decided to send Minister of Health Malcolm MacDonald to Dublin. The Cabinet had a fall-back plan for when, as expected, de Valera rejected the offer to join the war owing to the continued partition of the island. In response,

MacDonald was instructed to suggest an All-Ireland Defence Council that 'would form a bridge for the eventual discussions on partition', but would immediately begin a formal and public defence policy. If de Valera approved, and the Cabinet again thought it unlikely, then MacDonald was to go to Belfast and attempt to get Lord Craigavon and the Northern Ireland government he led to agree as well.[38]

MacDonald had a very long meeting with de Valera on 17 June in Dublin. De Valera rejected the initial British proposal 'emphatically', stressing his ongoing actions in support of Britain and the unacceptable situation of partition. MacDonald urged de Valera to at least give up the use of the Treaty ports so that the British could patrol more efficiently and give Ireland advance warning of any impending German invasion. Quite disingenuously, MacDonald also claimed that all of his pleadings were for the benefit of Ireland alone, that Britain could take care of itself. Citing Irish public opinion, de Valera emphasized that if partition had been ended before the war, Ireland might have already become a belligerent at Great Britain's side, but now that the war was on and partition remained, neutrality was the only policy that united the people. He told MacDonald that only a united people could mount even a remotely effective resistance to any possible German aggression. Abandoning neutrality now would only make matters worse for the British.

MacDonald then moved to the backup plan, the offer of an All-Ireland Defence Council, with the dangling of some future unification of the island that 'would be difficult to break down' in peace after a period of cooperation during war. De Valera responded that it was premature to establish such a council, but that if Ireland and Ulster found themselves fighting together then Great Britain could immediately announce that Ireland was united for the war and 'henceforth for the whole business of government'. Now it was MacDonald's turn to reject the discussion out of hand.[39]

When MacDonald reported to the War Cabinet on 20 June, there was much discussion about the possibility of using force to gain control of the Treaty ports and to what extent Northern Ireland could be persuaded or forced into discussion about Irish unity.[40] Upon hearing the news of the Dublin meeting, Churchill was 'deeply disappointed, and deeply critical of de Valera', but years later, MacDonald wrote that de Valera 'could scarcely have promised more benevolent cooperation short of declaring war against the enemy'.[41] Chamberlain wanted to pursue the Northern Ireland option as far as possible, but the Cabinet decided to approach Craigavon on the issue only after the rather unlikely event that de Valera accepted it first. MacDonald, however, was to give de Valera the impression that the offer was already finalized.[42] The British Chiefs of Staff had argued that the government must bring 'the strongest possible pressure' on the Northern Ireland government and that the 'people of the North should be told in the plainest terms that if we win the war we shall see to it that a united Ireland is ruled within the Empire', but that if they do not cooperate, 'they will have a unified Ireland in any event, but … under the German jackboot'. Churchill rejected this approach, claiming that he 'could never be a party to coercion of Ulster to join the Southern counties'.[43]

MacDonald presented de Valera with a new series of proposals at their next meetings on 21, 22 and 26 June. The main carrot involved the British government 'accepting the principle' of a united Ireland, with a committee from Northern Ireland and Ireland to work out the constitutional and 'other practical details' over time. In return, Ireland was to declare war immediately and allow British forces to take positions throughout Ireland, including the Treaty ports. De Valera rejected the proposals in their entirety. He realized that it would be almost impossible for Craigavon to agree to the unification of the island and that the British government, by only offering the acceptance of the *principle* of a unification, was not going to demand or pressure Northern Ireland into the agreement. Chamberlain countered with a draft that declared the agreement 'would take the form of a solemn undertaking that the Union is to become at an early date an accomplished fact from which there shall be no turning back'. De Valera rejected this as well. The Taoiseach stated that only a united Ireland would be able to vote to enter the war, and that as long as partition remained he would not bring Ireland into the war. He called for an immediate reunification of Ireland, with its neutrality guaranteed by both the United States and Great Britain, and suggested that American armed forces take up positions in Ireland.[44]

Churchill and the War Cabinet understood the consequences of their options on American opinion, but failed to realize the depth of importance that neutrality held for Irish identity. American officials made it clear that any British effort to take the Treaty ports by force would 'embarrass American efforts to aid Britain'.[45] Later that autumn, Maffey made it clear to Walshe that Irish matters were the most difficult for the British government to tackle because they 'had to consider above all the feelings of the United States and the disastrous repercussions which would inevitably be caused over there'.[46] For de Valera and the Irish government, neutrality simply was not a policy that could be negotiated away as part of some overall political or strategic process unless partition was first eliminated and the Irish people freely decided to join the war, not merely as means to return the favour of unification. Walshe summarized the importance of neutrality in the internal debates over the official response to the British offers:

> Neutrality has given the people more faith in what the Government has achieved for the independence of this country than any other act of theirs. They regard it as a sign and symbol of our independence, and, if it goes, they will believe – and rightly – that our independence has gone with it.[47]

What also may have played a part in de Valera's thinking in the summer of 1940, after the British retreat at Dunkirk and the fall of France, was a suspicion that Britain was going to lose the war. Walshe wrote to him that 'England is already conquered.'[48] If Britain did go down to defeat, and de Valera calculated that Irish participation in the war would not increase measurably the likelihood of a British victory, then abandoning neutrality would only open up Ireland to the destruction of war and the enmity of the eventual victor. That would have been a high price to pay even if Churchill were willing or able to unify Ireland. As with most events concerning British–Irish relations, de Valera was quick to bring the American public, especially Irish Americans, into the policy mix. The day he forwarded his formal rejection of the British proposals de Valera arranged an interview with the *New York Times*, during which he made it clear that Ireland was determined to stay neutral and deter any aggressor. While he did not mention either Germany or Britain, he stressed that he did not intend for Ireland to be used as a base for operations against any belligerent. Again, he stressed that Ireland wanted cordial relations with Britain, but that the lone outstanding obstacle to the bilateral relationship, was the 'most important' issue of partition.[49]

In order to reinforce the message, Frank Aiken, the Irish Minister for Co-ordination of Defensive Measures, arranged an interview on that same day with the National Broadcasting Company that was broadcast in the United States. When asked what Ireland's reaction would be if attacked by Germany, he responded that if Ireland were attacked by 'anyone', being careful not to specify either Germany or Britain, Ireland would 'certainly [be] helped by the other'. It was not a new formulation for Irish policy makers, as the year before, in front of an Irish Day celebration in Scranton, Pennsylvania, Brennan had told the crowd that if any power 'even touched Ireland' the Irish would take every measure to mount a resistance.[50] Aiken's implication that Ireland would call on Germany's aid if Britain tried to seize the ports drew the attention of Washington. Two days later, Secretary of State Cordell Hull cautioned the British against attacking Ireland.[51]

Faced with the fact of Roosevelt's refusal to defend a British seizure of the ports, Churchill hoped that Irish fears of a German invasion would compel de Valera to accept at least an American occupation of Berehaven. An American naval presence there, the most southern and western of the Treaty ports, might be an asset in the continuing fight against German U-boats. When Churchill made the request to Washington, FDR declined, citing the importance of maintaining the fleet in Hawaii.[52] Again, Roosevelt refused to be brought into the conflict by either side.

During this flurry of official and unofficial tension, the German Minister in Dublin worked behind the scenes to allay de Valera's concerns about German intentions. On 1 July he reported to Berlin on his attempts to convince de Valera that there would be no German attack and on his broader efforts to 'minimize suspicion' of German espionage activities. Unaware of the numerous ways the Irish were already aiding the Allies, the Germans did not want Ireland to join the war. As far as Berlin was concerned, even though Hempel knew or suspected some of the ways the Irish government was helping the Allies, Ireland was simply waiting out the war.[53]

In the midst of this tension, the Irish opposition parties began to rally even more strongly around de Valera. Dr T.F. O'Higgins, the vice president of the main opposition party, Fine Gael, wrote to the Defence Council: 'Our present policy is one of ABSOLUTE NEUTRALITY with meticulous attention to very correct balance.' He went on that the Irish should shoot the British, the Germans, or the Americans if they tried to take the ports, but that the British would be shot with 'greater relish' than the Americans. There were only a few opposition members in favour of forming a closer alliance with the British in order to stave off a German invasion, but de Valera responded that the best way to maintain Irish security and independence was with strict neutrality.[54]

In July 1940 there were a series of articles and editorials in the American and British press condemning Ireland's refusal of the British offers to work towards unification if Ireland joined the war. Realizing that much of his ability to maintain neutrality rested on whatever restraint the American and British public, especially the Irish-American community, put on Churchill, de Valera worked hard to counter the attacks. Meeting with the opposition, de Valera expressed his concern over the 'vigorous effort ... to influence public opinion against us in the United States' because he had turned down the British offer.[55] De Valera felt that Gray was behind the press barrage, in part because Gray did little to hide his pleasure in reading the tone of the articles. In late July he wrote to Walshe that Irish-American groups in the United States had lost their effectiveness because they were now associated 'in the public mind with Nazis and Fascists'.[56]

Dublin was therefore eager to get its side of the story to the American press. Walshe and de Valera felt that 'American public opinion seems ... to be the only effective weapon left to us against an early occupation by the British Army as soon as British political intrigues prove unsuccessful.' On 21 July 1940, Walshe instructed Brennan to get the following explanation of Irish neutrality out to American newspapers:

> Neutrality is of the very essence of Irish independence. It is based on the fundamental and universal will of our people, so much so that no Government could depart from it without at once being overthrown. It was not adopted as a bargaining factor but as the fullest expression of our independence in time of war. We are determined to defend it against all invaders to the bitter end. The hostile attitude of certain Americans to Ireland is completely opposed to American statements about small nations and self-determination.[57]

In addition to the public diplomacy efforts, Brennan supplied sympathetic Irish-American senators with information designed to influence the Roosevelt administration and British representatives in Washington. During this crisis, Senator James Murray of Montana acted almost as an agent of the Irish government. He met with the British ambassador to warn him that any British attempt to take the ports would split the Democratic Party and seriously threaten any aid packages to Great Britain. Murray also met with Secretary of State Cordell Hull and other Democratic leaders to warn them of the consequences of unilateral British actions on the ports.[58]

In August 1940, Walshe took his concerns over the press campaign directly to Gray. Walshe received a letter from Gray on 6 August saying that he was surprised that the Irish were worried at all about Britain seizing the ports and therefore had nothing to fear from a press campaign. Walshe responded by sending Gray a series of clippings from British and American newspapers in an attempt to outline a coordinated anti-Irish campaign. Walshe quoted Churchill's comments on the ports in the 1938 debate in the British House of Commons: 'Now we give up the ports to an Irish Government led by men whose rise to power is proportioned by the animosity with which they have acted against this country.' He also noted the similarities in the British and American press campaigns, remarking that 'the mere coincidence gives one furiously to think'.[59]

It is clear that Gray had no real understanding of Irish concerns and did not sympathize with a fellow neutral country's desire to remain neutral. His total lack of understanding can be found in his August 1940 report to Washington on Irish political conditions:

> There is, of course, the question of Partition which all political parties in Eire make much of, but it affects so little the individual life of most of the citizens of Eire and is so complicated with countervailing equities that it cannot account for the acute state of mind that comprises public opinion.

It is difficult to imagine whom Gray relied upon for the basis of this report, but he closed with such a shocking quotation that it is easy to speculate that he fabricated it: 'One observer has said to me, "the best thing that could happen to Ireland would be to have Hitler invade us".'[60]

In the autumn of 1940 a number of developments made Churchill eager to press Ireland again over joining the war or making the Treaty ports available to the British Navy. After the fall of France in June 1940, the German Navy began to base U-boats on the French coast. Even though only ten U-boats were ever on patrol at a time, their shorter distance to targets in the Atlantic, and the British need to keep vessels in the English Channel to guard against an invasion, allowed the Germans to sink a significant amount of British shipping. October 1940 was the worst month of the war for the British in the Battle of the Atlantic, and almost all of the losses came within 250 miles of the north-west corner of Ireland. It is doubtful, however, what difference the British use of the Treaty ports could have made. The ports were in a state of disrepair, located far from the convoy routes and perilously close to the French coast. It is telling that even in the middle of the worst British shipping losses, there is no evidence that the British Navy was pressing the government to gain access to the ports.[61]

Without prior consultation with the Cabinet, on 5 November 1940 Churchill made his first public speech about the role of the Treaty ports in Britain's war effort. It was also election day in the United States, so it is possible that Churchill had been waiting so Roosevelt would not have to worry about an Irish-American backlash. After recounting the success of Britain in weathering the German air assaults over the summer, Churchill turned to Ireland:

> More serious than the air raids has been the recent recrudescence of U-boat sinkings in the Atlantic approaches to our islands. The fact that we cannot use the South and West Coasts of Ireland to refuel our flotillas and aircraft and thus protect the trade by which Ireland as well as Great Britain lives, is a most heavy and grievous burden and one which should never have been placed on our shoulders, broad though they be.[62]

Yet Churchill also went on to stress that perhaps the worst part of the naval situation had passed. During question time, Mr Lees-Smith commented on the American role in keeping Ireland neutral:

> Every month we watch the spectacle of hundreds of thousands of tons being sunk and of hundreds of British sailors being drowned because we cannot get the ports ... Ireland pays a good deal of attention to public opinion in the United States, and it is worth while calling the attention of the United States, who have influence, to what we are paying for our principles.

Other members urged direct action against Ireland, with Sir Southby urging cutting off all trade with Ireland unless the Irish government turned over the ports. Mr Price discussed how the Irish government must be hoping to use the ports 'to secure their dream of a united Ireland and to utilize American opinion to bring that about'. Mr Tinker warned de Valera that continued refusal regarding British use of the ports would mean that after the war any goodwill towards Ireland in resolving partition would be replaced with 'hostility'.[63]

Churchill's comments encouraged Gray to continue the pressure on the Irish government. On 7 November he advised Walshe that American public opinion, far from holding back the British from action, would support Churchill if he took the Treaty ports by force. Gray also wrote to Washington that part of the support would come from 'what is reported to be Chamberlain's undocumented understanding' that the ports would be available to Britain in an emergency. This is one of the rationales that Gray suggested back in May that the British use as a post facto defence of seizing the ports, but there is no evidence that Chamberlain believed there was an understanding that the ports would be available to the British forces. Gray concluded his note by claiming that de Valera had the qualities of a 'fanatic and Machiavelli' and that he would 'do business on his own terms or must be overcome by force'. Ever aware of the need for American support, and concerned about Gray's actions, Walshe instructed Brennan in Washington to work diligently to put the Irish case in front of American officials and newspaper editors.[64]

De Valera's public response to Churchill focused on the positive aspects of the British–Irish relationship. He insisted that he would not have graced Churchill's comments with any response if they had not been followed by a series of speeches in Parliament and a press campaign in Britain and the United States. De Valera emphasized the importance of friendly relations with Britain, and that save for the issue of partition, since the end of the Economic War the bilateral relationship had never been stronger. He also stressed again how he had for more than twenty years given assurances that Ireland would never be a base against Britain. Of course, he did not disclose the extensive covert aid that Ireland had been giving the Allies. He concluded, however, with a stern warning that for the first time mentioned Britain specifically as a potential enemy of Ireland:

> There can be no question of the handing over of these ports so long as this State remains neutral. There can be no question of leasing these ports. They are ours. They are within our sovereignty, and there can be no question, as long as we remain neutral, of handing them over on any condition whatsoever. Any attempt to bring pressure to bear on us by any side – by any of the belligerents – by Britain – could only lead to bloodshed.[65]

In Washington, Brennan emphasized Irish displeasure with the official and unofficial pressure on the ports. He presented a copy of de Valera's speech to Under Secretary of State Sumner Welles, along with an official note stating that Ireland would 'resist by force' either Germany or Britain should Ireland's neutrality be violated. The note also complained that a semi-official press campaign in Britain was being 'echoed' in the United States. When Welles pressed Brennan on how Ireland would fare if Germany defeated Britain, Brennan countered that if the Irish surrendered the ports to the British in an effort to prevent a German victory, 'it was highly probable that revolution would develop within the Irish Free State'.[66]

De Valera felt that the only real obstacle to unilateral British action against Ireland was the War Cabinet's concern that ensuing negative American and Irish-American public opinion might limit Roosevelt's ability to assist in the war. Consequently, he initiated a press and organizational campaign of his own, having Brennan write to and meet with dozens of newspaper editorial offices across the United States.[67] De Valera also sent a telegram to the New York meeting of the American Association for the Recognition of an Irish Republic urging a massive effort 'to put the Irish case, including partition, clearly before the American public'. Pointing to the rights of neutrals and drawing parallels between the American and Irish rights to decide for themselves issues of war and peace, de Valera argued that it would be an 'inhuman outrage' to pressure a woefully unprepared Ireland into war.[68] On 19 November, de Valera gave a widely published interview to Wallace Carroll of United Press International, in which he again insisted that maintaining neutrality and not allowing Britain to use or lease the ports was a matter of sovereignty. He also emphasized the familiar assurance that Britain had no need to fear Ireland being a base against it.[69] The Irish-American press took up the call. The *Irish Echo* called for a meeting of 'all people interested in assisting Ireland in preserving her neutrality'.[70] Almost 2,500 people arrived in a New York hotel on 24 November for what became the organizational meeting of the American Friends of Irish Neutrality (AFIN). AFIN hired a staff whose primary mission was to submit articles and organize letter-writing campaigns across the country. They also published a monthly newsletter, 'Neutrality News'.[71]

Brennan was careful to remain behind the scenes of Irish-American groups such as AFIN for fear that any official Irish government representation, aid or sanction would be seen as foreign interference in American domestic politics. He did, however, maintain extensive informal contact with prominent Irish Americans. In December, Dennis Cardinal Dougherty in Philadelphia notified him that an 'English emissary' had been visiting Irish-American bishops asking them to influence de Valera to yield on the ports.[72] The emissary was Rossa Downing, who headed the Irish group of the Committee to Defend America by Aiding the Allies (CDFAA). Brennan worried that an open split among Irish Americans would deprive him 'of the only weapon I had to save Ireland in the course of the administration's headlong race to save Britain'.[73] In an effort to prevent that, Brennan met with Welles to officially protest against the actions of the Irish group of the CDFAA. Brennan told Welles that already there was a backlash among many Irish Americans and threatened that there might soon appear 'Irish-American propaganda to the effect that the British were seeking these bases in Eire solely as a means of restoring British domination over Ireland'.[74]

The British and American governments took note of de Valera's campaign. There was some discussion in the British Cabinet that perhaps the government should ease the pressure on Ireland out of fear of an American backlash. Churchill, however, would not be moved. He wrote to Maffey, who was advocating an ease of tension, that de Valera 'should stew in his own juice for a while' and that 'certainly nothing must be said to reassure him'. In Washington, Secretary of the Navy Frank Knox was lobbying FDR to join Britain in putting pressure on de Valera, but Roosevelt still resisted getting actively involved. It is probable that he was quite content with Gray's efforts in Dublin, where Gray was telling de Valera that American public opinion would soon more clearly see that the Irish were enjoying their continued safety and standard of living only at the expense of British lives. Gray told de Valera on 21 November that he knew of the 'many friendly ways' the Irish were cooperating with British officials, but that American opinion was turning against the Irish. By January 1941 Gray was telling de Valera that if the survival of Britain meant it had to seize the Treaty ports, then American opinion 'might be expected not to criticize too severely an act which unquestionably was technically wrong'.[75]

The seeds of the autumn's British propaganda campaign against Irish neutrality bore fruit throughout the winter of 1940/1 in the press, but it did not change de Valera's position.[76] Reviewing the nature of the articles about Irish neutrality during the time, historian T. Ryle Dwyer concluded that there were four main areas of 'distortions and misrepresentations' about Ireland: that numerous German agents were in Dublin; that the German diplomatic staff in Dublin was excessively large; that U-Boats were refuelling in Irish ports; and that the lights of Irish cities aided German pilots.[77] Not all of the press was negative. The *New York Times* outlined the errors in articles in the *London Daily Telegraph* and the *London Evening Standard*.[78]

When the propaganda campaign failed, Churchill turned to a two-pronged strategy in December 1940: exerting economic pressure on Ireland; and enlisting American diplomatic aid.[79] While he rejected a more serious proposal to curtail trade with Ireland for fear that the backlash would only strengthen de Valera's hand, the halfway measures he imposed, mostly the reduction in the amount of goods shipped to Ireland, were not strong enough to force a change in the Irish position. Not wanting even these measures to appear as sanctions for Irish intransigence, the Ministry of Information portrayed them as merely unfortunate consequences of the war. Churchill also took his case on Ireland directly to Roosevelt. In the same letter in which he suggested the outline of what became Lend–Lease, Churchill asked for the 'good office of the United States, and the whole influence of its Government' to secure for Britain the Treaty ports and air facilities in southern and western Ireland. Acknowledging the importance of Irish-American politics, he continued:

> If it were proclaimed an American interest that the resistance of Great Britain should be prolonged and the Atlantic route kept open ... the Irish in the United States might be willing to point out to the Government of Eire the dangers which its present policy is creating for the United States itself.

In spite of the need, however, Churchill made it clear that he would not compel Northern Ireland into any union with Ireland. Seemingly out of a realization that he would not get Roosevelt's approval for a British military takeover of the ports, Churchill deleted a line that was included in an earlier draft of the message: 'It must be emphasized that failing any agreement about Eire bases, it may become necessary as a measure of self-preservation, to secure these bases.' Roosevelt did not respond directly to the issue of Ireland.[80]

For his part, de Valera suspected that much of the British agitation for the ports rested not on sound military judgement, but on the need for a scapegoat. Writing to Brennan on 5 December, he outlined how the ports were in such an unprepared condition that it would take months to get them ready, that concerns about the Irish Army and the IRA would force the British to occupy the entire country, and that most of the shipping traffic and sinkings were occurring to the north and west of Northern Ireland, not along Ireland's southern coast. In spite of this, and in a veiled reference to Churchill, de Valera noted that the 'composition of [the British] Cabinet makes [the] situation uncertain and dangerous'.[81]

On 13 December Churchill gave Roosevelt a warning that Great Britain was about to limit the amount of shipping going to Ireland. The effect, according to Churchill, was that Ireland would still have enough to survive, but not enough to have 'the prosperous trading they are making now'. About a week later Churchill also asked Roosevelt what his reaction would be to a complete cessation of shipping to Ireland, because British public opinion could not sustain trade with Ireland much longer while 'de Valera is quite content to sit happy and see us strangled'. Churchill asked Roosevelt to respond 'quite privately'. Roosevelt may have spoken to Churchill about it, but there is no record of any response. Churchill did continue the economic pressure, but he never halted shipping to Ireland.[82]

In his 1940 Christmas message to the United States, carried by the

Columbia Broadcasting System, de Valera complained about the recent British actions and the 'false picture' that the press in Britain and the United States were painting about life in Ireland. Citing a long list of privations endured by the Irish, de Valera claimed that Ireland was blockaded more than any other country in Europe, including by Britain. Again stressing the commitment to neutrality and the reports about the possible seizure of the Treaty ports, he said that the Irish people would 'defend ourselves to the utmost'. Gray complained to de Valera that the speech was designed to 'put the pressure on the Irish-American vote', and that it was not so much the fact of Irish neutrality, but the 'attitude of Irish opinion' as it was being reported that caused problems in the United States. Of course, Gray was attempting to influence that opinion despite the fact that he knew the Irish were cooperating with the British on several issues.[83]

Roosevelt reacted strongly to de Valera's plea. The president was already deeply involved in moving the American public towards a new stage of support for Britain and in laying the groundwork for Lend–Lease and did not appreciate de Valera's public criticism of British naval and shipping policy. During his radio address of 29 December in which he called on the United States to be the 'great arsenal of democracy', he posited that a defeated Britain would mean ruin for Ireland. Clearly addressing de Valera and the majority of Irish Americans, Roosevelt asked dismissively if 'Irish freedom [would] be permitted as an amazing exception in an unfree world'.[84] Gray got the message. In February 1941 he wrote to 'My Dear Franklin' that he intended to get tougher with the Irish government, but that if FDR wanted him to back down he merely had to send him a telegram saying 'be careful'. Gray also wrote that the Irish government was only as good as the Dutchess County Board of Supervisors. (FDR's home was in Dutchess County in New York.) Roosevelt wrote back that Gray was being 'unfair' to the supervisors, 'almost all of whom are practical people', and that Gray had no need to be careful.[85]

Although Roosevelt was unwilling to put any direct personal pressure on de Valera, the British economic pressure and publicity campaign began to have an effect on non-Irish-American public opinion at the start of 1941. The Gallup Poll asked Americans in the first week of January: 'Would you like to see the Irish give up their neutrality and let the English use war bases along the Irish coast?' Among all Americans, 63 per cent said yes, 16 per cent no, with 21 per cent undecided. Among those who identified themselves as Irish Americans, the results were 40 per cent yes, 52 per cent no, and only 8 per cent undecided.[86]

In Dublin, Maffey renewed his warnings to London about possible backlash to the continued pressure and reminded the government about the true nature of Irish neutrality. He noted that the best hope for accomplishing British goals 'always will lie in the actions and thoughts of Irishmen overseas'. He continued:

> Hateful as their neutrality is, it has been a neutrality friendly to our cause. I need not give in detail what we have got and are getting in the way of intelligence reports, prompt reports of submarine movements, free use of Lough Foyle ... etc. ... The catastrophic fall of France stiffened the country's resolve to maintain neutrality, but the Éire government continued to help in every way which did not expose them to German action.[87]

The end result of the British proposals, propaganda campaigns, appeals to Roosevelt and the economic pressure of 1940 was that they created no change in de Valera's policy of neutrality, nor in its pro-British bias. They had, however, created consternation and exasperation for Irish policy makers, especially owing to the way Gray was handling it privately and FDR and Churchill were handling it publicly. Walshe wrote in January 1941 that 'the sacrifices which are still open to America to make before she reaches the magnitude of those involved for us in handing over the ports are enormous, and we are getting tired of America's vicarious heroism at our expense'.[88]

THE AIKEN MISSION

By early 1941 de Valera was concerned enough that Germany may invade Ireland that he moved to enhance the Irish military position.[89] He did not believe Hempel's assurances to the contrary, and the strategy seemed to him the best way for Germany to advance its strategic position against Britain. With Churchill continuing the public pressure on him and with Roosevelt publicly deriding Irish neutrality, de Valera felt that in addition to the public diplomacy efforts in the United States and Great Britain, Ireland needed to improve its defence capabilities. Doing so might at least give the Germans or the British some unease before an attack, or at least more than he expected they would have, given the state of the Irish military. More important, it might give credence to his oft-repeated assurances to the British that Ireland would not be a base against Great Britain, thus forestalling a pre-emptory British invasion. Unable to secure arms from Britain, he turned to the United States both for weapons and for additional ships to offset the loss of British shipping trade. De Valera realized, however, that his relationship with Gray had deteriorated to such a point that there was little prospect of successful negotiations in Dublin, so he decided to send a special envoy to Washington.[90]

De Valera tapped the Minister for Co-ordination of Defensive Measures, Frank Aiken, for the mission. Aiken had a long and distinguished reputation among Irish nationalists, an asset that de Valera hoped would help him establish an immediate connection with Irish Americans. He had served in the Irish Republican Army during the Anglo-Irish War, and as IRA Chief of Staff in 1923 gave the ceasefire and the 'dump arms' orders that ended the civil war. He was instrumental in the founding of Fianna Fáil and served as Minister of Defence from 1932 until the start of the Emergency in 1939.[91]

Aiken's reputation, or at least a version of it, preceded him and impeded his talks with American officials. On 10 March, Bill Donovan from the Office of Strategic Services (OSS) sent a note to Roosevelt that concluded: 'Aiken is possibly in America for other reasons; he is of the extreme left.' Soon this information made it into the briefings being prepared for State Department officials. Gray had also written to Washington that Aiken needed to become 'more fully aware of the American situation', in the hope that if Aiken could see that American and Irish-American public opinion was not supporting Ireland then de Valera would give up neutrality.[92]

Aiken's mission took on an added importance for de Valera after Maffey told him on 14 March that Britain could not give a guarantee similar to the one that Germany gave about not invading Ireland. De Valera later recalled Maffey saying the time might come when Britain or America or both would be pressed to bring 'serious pressure' on Ireland. Maffey felt that he could not give de Valera a guarantee not to invade 'without a mental reservation'.[93] Faced with this knowledge, de Valera used his traditional St Patrick's Day message to the United States to set the stage for Aiken's visit. He directed Americans seeking to understand Irish neutrality to look to George Washington's declaration of neutrality in 1793. He then argued that the real problem was that at the start of the war the Irish and British governments had agreed that if Ireland agreed not to pursue independent shipping charters, Britain would then supply Ireland. Now that Britain was beginning to reduce those supplies, however, the hardship facing the Irish was that there was no longer any independent shipping charters available. Therefore, according to de Valera, 'Both sides in blockading each other ... were blockading us.' He also reiterated his stand that he would never allow Ireland to be used as a base of attack against Britain.[94]

Aiken arrived in New York on 18 March 1941 and spent some weeks touring American military facilities while Brennan tried to arrange meetings for him with Roosevelt and the State Department. On 2 April, Assistant Secretary of State Dean Acheson pressed Aiken on the existence of cooperation between Ireland and Britain on security matters. Acheson wanted some assurances that any arms the United States gave to Ireland would not be used against the British. Clearly the British had not informed Washington about the British–Irish military liaisons; to have done so would have weakened their argument about Ireland's lack of cooperation in the war effort. Aiken and de Valera were also determined to keep the talks secret. They did not want the Germans to learn about them and use them as a pretext for invasion. Aiken, therefore, denied that there were any British–Irish arrangements. Acheson then informed Aiken that he saw no way to sell arms to Ireland without there first being a prior arrangement with Britain for a defensive plan. Aiken said that Ireland would never abandon neutrality, but that it needed arms in order to defend its right to remain neutral. He told Acheson that neutrality was the 'crown and symbol of Irish independence'.[95]

Aiken, accompanied by Brennan, finally met with Roosevelt on 7 April 1941. Immediately prior to receiving the Irish representatives, Roosevelt met with Lord Halifax, the British ambassador, who told Roosevelt that Aiken was anti-British and hoped for a German victory.[96] According to Brennan's account of the latter meeting, Roosevelt talked for about twenty minutes about his love for Ireland and the Irish people. As Roosevelt was finishing up, his aide entered the room as the unofficial signal that the meeting was over. Aiken did not politely rise, though, and told Roosevelt that the position of the Irish towards fascism should be clear to all, for Ireland was the only nation to defeat an internal fascist threat.[97] All Ireland was asking for was the opportunity to buy arms and ships to defeat any invader. Roosevelt interrupted with 'I believe in talking straight. You are reported as having said that it does not matter to Ireland whether England or Germany wins the war.' When Brennan and Aiken both told Roosevelt that Aiken had never made such a comment, Roosevelt continued to lecture them on the global and Irish consequences of a German victory. Aiken then asked the president if the Irish people would have his sympathy in case of aggression. Roosevelt replied: 'Yes. German aggression.' When Aiken suggested that Ireland might also be the target of British aggression, FDR said that was preposterous, emphasizing: 'What you have to fear is German aggression.' Aiken then appended, 'or British aggression', at which point, according to Brennan, Roosevelt jerked the tablecloth for lunch that aides had just placed before him, sending the silverware flying across the Oval Office. When Aiken asked why the British would not guarantee it, FDR said he could get it the next day from Churchill. A few days later, Brennan asked Welles about the promise, but Welles told him that it was a matter between Brennan and Roosevelt.[98] Years later, Aiken said he knew right after the meeting that he would not be able to persuade Roosevelt: 'Churchill had been at him to put the screw to us.'[99]

Although Roosevelt realized that it would not be good public relations to deny everything the Irish asked for, he was determined not to have Aiken's mission be a success. On 25 April the State Department told Gray to inform de Valera that the United States would negotiate with him, not Aiken, for the transfer of two ships to Ireland. Gray was told to add that 'the Government of the United States does not question the right of neutrality', but there is a difference between neutrality and a policy that 'at least potentially provides real encouragement to the German Government'.[100]

After his visit to Washington, Aiken continued the Irish effort to secure Irish-American opinion by touring the country over the next few weeks as a guest of the American Friends of Irish Neutrality. His standard speech began with the argument that a free and neutral Ireland was simply trying to purchase weapons to defend itself. Ireland would pay for those weapons in currency, not by bartering away 'the sovereign rights of the Irish people' by giving up neutrality. 'One of the first principles of democracy is that the people concerned shall have the right to decide for themselves the vital question of war and peace.' He stressed that Ireland's position was not taken out of resentment over years of conflict with Britain. Apart from the continuing injustice of partition, according to Aiken, the countries were closer than ever. He closed by reiterating de Valera's positions on the inability of small nations to control war and peace, and asked for his audience's 'moral support against aggression'. In his farewell, Aiken said that Ireland's survival depended on neutrality, which in turn depended on the 'moral support of … friends abroad'.[101]

As instructed, Gray met with de Valera on 28 April to deliver the news about the sale of the ships. Gray began by criticizing de Valera's St Patrick's Day message to the United States, specifically the part about Britain blockading Ireland. According to Gray, de Valera 'flushed angrily and shouted that it was impertinent to question the statements of a head of state'. Gray's response was that at the time of the

Taoiseach's statements that there had been considerable pressure from the 'anti-British elements to whom he [de Valera] had chiefly appealed' that were trying to defeat Lend–Lease and 'sabotaging' the Roosevelt administration's efforts to aid Britain. According to de Valera's notes, Gray also complained that the AFIN was 'composed largely of German sympathizers and very probably financed by German funds', but Gray later backtracked from that allegation. Gray reported back to Washington:

> I no longer hope to get anything from him by generosity and conciliation. He must be made to realize that it is possible that a situation is approaching in which if it be essential to survival his ports will be seized with the liberal sentiment of the world, that he will have only the choice of fighting on the side of Great Britain or Germany.[102]

De Valera was torn between supporting his old friend Aiken and getting some badly needed ships. His first move was to have Brennan discuss the matter with Welles. When Welles again pressed Brennan on the issue of British–Irish security cooperation, Brennan continued to deny that there was any. Welles argued that given that condition, the offer on the table was the best the United States could do. De Valera rejected it and told Roosevelt that Irish neutrality 'has been a benevolent one, and consequently we have leaned on the side of helpful and sympathetic understanding'. Not content to lose the opportunity to gain a public relations boon among Irish Americans by showing support for Ireland, even if it did involve only a relatively minor transaction, Roosevelt simply ignored de Valera's rejection and told a press conference on 20 May that plans were being made to sell Ireland two ships. De Valera, content that his point had been made at the official level, quietly agreed to the sale.[103]

THE 1941 CONSCRIPTION CRISIS

Churchill's devotion to the loyalists in Northern Ireland was, if measured in either war production or volunteers for the British armed forces, often unrequited. Lord Craigavon noted in May 1940 the 'unsatisfactory position' of Northern Ireland with regard to recruiting. Craigavon could not have argued that the lack of recruits was the result of a massive and growing wartime economy, as by November 1940 the unemployment rate in the province topped 21 per cent. In a December 1940 report by Harold Wilson, future British prime minister and then with the Manpower Requirements Committee, 'at the end of fifteen months of war ... Ulster, far from becoming an important centre of munitions production, has become a depressed area ... Ulster has not seen the construction of a single new factory'. In March 1941 Churchill wrote of his concern about the 'limited extent of Northern Ireland's contribution to the nation's industrial war effort'.[104]

The first movement to introduce conscription in 1941 came from the Northern Ireland government, which hoped to use it to bolster the wartime contribution of the province. Churchill's announcement in the House of Commons on 20 May that the government might extend military conscription to Northern Ireland raised a firestorm of protest.[105] Canadian Prime Minister Mackenzie King wrote to Churchill that the move would have negative effects on Canadian unity. He also urged Churchill to talk with the American Ambassador to London, John Winant, on the possible effects of the move on Irish-American opinion.[106]

Churchill and John Dulanty, the Irish High Commissioner in London, met twice over the next few days to discuss the issue. The Irish argument was that Ireland was already helping Britain on many fronts, including allowing Irish men to enlist in British forces, and that conscripting Catholics in Northern Ireland would make it more difficult to maintain that level of involvement. The IRA would surely gain support, and the British would then be faced with a whole new set of problems. Churchill responded that if the Catholics did not want to be a part of the British Army they could simply escape to Ireland; 'we will put no obstacle in their path'. De Valera's formal complaint included the argument that 'there was no more grievous attack on any fundamental human right' than to make a person fight for a nation to which he objected being a citizen. Churchill replied: 'It makes my blood boil to think of your present position. Ireland has lost its soul.'[107]

The strong arguments by de Valera and opposition leaders about the consequences of Churchill's plans convinced Gray that in this instance Irish and American interests converged, and he urged Roosevelt to try to restrain Churchill. Gray felt that conscription was a tool of the 'weak and failing' Ulster government to provoke a crisis that would forestall any efforts to coerce it to leave the United Kingdom. Fine Gael leaders, whom Gray trusted much more than he did de Valera, convinced Gray that conscription in the North would lead to a number of problems, including draft riots and draft dodgers being welcomed in Ireland. It was the only time that Gray and the American Friends of Irish Neutrality agreed on anything.[108]

In the end Churchill realized the folly of the proposal and on 27 May he told the House of Commons that while Britain had the right to do so, enforcing conscription in Northern Ireland would be 'more trouble than it is worth'. It was the prudent decision. If conscription had been carried out in Northern Ireland there would have been no end to the difficulties it would have brought on de Valera and to British–Irish relations. Nationalist MPs from Northern Ireland had already drawn up a pledge for all Catholics to sign, vowing to 'resist conscription with the most effective means at our disposal'.[109] It was also likely that the Irish Republican Army would get involved in rallying the Nationalist cause, creating further difficulties for de Valera. If the British resorted to imprisoning those resisting the draft, the prospect of hunger strikes, long a tool of Irish nationalists, would have become a rallying cry for the Irish and for Irish Americans.

DECLINING AMERICAN–IRISH RELATIONS

In spite of the two governments' cooperation over the conscription crisis, American–Irish relations continued a steady decline during the summer and autumn of 1941, while, ironically, British–Irish relations improved. The official and unofficial pressure from Britain to relinquish the ports began to subside after the German invasion of the Soviet Union in June. After German attention turned away from the British Isles and the American Navy extended its patrols farther into the Atlantic, the British were able to minimize the shipping losses caused by the U-boat campaign. As a result, there was much less need for the ports. In addition, the flap over the conscription crisis in May hammered home to most British policy makers and military leaders that any overt actions to gain the ports without the support of the Irish government and people would be a disaster. Gray, however, believing it his mission from Roosevelt to keep up the pressure on Ireland, continued his assaults on de Valera and Irish neutrality.

A rare public debate in Ireland about neutrality probably encouraged Gray to think that his actions might bear fruit. On 17 July James Dillon, the deputy leader of the opposition party Fine Gael, stated in the Dáil that Ireland should stand up to the Nazi tyranny. He argued that it was wrong for Ireland to 'sell its honour and stake its whole material future on the vain hope that it may be spared the passing pain of effort now'. The best option for Ireland was to find out what Britain and the United States needed in order to respond to the Nazi threat and then to give them 'cooperation to the limit of our resources'. Dillon was not urging that Ireland enter the war, only that it move further in its cooperation with the Allies. He was certainly advocating giving Britain use of the

Treaty ports.[110] De Valera's response turned the fire-fighting analogy Roosevelt used to defend Lend–Lease on its head. FDR explained Lend–Lease, which supplied Great Britain with weapons, as analogous to loaning your neighbour a garden hose when his house was on fire. It was a practical effort to prevent your own house from burning. De Valera commented:

> I was speaking to one person who happened to visit us here and he asked … 'If a neighbour's house was on fire, surely you would allow the firemen to get up on your roof to put out the fire next door?' Of course we would, but that is not an analogy to what we are being asked to do. What we have been asked to do is to set our own house on fire in company with the other house. We have been asked to throw ourselves into the flames – that is what it amounts to.[111]

Gray hoped the British would exploit this first open rift in Irish support for neutrality. Churchill, however, had begun to understand the dangers involved in pursuing further action against de Valera. In August Gray wrote to Roosevelt that the British should cut off all supplies to Ireland in order to 'explode this nationalistic dream of self-sufficiency'. Roosevelt did not indicate that he would pursue the matter with Churchill, but he did reply that 'people, frankly, are getting pretty fed up with my old friend Dev'.[112]

Gray then implemented a policy of unofficial public diplomacy pressure on Ireland. Over the summer and autumn of 1941 he gave a series of 'off the record' interviews with American correspondents about Axis espionage activities in Ireland. He sent a note in September 1941 to Joseph Walshe at External Affairs outlining his talking points to the reporters. Gray had been telling the reporters that he had infor-mation from 'several likely sources' that Germany had made a deal with the Irish Republican Army in which in exchange for cooperation against the British, Ireland would be reunited and given two English counties 'as a bridgehead for control of England'. He claimed that there were probably many agents in Ireland operating freely. In the United States, Gray argued that the activities of Irish Americans in defence of Irish neutrality were part of an Axis propaganda plan.[113]

Walshe drafted a response to Gray that challenged his conclusions point by point, but never sent it. Perhaps, given the tone of his draft, he either wrote it as a cathartic exercise or realized after the fact that sending it would have devastating consequences for American–Irish relations. He began by complaining that Gray's assertions that the comments were off the record did not mitigate the harm they were doing to the bilateral relationship. Walshe complained bitterly that all of Gray's points were 'in the realm of assumption and opinion'. With regard to Irish-American activities, Walshe wrote:

> Is it possible that because they sympathise with the aspirations of this county to govern its own destiny, Irish-Americans must be branded by you as pro-German or anti-British? … The freedom of the human spirit about which you spoke to me must provide for even Irish-Americans being Irish and American without being pro-German … You can hardly mean to insinuate … that ex-President Hoover and a great many other distinguished Isolationsists are one whit less American than you are.

In conclusion, Walshe wrote that Gray's entire account was merely 'insinuation and innuendo' that was 'founded on acknowledged ignorance'. Given Gray's views, Walshe doubted that Gray's 'prejudices' would ever allow him to be an instrument of goodwill between the American and Irish governments.[114]

Gray's portrayal of German espionage in Ireland was off the mark. In recent times historians have begun to learn how large, extensive and effective was the cooperation between the Irish and British intelligence agencies during the war. In the most current and complete review of German intelligence efforts in Ireland during the war, Mark Hull concludes that the entire German espionage effort was an 'absolute failure', primarily because of 'the system of brilliantly effective counterintelligence operations run by both Ireland and Britain'.[115]

The case of Walter Simon is a typical example of the quality of German intelligence activities in Ireland. Simon travelled to Ireland in U-38, which had entered Dingle Bay on the night of 12 June 1940. After walking along a rusted railway track for several hours, Simon asked some locals about when the next train would be around. After having been informed that no train had run on the track for over ten years, Simon waited in a pub before taking a bus to Tralee, hoping to catch a train to Dublin from there. Simon got drunk while he waited, explaining to all who would listen that the conditions in Ireland would improve as soon as Hitler landed. His actions and accent brought him to the attention of two plain clothes officers who followed him on to the train. Simon told the officers that he had been in Dingle, but had been in German-controlled Rotterdam before that. The officers asked, jokingly, if he was looking for the Irish Republican Army, and Simon asked them if they were in the IRA and if they knew any of the commanders. The officers called ahead to Dublin and the police arrested Simon when the train arrived.[116]

CONCLUSION

De Valera, with some help from Irish Americans and the spectre of an angry Irish American and American public opinion, successfully managed the first difficult years of Irish neutrality. His effort was a study in pragmatism, but it grew out of his desire to create a unique Irish identity against a history of dominance by Britain over Ireland. While Churchill certainly did not see it then or later, de Valera's efforts also aided Britain. If Ireland had joined the war, many, if not most, of the Irish volunteers going to the British Army would have stayed in Ireland, draining the British forces of troops, arms and munitions, and forcing them to extend air coverage to Ireland during the Battle of Britain.

Before the United States entered the war, Irish Americans were willing to work hard to help de Valera and the Irish maintain their neutrality. All of that would change after the attack on Pearl Harbor. On 16 December 1941 Brennan reported to Dublin that the AFIN had disbanded in order to concentrate 'every effort on the successful prosecution of the war'. Two days later he reported that the Irish legation in Washington was getting 'abusive letters and telephone messages'. For the next four years the New York City St Patrick's Day Parade avoided celebrating Ireland, concentrating instead on the accomplishments of Irish Americans.[117]

NOTES

1. Louis MacNeice, *Collected Poems, 1925–1948* (London: Faber & Faber, 1949). The poem was written in 1942 and first published in 1944, but the sentiments it expresses took root for many in the period right after the start of the war. MacNeice wrote the poem soon after a friend died in the North Atlantic; see Brian Girvin, *The Emergency: Neutral Ireland, 1939–1945* (London: Macmillan, 2006), 28, and also Clair Wills, *That Neutral Island: A Cultural History of Ireland During the Second World War* (London: Faber & Faber, 2007), 127–8. For a comparison of MacNeice and Yeats, see Richard Danson Brown, 'Neutrality and Commitment: MacNeice, Yeats, Ireland and the Second World War', *Journal of Modern Literature* 28, no. 3 (2005): 109–29.
2. 'Hearne to Skelton', 22 December 1939, Royal Irish Academy and Department of Foreign Affairs, *Documents on Irish Foreign Policy*, vol. 6, *1939–1941*, ed. Catriona Crowe *et al.* (Dublin: Royal Irish Academy, 2008), doc. 121 (hereafter given as *DIFP*, vol. number, document number).
3. 'Notes for a Conversation with the Representative of Germany Concerning Ireland's Neutrality', 25 August 1939, University College Dublin archives, De Valera Papers, P150/2571 (hereafter manuscript collections from the Archives at University College Dublin will be cited as UCD, collection name, file number).
4. Joseph Walshe, 15 May 1945, National Archives of Ireland, Department of Foreign Affairs, A2 (hereafter NAI/DFA/file number). The Department of External Affairs became the Department of Foreign Affairs in 1971. See also Dermot Keogh, *Ireland and Europe, 1919–1948* (Dublin: Gill & Macmillan, 1988), 163–4.
5. T. Ryle Dwyer, *Irish Neutrality and the USA, 1939–47* (Dublin: Rowman & Littlefield, 1977),

2–3.

6. Trevor Salmon, *Unneutral Ireland: An Ambivalent and Unique Security Policy* (New York: Oxford University Press, 1989), 152.

7. See especially his speech to the League on 26 September 1932, in Éamon de Valera, *Speeches and Statements by Eamon de Valera, 1917–1973*, ed. Maurice Moynihan (New York: St Martin's Press, 1980), 220–3.

8. 'De Valera Arrives to Aid Press Fund', *New York Times*, 11 December 1929.

9. Michael Kennedy, *Ireland and the League of Nations, 1919–1946: International Relations, Diplomacy, and Politics* (Dublin: Irish Academic Press, 1996), 222.

10. 'Withdrawal of Sanctions', 2 July 1936, Special Session of the League of Nations Assembly, in Éamon de Valera, *Peace and War: Speeches by Mr de Valera on International Affairs* (Dublin: M.H. Gill & Son, 1944), 59. The Irish government's position on the legal basis of its neutrality policies is outlined in 'Ireland's Neutrality in Practice', 1 September 1939, NAI/DFA, Legal Adviser's Papers.

11. Brian Girvin, 'Politics in Wartime: Governing, Neutrality and Elections', in *Ireland and the Second World War: Politics, Society and Remembrance*, ed. Brian Girvin and Geoffrey Roberts (Dublin: Four Courts Press, 2000), 24–46.

12. 'First Amendment of the Constitution Bill, 1939'. All Irish legislation is available at http://www.irishstatutebook.ie/.

13. 'Emergency Powers Bill, 1939'. The primary philosophical and practical points of Irish censorship are in 'Censorship of War News, Espionage, etc. in a Neutral Country During War', 7 March 1939, UCD, Aiken Papers, P104/3429. For an excellent recent review of Irish censorship see Robert Cole, *Propaganda, Censorship and Irish Neutrality in the Second World War* (Edinburgh: Edinburgh University Press, 2006).

14. Brennan informed the US State Department on 3 September 1939; see Robert Brennan, *Ireland Standing Firm: My Wartime Mission in Washington* (Dublin: University College Dublin Press, 2002), 20; 'Open Letter to President Wilson', 27 October 1920, in de Valera, *Speeches and Statements*, 41; *Dáil Debates*, 13 July 1938, col. 691. All Dáil debates are available at http://www.historical-debates.oireachtas.ie/.

15. Seán Cronin, *Washington's Irish Policy, 1916–1986: Independence, Partition, Neutrality* (Dublin: Anvil Books, 1987), 72; 'The Minister in Eire to the Foreign Minister', 14 November 1939, doc. 355; 'Hempel to Foreign Minister', 8 October 1939, doc. 216, in *Documents on German Foreign Policy*, vol. 9, Series D (Washington, DC: Government Printing Office, 1956).

16. 'Visit of the Secretary of the Dept of External Affairs to London, 6th to 10th September, 1939', undated, UCD, De Valera Papers, P150/2571.

17. *DIFP*, vol. 6, doc. 19; 'Maffey to Eden', 24 September 1939, Public Record Office (London), Records of the Prime Minister's Office, PREM 1/340 (hereafter cited as PRO, PREM and file number); 'Churchill to Halifax', Public Record Office (London), Records of the Foreign Office, 800/310 (hereafter cited as PRO, FO and file number).

18. *DIFP*, vol. 6, doc. 32. De Valera rejected the British preference for the title of 'High Commissioner'. In his official biography, the controversy is described as follows: 'The title "high commissioner", with its imperial history, was unacceptable in Ireland while, for Britain, the appointment of an "ambassador" or "minister" might be considered a recognition of Irish independence.' See Frank Pakenham Longford and Thomas P. O'Neill, *Éamon de Valera* (London: Arrow Books, 1974), 350.

19. Paul Canning, *British Policy Towards Ireland, 1921–1941* (New York: Oxford University Press, 1985), 353.

20. Robert Brennan, *Allegiance* (Dublin: Browne & Nolan, 1950).

21. For an example of Brennan's activities, see his report on his trip to Boston in December 1939, where he met with the mayor, Cardinal O'Connell, and with the president of Harvard University and was hosted a dinner of the Clover Club; 'Brennan to Walshe', 12 December 1939, *DIFP*, vol. 6, doc. 87.

22. Dermot Keogh, *Twentieth-Century Ireland: Nation and State* (New York: St Martin's Press, 1995), 120–4 and Salmon, *Unneutral Ireland*, 129. Near the end of the war, Viscount Cranborne, the British Dominions' secretary, outlined fourteen of the most helpful Irish efforts. See Ronan Fanning, *Independent Ireland* (Dublin: Helicon, 1983), 124–5.

23. Eunan O'Halpin, 'Intelligence and Security in Ireland, 1922–45', *Intelligence and National Security 5*, no. 1 (1990): 50.

24. The list is undated, but it was attached to a memo dated 24 May 1941, 'Help Given by the

Irish Government to the British in Relation to the Actual Waging of the War (Most Secret)', NAI/DFA/A3.

25. Richard Doherty, *Irish Men and Women in the Second World War* (Dublin: Four Courts Press, 1999), 15–26.
26. Keogh, *Nation and State*, 108.
27. Eunan O'Halpin, ed., *MI5 and Ireland, 1939–1945: The Official History* (Dublin: Irish Academic Press, 2003), 31.
28. 'Gray to State', 26 November 1945, FDR Library, David Gray Papers, box 10. For Cudahy's desire to move, see Dwyer, *Irish Neutrality*, 23.
29. T. Ryle Dwyer describes Maude Gray's relationship with Eleanor Roosevelt as follows: 'Maud [*sic*] was the youngest sister of Eleanor Roosevelt's mother, who died when Eleanor was a child. Subsequently Eleanor was raised by her grandmother in the same home as Maud, who was only six years her senior, with the result that the relationship between them was more akin to that between younger and older sisters than between aunt and niece.'Dwyer, *Irish Neutrality*, 48. There is some evidence that Eleanor pushed her husband to appoint Gray. See Raymond James, 'David Gray, the Aiken Mission and Irish Neutrality, 1940–41', *Diplomatic History* 9, no. 1 (1985): 56; David Gray, 'Behind the Green Curtain', unpublished manuscript, p. 66, University of Wyoming, American Heritage Center, David Gray Papers, box 1 (hereafter UW, AHC, box number). See also 'Geneology', UW, AHC, box 23 and 'Family Scrapbook', UW, AHC, box 2. For the Eleanor Roosevelt correspondence, see FDR Library, David Gray Papers, boxes 5 and 6.
30. Gray presented his credentials to the Irish government on 15 April 1940; see National Archives of Ireland, Department of the Taoiseach, 5252B (hereafter NAI/DT/file number); 'Gray to Roosevelt', 8 April 1940, quoted in Dwyer, *Irish Neutrality*, 49.
31. *DIFP*, vol. 6, docs. 96, 112, 121.
32. Joseph T. Carroll, *Ireland in the War Years, 1939–1945* (San Francisco, Calif.: International Scholars Publications, 1998), 39–41; Canning, *British Policy Towards Ireland*, 266.
33. 'German Attack on Neutral States', Galway, 12 May 1940, *Speeches and Statements*, 434–5; 'Report from Walshe to de Valera (Most Secret)', 6 May 1940, UCD, De Valera Papers, P150/2571.
34. Canning, *British Policy Towards Ireland*, 290.
35. 'Gray to Secretary of State', 18 May 1940, in *Foreign Relations of the United States: Diplomatic Papers, 1940*, vol. 3, *The British Commonwealth, the Soviet Union, the Near East and Africa* (Washington, D.C.: US Government Printing Office, 1958), 160 (hereafter citations from *Foreign Relations of the United States* will be cited as *FRUS*, year, vol. number: page number); 'Secretary of State to Gray', 22 May 1940, *FRUS*, 1940, 3: 160–1. See also Cordell Hull, *The Memoirs of Cordell Hull* (New York: Macmillan Co., 1948), vol. 2, 1352.
36. 'Gray to Cooper', 30 May 1940, in Dwyer, *Irish Neutrality*, 54; *Dáil Debates*, 27 April 1938, cols. 35–7.
37. 'Minutes of Meeting between Representatives of the Government of Éire and Representatives of the Dominions Office and Service Departments of the United Kingdom (Secret)', 23 and 24 May 1940, NAI/DFA/A3; 'Gray to State', 23 October 1940, National Archives of the United States, Record Group 84 (Foreign Service Post Files), Dublin Legation Classified Records, DF 711 (hereafter NAUS/RG84/DLCR/file number).
38. 'Chamberlain to Churchill', 12 June 1940, PRO, PREM 3/131/2; Most of the reports of a possible German invasion came from Sir Charles Tegart, who had been reporting from Ireland. One of his wildly inaccurate reports stated that 'up to 2,000 [German] leaders have been landed in Eire from German U-Boats and by other methods since the outbreak of the war'(quoted in Coogan, *Eamon de Valera: The Man Who Was Ireland* [New York: HarperCollins, 1995], 549). The British position also rested on an interpretation of some documents that the Irish found in a raid looking for German agents. See Girvin, *The Emergency*, 111. Lord Halifax, the British Foreign Secretary, had also proposed to Churchill that some movement on the partition issue might get Ireland into the war; see Robert Fisk, *In Time of War: Ireland, Ulster and the Price of Neutrality*, 1939–45 (Dublin: Gill & Macmillan, 1983), 184–5.
39. 'MacDonald Notes', 17 June 1940, PRO, PREM 3/131/1.
40. 'Cabinet Minutes', 20 June 1940, PRO, CAB 66/9.
41. Malcolm MacDonald, *Titans & Others* (London: Collins, 1972), 85.
42. Dwyer, *Irish Neutrality*, 60.
43. Canning, *British Policy Towards Ireland*, 279.

44. 'Notes of Conversation between de Valera and MacDonald', 23 June 1940, PRO, PREM 3/131/1; 'Memorandum of Talks between de Valera and MacDonald', 28 June 1940, NAI/DFA/P3; 'Chamberlain to de Valera', 29 June 1940, NAI, DFA/P13; 'De Valera to Chamberlain', 4 July 1940, UCD, De Valera Papers, P150/2548; 'Dulanty to Walshe', 8 July 1940, NAI/DFA/P13.
45. Dwyer, *Irish Neutrality*, 60.
46. 'Walshe to de Valera (Secret)', 18 October 1940, NAI/DFA/A2.
47. 'Walshe to de Valera', 1 July 1940, NAI/DFA/P13.
48. 'Memorandum by Walshe for de Valera', 11 July 1940, NAI/DFA/A2.
49. 'Dublin Arms to Bar an Invasion, Whether from Britain or Reich', *New York Times*, 6 July 1940.
50. 'Text of Interview', 6 July 1940, UCD, Aiken Papers, P104/3577; 'Brennan to Walshe', 1 September 1939, NAI/DFA/219/3; *Scranton Tribune*, 28 August 1939.
51. Dwyer, *Irish Neutrality*, 77.
52. 'Churchill to Roosevelt'and 'Roosevelt to Churchill', 13 June 1940, in Warren F. Kimball, ed., *Churchill and Roosevelt: The Complete Correspondence*, vol. 1, *Alliance Emerging* (Princeton, N.J.: Princeton University Press, 1984), 45–6.
53. 'SECRET: Hempel to Berlin', 1 July 1940, *Documents on German Foreign Policy*, 89; the Department of External Affairs admonished all foreign missions to work actively against any mention of secret collaboration between Ireland and Great Britain. See 'Telegram from External Affairs to All Missions Abroad', 5 July 1940, NAI/DFA/P14.
54. 'Memorandum to Defence Council', 3 July 1940, UCD, Mulcahy Papers, P7/A/215 (emphasis in the original); 'Cosgrave to de Valera, 9 July 1940', NAI/DT/S14213; 'De Valera to Cosgrave', 13 July 1940, UCD, Mulcahy Papers, P7/C/112.
55. 'Notes on Conference Held in Taoiseach's Room on Morning of July 16th, 1940', NAI/DT/S14213.
56. Gray to Walshe, 25 July 1940, NAI/DFA/P10.
57. 'Walshe to de Valera (Most Secret)', 15 July 1940, NAI/DFA/A2; 'Dublin to Washington, Personal and Most Secret', 21 July 1940, NAI/DFA/P2.
58. 'Brennan to Walshe', 8 July 1940, NAI/DFA/P2. For more on Murray, see William B. Evans, 'Senator James E. Murray: A Voice of the People in Foreign Affairs', *Montana: The Magazine of Western History* 32, no. 1 (winter 1982): 24–35. Brennan gave a 'long speech'to Senator Murray in support of Irish neutrality in January 1941; see 'Brennan to Walshe', 22 January 1941, NAI/DFA/P2.
59. 'Walshe to Gray', 9 August 1940, NAI, DFA/P10.
60. 'The Irish Political Situation as of August 28, 1940', 28 August 1940, NAUS/RG84/DLCR/850.2.
61. See Williamson Murray and Allan Millett, *A War to Be Won: Fighting the Second World War* (Cambridge, Mass.: Belknap Press, Harvard University Press, 2000), 234–61.
62. *Commons Debates*, 5 November 1940, col. 1243. All debates in the House of Commons are available at http://www.hansard.millbanksystems.com/commons/C20.
63. *Commons Debates*, 5 November 1940, cols. 1252, 1262–3, 1271, 1289.
64. Ironically, on 5 November Brennan reported to Dublin that 'during the past few weeks we find there is now far better understanding of Ireland's position'. 'Washington to Dublin', 5 November 1941, NAI/DFA/2; 'Gray to the Secretary of State', 10 November 1940, *FRUS*, 1940, 3: 168–70; 'Walshe to Brennan', 7 November 1940, NAI/DFA/P2. Gray had earlier written to the State Department's Division of European Affairs asking to be kept aware of 'Irish interference with American domestic policy'; see 'Gray to Stewart', 4 November 1941, University of Wyoming, American Heritage Center, Gray Papers, box 23 (hereafter cited as UW/AHC, box number).
65. *Dáil Debates*, 7 November 1940, cols. 583–4.
66. *DIFP*, vol. 6, doc. 329; Welles wrote to Gray about the meeting on 19 November 1940, see 'Acting Secretary of State to the Minister in Ireland', 19 November 1940, and 'Irish Legation to the Department of State', 9 November 1940, NAI/DFA/P10.
67. Brennan, *Ireland Standing Firm*, 9–10, 36–9.
68. 'Telegram from De Valera to AARIR', 8 November 1940, NAI/DFA/P2.
69. 'Interview with US Journalist', 19 November 1940, in Éamon de Valera, *Ireland's Stand: Being a Selection of Speeches of Éamon de Valera During the War* (Dublin: Stationery Office, 1946), 28–33.
70. *Irish Echo*, 18 November 1940.

71. *Neutrality News*, 1 July 1941, UCD, Aiken Papers, P104/3607.
72. When the AFIN was running out of money, Brennan refused to provide a subsidy; see 'Washington to Dublin', 29 September 1941, NAI/DFA/2; 'Washington to Dublin', 9 December 1940, NAI/DFA/2.
73. Brennan, *Ireland Standing Firm*, 24.
74. Sumner Welles, 'Memorandum of Conversation', 9 December 1940, *FRUS*, 1940, 3: 173–5.
75. Churchill quoted in Dwyer, *Irish Neutrality*, 93; 'Gray to de Valera', 21 November 1940 and 'Gray to de Valera', 14 January 1941, UCD, De Valera Papers, P150/2589.
76. Clippings sent by Brennan to Dublin are contained in NAI/DFA/P10, 'British and American Press and Radio Campaign Against Irish Neutrality'.
77. Dwyer, *Irish Neutrality*, 97.
78. 'Ireland Disturbed at Issue of Bases', *New York Times*, 10 November 1940.
79. Canning, *British Policy Towards Ireland*, 295–307.
80. 'Churchill to Roosevelt', 7 December 1940, and 'Printed for the War Cabinet', November 1940, in Kimball, *Churchill and Roosevelt*, 99–111.
81. 'Dublin to Washington', 5 December 1940, NAI/DFA/2.
82. 'Confidential and Personal for the President from Former Naval Person', 13 December 1940, Kimball, *Churchill and Roosevelt*, 113.
83. 'Taoiseach's Broadcast to US Christmas, 1940', 25 December 1940, NAI/DT/S10701A; 'Gray to the Secretary of State', 7 January 1941, *FRUS*, 1941, 3: 215–16.
84. 'National Security Address of President Roosevelt', 29 December 1940, Department of State *Bulletin* 4, no. 80, 4 January 1941.
85. 'Gray to FDR', 4 February 1941 and 'FDR to Gray', 6 March 1941, FDR Library, David Gray Papers, box 6.
86. George Gallup, *The Gallup Poll: Public Opinion, 1935–1971*, vol. 1, *1935–1948* (New York: Random House, 1972), 260. The poll was conducted 2–7 January 1941.
87. 'Maffey to Cranborne', 19 January 1941, quoted in Dwyer, *De Valera*, 254.
88. 'Mr Gray's Memorandum: Notes Thereon', 17 January 1941, NAI/DFA/P48; also in UCD, De Valera Papers, P150/2571.
89. The legal advisor in the Department of External Affairs drafted a note in January 1941 to be sent to foreign governments in case of an attack. See NAI/DFA/P22.
90. Gray's relationship with de Valera and Walshe was almost completely soured by November 1940. Walshe wrote to Brennan that 'Gray thinks on exclusively British lines and believes the Germans are really going to invade America.' See 'Dublin to Washington', 26 November 1940, NAI/DFA/P2.
91. Maffey wrote to London that Gray first suggested a special envoy during a meeting with de Valera on 6 January; see 'Maffey to Foreign Office', 24 February 1941, quoted in Carroll, *Ireland in the War Years*, 101–2. De Valera informed Gray about the mission and the choice of Aiken in a meeting on 22 February 1941: 'Gray to Secretary of State', 24 February 1941, *FRUS*, 1941, 3: 218–19. In a 1979 interview Aiken told Robert Fisk that he proposed the mission to de Valera after Churchill's 5 November 1940 speech on the ports. See Fisk, *In Time of War*, 264. Joseph Carroll has argued that Gray 'deliberately set a trap' for de Valera by suggesting the sending of an emissary, see Carroll, *Ireland in the War Years*, 101.
92. 'Donovan to Roosevelt', 11 March 1941, Franklin Delano Roosevelt Library, President's Secretary Files 4 (hereafter cited as FDR/PSF/file number). Gray's views of Donovan's visit are in 'Gray to the Secretary of State', 10 March 1941, *FRUS*, 1941, 3: 222; 'Gray to Welles', 7 March 1941, National Archives of the United States, Record Group 59 (State Department Central File), 841D.00/1306 (hereafter cited as NAUS/RG59/file number). De Valera had tried to dissuade Gray of the opinion that Aiken was pro-German some weeks earlier; see 'Memorandum of Conversation', 26 February 1941, UCD, De Valera Papers, P150/2589.
93. Longford and O'Neill, *De Valera*, 377.
94. 'Ireland's Position in a World at War', 17 March 1941, *Speeches and Statements*, 452–5.
95. Acheson, 'Memorandum of Conversation', 2 April 1941, *FRUS*, 1941, 3: 223–5.
96. Fisk, *In Time of War*, 309. Maffey had written Halifax back in March that 'it is important that he [Aiken] return in a chastened mood'. See Carroll, *Ireland in the War Years*, 102.
97. De Valera repressed the 'Blueshirts', the popular name of a quasi-fascist organization, the Army Comrades Association, in the early 1930s through use of the Offences Against the State Act. See Mike Cronin, *The Blueshirts and Irish Politics* (Dublin: Four Courts Press, 1997) and Keogh, *Nation and State*, 81–7.

98. Robert Brennan, 'Report on Mr Aiken's Interview with President Roosevelt', 10 April 1940, UCD, De Valera Papers, P150/2604; Brennan, *Ireland Standing Firm*, 45–8. Aiken gave a similar account of the meeting (except without the table clearing dramatics) during a 24 May 1941 dinner with Charles Lindbergh; see Charles A. Lindbergh, *The Wartime Journals of Charles A. Lindbergh* (New York: Harcourt Brace Jovanovich, 1970), 495. For more on the Aiken's visit, see 'Cablegrams from Washington Regarding Mr Aiken's Activities in the USA', UCD De Valera Papers, P150/2615. Brian Girvin argues that the lack of corroborating evidence places the table-clearing part of the meeting in doubt; see Girvin, *The Emergency*, 210–12. Girvin's evaluation of Gray's motivation, especially Gray's efforts to influence Aiken's trip, is flawed. Girvin misses much of Gray's concern about postwar Irish-American political action. See especially Girvin, *The Emergency*, 181–219.
 99. Interview with Robert Fisk, December 1979, quoted in Fisk, *In Time of War*, 266.
100. 'Secretary of State to Gray', 25 April 1941, *FRUS*, 1941, 3: 226–7; 'Walshe to de Valera', 1 May 1941, NAI/DFA/A24.
101. His major stops included New York, Boston, Chicago, Philadelphia, Minneapolis, Seattle, and Los Angeles. See 'Names and Addresses', 25 October 1941, UCD, Aiken Papers, P104/3576; 'Speech Made by Mr Aiken at Boston on 18th April, 1941', UCD, Aiken Papers, P104/3569. 'Mr Aiken's Farewell Speech', 23 June 1941, UCD, Aiken Papers, P104/3583. The text of Judge Cohalan's speech at the dinner is in UCD, Aiken Papers, P104/3572. Aiken made similar remarks to a national radio audience on CBS on 21 June 1941; see 'Speech Delivered by General Frank Aiken', 21 June 1941, UCD, Aiken Papers, P104/3576. For the general tone of all of his speeches, see 'Basic Speech Delivered by Mr. Aiken', UCD, Aiken Papers, P104/3582.
102. 'Gray to Secretary of State', 1 May 1941, *FRUS*, 1941, 3: 229–32. De Valera noted that he wanted to express his displeasure at Gray 'as vividly as I could'. See 'Memorandum by E. de V. of interview with D. Gray', 28 April 1941, UCD, De Valera Papers, P150/2589. For Gray's backtrack on the AFIN, see 'Gray to de Valera', 12 May 1941, UCD, De Valera Papers, P150/2589.
103. Welles, 'Memorandum of Conversation', 29 April 1941, *FRUS*, 1941, 3: 228–9; 'Irish Legation to the Department of State', 15 May 1941, *FRUS*, 1941, 3: 232–3; Brennan, *Ireland Standing Firm*, 51–6.
104. Fisk, *In Time of War*, 386–409. Maffey related his thoughts to Gray on 25 May 1941 that the Belfast air raids and the ensuing lack of recruits embarrassed the Northern Ireland government; see 'Gray to Secretary of State', 25 May 1941, *FRUS*, 1941, 3: 238.
105. *Commons Debates*, 20 May 1941, cols. 1390–1.
106. Canning, *British Policy Towards Ireland*, 309.
107. 'Dulanty to Walshe', 22 and 26 May 1941, NAI/DFA/P12/14.
108. 'Gray to Secretary of State', 24 May 1941, *FRUS*, 1941, 3: 235–6. The AFIN issued a call for the American government to intervene with Great Britain; see 'America and Conscription', UCD, De Valera Papers, P150/2621.
109. *Commons Debates*, 27 May 1941, col. 1718. De Valera's official biographers note that 'de Valera would have been compelled to take the part of the conscripted Nationalists'. Longford and O'Neill, *De Valera*, 385, quoted in Fisk, *In Time of War*, 445.
110. *Dáil Debates*, 17 July 1941, col. 1864.
111. *Dáil Debates*, 17 July 1941, cols. 1913–14.
112. Dwyer, *Irish Neutrality*, 133.
113. 'Notes on Axis Activities in Ireland', 3 September 1941, UCD, De Valera Papers, P150/2589.
114. 'Walshe to Gray', 11 September 1941, NAI/DFA/A4.
115. Mark Hull, *Irish Secrets: German Espionage in Wartime Ireland, 1939–1945* (Dublin: Irish Academic Press, 2003), 278, 275. Eunan O'Halpin writes that at times the British–Irish relationship with regard to security and counter-espionage was close to a 'full alliance'. See O'Halpin, *Spying on Ireland: British Intelligence and Irish Neutrality During the Second World War* (New York: Oxford University Press, 2008), 300.
116. Hull, *Irish Secrets*, 107–13.
117. 'Brennan to Walshe', 16 and 18 December 1941, NAI/DFA/P2; Mike Cronin and Daryl Adair, *The Wearing of the Green: A History of St Patrick's Day* (New York: Routledge, 2002), 155.

4

War, Demands and Distortions: 1941–1945

Personal. Private and Secret.
Begins.
Now is your chance, Now or never. 'A Nation once again'. Am very ready to meet you at any time.
Ends. (Churchill to de Valera, 8 December 1941)[1]

This assertion of her neutrality is Eire's first *free* self-assertion: as such alone it would mean a great deal to her ... She has invested her self-respect in it. It is typical of her intense and narrow view of herself that she cannot see that her attitude must appear to England an affair of blindness, egotism, escapism or sheer funk. (Elizabeth Bowen)[2]

The relationships among the American, Irish and British governments, as well as their interactions with Irish Americans, changed dramatically after 7 December 1941. No longer would Irish Americans organize around the issue of protecting Irish neutrality, with the American Friends of Irish Neutrality disbanding the day after the attack on Pearl Harbor. David Gray need no longer dance around the issue of one neutral pressuring another neutral to enter the war. Winston Churchill could now present his appeals to Ireland in light of a worldwide struggle, no longer afraid of alienating American public opinion by antagonizing its Irish-American elements. Éamon de Valera no longer had a ready flank of Irish Americans to support his positions, but he did have an even more supportive Irish public committed to staying out of the war. The political, diplomatic and military manoeuvres of the three governments played the central role in the story of Ireland's neutrality during the war. While Irish Americans eagerly joined the national war effort, putting their own assertions of cultural identity on hold, David Gray wanted to take no chances that their later activities would diminish the postwar British–American relationship.

The American entry into the war also diminished considerably the strategic importance of the Treaty ports. The United States had gained considerable bases in Iceland, Greenland and the Azores in 1941, and now the Allies could use those bases to take more active roles in the defence of the Atlantic. Taken together with the expansion of bases in Northern Ireland, improvements in code-breaking of U-boat communications and the introduction of effective long-range anti-submarine aircraft, the new strategic situation meant that the Treaty ports were not nearly as important as they had been before December 1941. The real concern of British and American military leaders was that Ireland not be a base of espionage activities against Britain. With the American entry into the war, both American and British intelligence services kept a watch on Ireland and they were pleased with the cooperation of the Irish and the success of the operation. David Gray, the American Minister to Ireland, however, would not let the facts of Ireland's friendly neutrality get in his way.[3]

THE UNITED STATES ENTERS THE WAR

The Japanese attack on Pearl Harbor and the subsequent state of war between the United States and the Axis powers shifted the power dynamics of the world conflict and also among the American, Irish and British governments. In the early morning of 8 December 1941, after learning that Churchill had sent him an urgent telegram, de Valera assumed it was an ultimatum on the Treaty ports and ordered the Irish Army to assume a heightened state of readiness.[4] After reading the passage 'A Nation once again', both de Valera and Sir John Maffey, the British representative in Dublin, felt it was Churchill's renewed offer to unify the island if the Irish joined the war. De Valera rejected the supposed offer, just as he had the offers of June 1940. He did not think that Churchill would or could deliver on any promise to unify the island because there had been no indication of a willingness to pressure the Northern Ireland government to compromise. There was, however, no such offer on Churchill's mind when he sent it. He had used 'A Nation Once Again', which was the title of the anthem of the Irish Parliamentary Party years before, as a metaphor for Ireland's entry into the war being a chance for Ireland 'to regain her soul'. When alerted to the interpretation of Maffey and de Valera, Churchill wrote back that he 'certainly contemplated no deal over partition', adding that unification could only come with the agreement of Northern Ireland.[5]

De Valera outlined the Irish position given the new world situation

Who's Next?

4.1 *The Nation*, 31 January 1942.

in a speech in Cork one week after the attack on Pearl Harbor. He referred to the bonds that drew the Irish and American peoples together and that the attack on the United States brought 'a source of anxiety and sorrow to every part' of Ireland. Despite this new development, de Valera insisted that Ireland could only remain 'a friendly neutral'. He argued that 'our circumstances, our history, the incompleteness of our national freedom through the partition of our country, made any other policy impracticable'. The alternative would only divide the people and bring ruin to the country. Minister for Co-ordination of Defensive Measures, Frank Aiken focused on the practical matters of neutrality, but also placed it within the rights of sovereign states: 'We have the right and duty, that large Powers practice, to think first of the interests of our own people.'[6] In response, Roosevelt warned de Valera that the experience of the United States was that neutrals were not able to stay out of the war, and that neutrality merely allowed the aggressors the opportunity to name the time and place of their attack. He urged de Valera and the Irish people to ponder these 'stern facts'and to realize that their freedom too was at stake.[7]

The American press coverage of Ireland began to take a much more critical attitude towards Irish neutrality after the United States entered the war. The most comprehensive review of Irish neutrality and Irish–American relations in the influential press during America's war years was *The Nation*'s entire supplement devoted to Ireland on 31 January 1942. As if to establish the legitimacy of its critique, the lead editorial began with a review of how *The Nation* played a role in publicizing de Valera's calls for Irish independence during his stay in America in 1920. The consensus of the writers was that it would simply be a matter of time before Germany attacked Ireland, and that Ireland's best hope for survival would be to join the war before being attacked. For example, the editorial cartoons showed the neutral countries as being Hitler's next victims and the German Navy praising Ireland's neutrality until the eventual day when Hitler would invade. De Valera, meanwhile, argued that joining the Allies guaranteed a German attack and destruction, with little hope of making a difference in the course of the war. Many of the articles recounted the long history of support that Irish Americans and American liberals gave to Irish independence and assumed that 'rather than see tyranny triumph', Ireland would eventually either enter the war with the Allies or provide the Allies direct aid, including the use of the Treaty ports.[8] William Shirer, in his article on whether Germany would invade Ireland, speculated that one of the main reasons Hitler never attacked Ireland in 1940 to secure a base against Britain is that doing so would have brought the United States into the war.[9]

Maxwell Stewart's contribution to the issue focused on the perceived bias of Irish neutrality in favour of the Axis. It is emblematic of much reporting about Ireland during the war. He obviously could not know of the secret British–Irish defence preparations, so his discussion about 'the absence of coordination between north and south' was inaccurate. On the matter of espionage, the assumption was always that Ireland had numerous spies and that the German delegation was actively and effectively aiding them.

Writing about British defence drills, Stewart claimed that 'it is almost certain that the maneuvers were witnessed by enemy agents' who then slipped back to Dublin so their reports could be forwarded to Berlin by diplomatic pouch.[10] The next week *The Nation*'s lead editorial was entitled 'Irresponsible Neutrality', and it ended by arguing that Ireland's stance was cementing partition, because after the war the British and Americans would never offer a sympathetic hearing for independence as long as Ireland had been 'indifferent to the continued freedom of 46,000,000 English, Welsh, and Scots'.[11]

US TROOPS IN NORTHERN IRELAND

During the course of their meetings in December 1941 to plan grand war strategy, Roosevelt and Churchill agreed to have American troops relieve British troops in Northern Ireland.[12] There is no record that either anticipated the level of reaction from de Valera, but Gray knew immediately that de Valera would protest. Even though the 1937 Irish Constitution recognized that the de facto control of the Irish government did not extend to the six counties of Northern Ireland, it still claimed that the national territory included the whole island. Gray knew the Irish government was unlikely to allow the stationing of another nation's troops in Northern Ireland to go unchallenged.

The American troops arrived in January 1942 and de Valera's protest quickly followed. He was careful not to lodge an official protest with the American government, probably realizing that it would be ignored and only serve to alienate American public opinion on which he relied so heavily. Instead, he released a press statement that focused on the continuing injustice of partition. While the Irish had no quarrel with the United States, he argued that 'no matter what troops occupy the Six Counties [Northern Ireland], the Irish people's claim for the union of the whole national territory' would continue. As he hoped, the *New York Times* ran a long story on the protest. In a later letter to Roosevelt, de Valera contended that the landing of American troops without first consulting the Irish government amounted to the United States 'taking sides'in the dispute over partition.[13]

Gray was happy to explain to de Valera the American position, which was that the US government felt no need to consult with any government about stationing its troops in the legal territory of an ally. Gray further explained that the United States had actually helped de Valera, because had the American government notified him and he made a public protest that went unanswered, his political fortunes would have been damaged with no gain.[14] Gray later made it clear to Frank Aiken that the Irish government's protest about the troops 'cost the Irish Government whatever sympathy American majority opinion may have cherished for the Irish viewpoint'on partition. In effect, Gray told him that partition was no longer on the table in American–Irish relations.[15]

Gray, however, was not yet ready to intensify the pressure on Ireland completely. He was very concerned in February 1942 about continued German propaganda that the landing of American troops in Northern Ireland was the first step towards an American invasion of Ireland on behalf of Britain. Eager to find ways to bolster Irish opinion of the United States, Gray wrote to Washington on 14 February that some 'token concessions highly publicized', such as limited arms sales, might reduce some Irish hostility. The United States did not send the arms, but FDR did send de Valera a note explicitly stating that American troops were not in Northern Ireland to prepare for an invasion of Ireland.[16]

Another of Gray's strategies to counter German activity in Ireland was the weekly publication of *Letter from America*.[17] Its first issue came out on 30 October 1942 and was thereafter published throughout the war. It was a subscription newsletter, sent via the Irish mail to about 15,000 subscribers by 1945. The first issue had a quotation from Al Smith to New York's Irish regiment, 'the fighting Sixty-Ninth'. He was quoted as telling them: 'American boys of every faith are fighting today for the same principles that freedom-loving and devout Irishmen themselves have fought for throughout the years.'

The newsletter concentrated on general war news, Voice of America radio broadcasts and a heavy dose of articles on Irish Americans involved in the war effort. Typical profiles included people with Irish surnames such as Captain Mike Moran and Rear Admiral Daniel Callaghan. The 4 December 1942 issue printed the full text of the statement of the American Catholic hierarchy on the American war aims. In the final issue, dated 20 April 1945, the editor wrote that the two reasons for the publication had been to 'make it clear it to you that the moral forces of right and armed might of the United Nations'would prevail and 'to combat lying German propaganda which has endeavoured to misrepresent to you every essential fact in recent history'.[18]

On 6 June 1942 Brennan met with Roosevelt in an effort to obtain weapons for the defence of Ireland. FDR's pleasantries at the start of the meeting included hopes that Brennan would convey good wishes to 'Davy Gray'. In the substance of the talk, FDR told Brennan that any diversion of war supplies to Ireland would be impossible. One possible alternative FDR proposed was that Irish forces train with shotguns, because 'it must be the case that every man in Ireland could use a shotgun'. According to Brennan's account, Roosevelt 'said he was sorry Mr DeValera had made the statement he did [about troops in Northern Ireland] but, of course, he knew he had to make a protest if only for appearance sake'. Brennan replied that it was not for the sake of appearances, but that 'we all felt deeply about partition'.[19]

As the concerns about American troops in the North died down in the summer of 1942, mostly because de Valera realized that a weak, unofficial protest was his only viable option, another potential flashpoint in

British–Irish–American relations developed. Six Irish Republican Army members killed a Belfast policeman during a street battle in June, and the court had scheduled their hangings for 18 August. Brennan called on Welles a few days before the scheduled executions to ask for American help in appealing to the British government to commute the sentences. Brennan stressed that the reactions to the executions by Nationalists in the North would create serious problems for the British authorities, as well as for the Irish government's efforts to rein in the IRA in Ireland, and that the ensuing street clashes might endanger American troops in Northern Ireland. In addition, there was a growing sense in Ireland that 'Germany was the real danger to Ireland and not Great Britain', according to Brennan. British executions of Irish nationals could jeopardize that trend. Brennan must have made a persuasive case because later that same day US Secretary of State Cordell Hull asked the American Ambassador in London, John Winant, to call on British officials to discuss the case.[20]

Hull also began to receive a flood of letters and calls about the scheduled executions. After some standard appeals, the British court set a new execution date of 2 September, giving Winant and the convicted more time. Hull wrote to Winant on 25 August, again urging the British government to commute the sentences. House Majority Leader McCormack and 'many others in both houses' had approached Hull about the case. Hull wrote: 'there is no question that Irish circles in this country are very active and that very wide and unquestionably undesirable publicity would be given to the executions if carried out'. Gray agreed, noting that 'hanging six for one would shock public opinion'. Perhaps as a consequence of American interest, five of the six had their sentences commuted, and only one, Thomas Williams, was executed. His death led to some sporadic rioting and the death of another police officer.[21]

Soon after that potential crisis had passed, two developments in the autumn of 1942 brought the stationing of American troops in Northern Ireland again to the centre stage in Irish–American relations. In October Cardinal McRory, the Catholic Primate of All Ireland and based in Northern Ireland, publicly condemned the presence of American troops and the continuation of partition. In response, Gray wrote to him that the American people had reacted with 'shock and surprise' when de Valera had protested earlier in the year and that McRory's recent comments would only serve 'to intensify the unhappy impressions' that Americans had towards Irish neutrality.[22]

A few weeks later Irish officials protested at the *Pocket Guide to*

Northern Ireland issued by American military authorities to American troops in Northern Ireland. The portion that caused particular concern to the Irish government stated:

> Eire's neutrality is a real danger to the Allied cause. There, just across the Irish Channel from embattled England, and not too far from your own billets in Ulster, the Axis nations maintain large legations and staffs. These Axis agents send out weather reports, find out by espionage what is going on in Ulster. The Ulster border is 600 miles long and hard to patrol. Axis spies sift back and forth across the border constantly.

When approached by Brennan over the offending passage, Welles implied that the Axis powers did in fact have large staffs in Dublin.[23] A few weeks later, Welles told Brennan that the War Department had certified that the information in its files substantiated the claims in the *Pocket Guide*.[24] The War Department's assurance about the size of the legations is curious. The German mission was under constant British and Irish surveillance, and both security services knew the mission did not have a large staff and had already determined that Hempel was avoiding espionage. Hempel also had little motivation to use the mission as a spy centre. He considered Irish neutrality an advantage to Germany and assisting in espionage efforts or making contact with the Irish Republican Army would only serve to bring Ireland into the war.[25]

The inaccuracies and stereotyping of the *Pocket Guide* might have originated in a July 1942 Office of War Information report. It concluded, with a heavy dose of conjecture, that 'information on the strength of the combined forces in Ireland, together with other military secrets, has allegedly been sought by IRA members, who may be cooperating with Nazi agents'. The report linked the IRA in Ireland with the 'thousands of IRA members' in Boston, mostly in the police force, and in New York, most conspicuously among 'city employees, utility workers, waterfront workers'. Even when not members of the IRA, the report concluded that Irish Americans, especially in Boston, at best did not understand the nature of the war:

> There is a pronounced tendency among the Irish in Boston to see the war in terms of narrow, sectional problems. The development of a foreign policy with which they are out of sympathy has been accompanied by an estrangement between the Administration and certain prominent Irish political leaders.[26]

It is possible that Gray might have been an additional source that the War Department relied upon. Walshe told him as far back as April that he had 'a very exaggerated idea about German agents and activities in Ireland'. In a hand-written note on his memorandum about the meeting, Walshe commented that Gray's 'spy mania has driven him to letting down his own nationals in favour of the Bs [British]'.[27] There had been a series of inflated and unsubstantiated press reports about the size of the embassies in Dublin, but it would have been very easy to have Gray or the British actually check on the Axis legations. If the War Department had done so, it would have discovered that the German and Japanese legations contained no more than a dozen people in total. If the War Department really had information to the contrary in its files, and there is no indication of any, then it was incorrect. The report's tone certainly matched Gray's outlook. A few months after its publication, Gray wrote to FDR with what one hopes was humorous advice about how to deal with political opponents: '[The] isolationist bastards are still trying to crucify you. Take a leaf out of Dev's book and start a good big concentration camp at Chi. [Chicago] with an annex in S. Boston.'[28]

An even more bizarre reading of the situation in Dublin came up at about the same time. John D. Hickerson, the Assistant Chief of the Division of European Affairs in the Department of State, contacted Brennan to clarify reports that 'hundreds of Japanese tourists' were in Ireland and posed a 'great danger to the interests of the United States'. Brennan told Welles that the Irish government was 'deeply irritated'and complained that the request proved that the American government was 'misinformed about Ireland' and that it blindly believed every false accusation about Irish complicity in Axis espionage. In spite of this irritation, Brennan asked Dublin to report the total number of Japanese in Ireland. The answer was four: the Japanese Chargé d'Affaires, his wife, the Japanese Consul and a stranded sailor.[29]

Gray was often the unquoted source for much of the misinformation in American reports. He had been telling American correspondents 'OFF the record' since 1941 that it was probable that the Axis intelligence system in Ireland was 'efficient and extremely important'. Brennan charged Leo McCauley, the Consul General for Ireland, to lead the rebuttals to the press reports about Irish neutrality and Axis espionage. Summing up the state of these reports in the autumn of 1942, McCauley took note of the number of articles falsely claiming that the staff of the German legation numbered over one hundred, that German submarines were refuelling in Irish ports and that Irish neutrality was only based on long-held grievances with the British.

McCauley repeatedly directed reporters to the investigations by the *New York Times* and *The Times* of London that refuted the reports about the German legation, the British government's denial about the refuelling of submarines and the repeated statements by de Valera that Irish neutrality was based on Ireland's desire 'to preserve her independence and integrity'.[30]

NEUTRALITY, IDENTITY, PRESSURE

The conflicts with Gray and with the British and American governments only served to reinforce for de Valera the value that Irish neutrality had in his dream of creating an Irish identity that was sovereign, independent, rural and Catholic. In the midst of fighting off pressures to join the war, he turned explicitly to his identity-forming project in his St Patrick's Day address of 1943. Perhaps motivated by the fiftieth anniversary of the Gaelic League, he began with the admonition that more people should learn Irish and use it daily. He continued by describing an Irish life 'that we all dreamed of', where people would live the life that God desired they live: 'satisfied with frugal comfort and devoted … to the things of the spirit'. The 'fields and villages'(he did not mention cities) would be filled with joy, community spirit, respect for elders, athletic contests and 'the laughter of comely maidens'. In many respects, the practical matters that took up his time during the Emergency were but tools to preserve the Irish nation so it could realize his dream.[31]

Gray, however, was becoming even more determined to end Irish neutrality. Even with the direction of the war clearly favouring the Allies in 1943, and the British less and less concerned with the ports because of the success in the Battle of the Atlantic, Gray was eager to find more effective means to pressure Ireland into the war, or at least to make de Valera relinquish the Treaty ports. When he became convinced that he would not succeed, he became determined to devise ways to discredit de Valera and distort the nature of Irish neutrality. He hoped that sufficient wartime pressure would sour American public opinion over Ireland so much that Irish Americans could not disrupt a postwar British–American partnership by agitating against partition. While visiting the United States in the summer of 1943, Gray told a member of the Irish legation in Washington that the United States and Great Britain would be working together in the postwar world. Any effort by the Irish to 'campaign for support' might bring up the 'usual resolutions' from Irish-American groups and politicians, possibly undermining that relationship.[32]

Gray laid out his plans on these matters in a long memorandum in May 1943.[33] He argued that considerations of Ireland's and Irish Americans' activities in the postwar world required that the Allies force Ireland to take a clear and convincing stand with regard to the war, above and beyond the myriad representations and explanations of neutrality heretofore offered by de Valera. While placing specific demands on Ireland might produce real military advantages for Britain and the United States, the real advantage of the request rested on its ability 'to clarify Eire's position in the post-war period'. For Gray, the three main British–American interests 'gravely prejudiced' by Irish neutrality were the 'withholding' of the ports, the maintenance of Axis Missions ('espionage centres') and the constitutional claim to *de jure* sovereignty over Northern Ireland. It was this final point that Gray felt de Valera would use during the war to impede the Allied war effort and after the war to sever the British–American alliance.

Gray started from the premise that because there had not been a specific request forwarded to Ireland for the use of the Treaty ports, after the war the Irish government could rightly claim that they never relinquished the ports because they were never asked to relinquish them. Without that direct veto of an Allied request, Gray was concerned that Ireland might point to the number of Irish volunteers serving in the British military as a cause for concessions on partition, 'benefits to which she ... [is] not entitled on the basis of her attitude during the war'. In the postwar world, Gray argued, an insufficiently stigmatized and isolated de Valera would use the 'alleged wrong' of partition to drive a wedge between Britain and the United States, using the 'sympathies and support of Irish-American groups to this end'. In Gray's thinking, this was not a possibility, but an eventuality unless the Allies took concrete steps to prevent it by embarrassing the Irish government during the war. Gray concentrated his argument on the practical arguments put forth in defence of Irish neutrality. While he conceded that 'prudence'might have played a role in Irish neutrality in 1939 and 1940, by 1943 neutrality was 'entirely voluntary and gratuitous'and could 'only be interpreted as a neutrality for material profit or a neutrality insensible to the moral issues of the war'. What he failed to account for fully was how neutrality, for de Valera and increasingly for the Irish people, fostered a fundamental Irish *identity*, separate from Britain.

Gray put forward two proposals in order to put pressure on de Valera over the ports and neutrality. The first involved using economic pressure to erode Irish popular support for neutrality. Gray argued that the Allies had the moral and legal right to withhold food and supplies to non-belligerents ('separatist nations who refuse to take responsibility for the common survival') if that action advanced the interests of the Allies. It is difficult to argue that the Allies had a responsibility to feed or supply Ireland if that action would have put undue burdens on their efforts to prosecute the war, but that effect is much different than an effort to punish Ireland during the war in order to forestall its potential political efforts in the postwar world. Gray felt, however, that gradual economic coercion alone would not work. His second proposal was to move quickly, before de Valera developed his 'skillful and mischievous intrigue', by making three demands, with the Irish refusal of any of them leading to the cessation of all shipping of raw materials. While the economic impact of the refusal might not change the wartime policy, in Gray's view, the open refusal would do real damage to Ireland's post-war hopes. The three demands were to lease the Treaty ports and other locations as needed to the Allies, remove the Axis missions, and clarify Ireland's position with regard to the British Commonwealth of Nations. Gray also argued that it would be helpful if the British enforced conscription in Northern Ireland. Although he admitted this would cause bloodshed, he argued that 'new bloodshed could hardly increase the political capital manufactured out of the executions of 1916'.

Gray concluded by stressing the importance of bringing to the notice of the American public the 'unfair and destructive'policy of de Valera and of obtaining a conclusive verdict of disapproval by American public opinion. Doing so, he argued, would remove the pressure of the Irish question from British–American relations and the ability of Irish Americans to inject themselves into the postwar discussions through American politics. He ended with a question:

> Can Eire as a geographical strategic keystone in the common defense of the British Isles and as the controlling area for the protection of Anglo–American communications again be permitted the right to refuse cooperation in time of crisis and endanger our existence?

Gray pointed to Robert Brennan's April 1943 article in the *New York Times* as one example in support of his claim that the Irish planned to lobby against partition after the war. In the article, Brennan claimed that all of the attacks on Irish neutrality, including historian Henry Steele Commager's March article in the *New York Times*, were based on the 'fallacy that the other nations went to war on moral issues'. In supporting the morality of the Irish position, Brennan argued that throughout the 1930s Ireland had advocated a vigorous international system to deter aggression, but that none of the major powers helped. He also wondered why the moral outrage of the world had not been directed at Britain for its implementation of partition.[34]

Brennan's article and his wider efforts to rally Irish-American public opinion had some early results. Irish-American organizations around the country held meetings about Irish neutrality on St Patrick's Day, 1943. Speaking at a dinner of the Charitable Irish Society in Boston, Father Edmund Walsh, the vice president of Georgetown University, defended the right of Ireland to remain neutral. Noting the 'severe criticism voiced in certain circles', Walsh said that the United States could not 'deny to Eire the same principle of self-determination of peace or war which the powerful United States maintained for so long'. If there were an invasion of Ireland by Britain, he continued, 'by the cold logic of reason ... [the Allies] would have to ask themselves how such aggression differs from Hitler's "preventative occupation" of Austria, Poland, Czechoslovakia and Luxembourg'.[35]

Soon after sending the memorandum, Gray went to the United States for consultations, visiting Roosevelt in Washington and Hyde Park.[36] In July he visited a series of Irish-American leaders in an attempt to gauge their potential response to postwar appeals over partition. During Gray's visit to Detroit, Archbishop Edward Mooney agreed that the appeals would have some currency among Irish Americans. Gray met with Frederick Sterling, who had preceded Cudahy as the American Minister in Ireland, and Sterling agreed as well. Gray was scheduled to meet with Joseph P. Kennedy, but it turned out to be the same day that the former Ambassador learned that John F. Kennedy was reported missing after the sinking of PT 109. On 14 August he discussed Ireland with Churchill and Roosevelt at a dinner in Hyde Park. No records exist of this meeting, but in a 1971 letter, Averell Harriman noted that Churchill 'seemed unimpressed' with Gray's plans to coerce Ireland into the war.[37]

Roosevelt, however, agreed with Gray that something had to be done to put de Valera on the record with regard to the ports.[38] Cordell Hull, in an effort to make the demand not appear as if the United States were simply trying to 'pull the British chestnuts out of the fire', asked the War Department to review the military aspects of the demand for Irish bases. Chairman of the Joint Chiefs of Staff George Marshall responded that air bases would not be of any advantage, but that naval bases might be of some benefit once it was possible to reroute shipping to the south of Ireland. The use of naval ports in Ireland, however, would not be a sufficient cause to reroute the shipping. Hull wrote to Gray that 'the War and Navy Departments believe that it is not possible to visualize just now what military value might lie in having bases in Eire or if we actually would want to utilize such bases as the war progresses'. Based on this finding, Roosevelt approved a draft proposal in September 1943 that called on de Valera to give *secret* approval allowing the United States to temporarily use the ports should the need arise.[39]

The British Cabinet had a mixed reaction to the State Department official draft, as did the Canadian Minister to Ireland, John Kearney. Some in the Cabinet felt that if de Valera agreed to the request, which they felt was unlikely but possible, he would be in an even more powerful position to request the end of partition at the conclusion of the war. Others felt that as long as de Valera was supporting the Allies as much as possible under the strict public reading of neutrality, it served no useful purpose to take a harsh approach with him that in all probability would have no direct benefit to the war effort. Kearney was baffled by the machinations in the note, which was designed for later consumption by the American public. He told Maffey that he agreed to the need for the note only because he had 'in the forefront of my mind the winning of the war'.[40]

Gray was not pleased with the State Department's draft, but for very different reasons. He felt that the request, couched in terms suggested by the War Department about the *possibility* of using the ports at a later date, would allow de Valera to declare that he could not possibly accede to such a request without knowing what other conditions might be in place at some future time. Gray became concerned that the note, as drafted, would 'inevitably lead us into a position where we get neither the promise of the desired facilities nor the record of a refusal'. Without a more specific demand, Gray felt that Irish-American 'pressure groups' would bring 'ceaseless agitation, disorder and growing bitterness' into American politics and British–American relations after the war. Gray also sensed that British interest in the ports and Irish neutrality was waning, but discounted it because the British also failed to anticipate the 1916 Easter Rising.[41]

When the British still had not approved the draft message by December, Gray drafted another note that was designed to put de Valera firmly on the record. Gray's new draft called for Ireland to expel the Axis delegations and deleted the secret demand for future use of the ports. In spite of the fact that the OSS and MI5 felt that the Axis had no successful intelligence successes or capabilities in Dublin, Gray argued the legations maintained 'highly organized' espionage rings that, despite any Irish successes in countering them, were by their nature 'impossible to suppress'. As the Axis powers did not have any military bases or planning within the area, allowing the Axis missions to remain amounted to aiding them while not aiding the Allies, a decidedly unneutral act.[42] It is this draft that became the 'American Note' that influenced British–Irish–American relations in 1944 and that Gray hoped would diminish the political influence of Irish Americans in the postwar world. He made his intentions explicit in a 20 January 1944 letter to John Winant, the American Ambassador in London: 'Our net gain would only be the advantage of having his refusal on record for defense against his raising of the Partition issue in the United States at some future time.'[43]

THE AMERICAN NOTE CRISIS

In early 1944 Brennan received a tip that 'an indictment' was being drawn up using false evidence of widespread Nazi espionage and lax efforts to counter it by the Irish government as a pretext for an Allied assault. Brennan never revealed the source of the information, but the news did prompt him to force a meeting with William (Bill) Donovan, the Director of the Office of Strategic Services (OSS). After Donovan told him that the American government knew there were 'a great many Nazi agents working in Ireland', Brennan asked him for a list so the Irish could arrest them. Donovan refused, saying it was the job of the Irish to round them up. Brennan concluded after the meeting: 'Wild Bill no more believed his own propaganda that [than] the sources from which it all emanated in Dublin. Their grievance was not that Ireland was overrun with spies, Nazi or otherwise. Their grievance was that Ireland was not in the war.'[44]

There was a high level of coordination between the American and Irish security services during the war, notwithstanding Gray's repeated mischaracterizations of Irish support for the Allied efforts in general and success in countering Axis intelligence operations in particular.[45] Gray knew as early as January 1942 that the Irish and British militaries were maintaining secret contacts and that the Irish authorities, under de Valera's specific direction, were releasing Allied airplanes and crews.[46] He also knew of the Irish–American military liaisons that were taking place across the Ireland/Northern Ireland border. In March 1942 he wrote that 'a mutual good feeling and confidence have been established between the Irish and British Military chiefs beyond what might be reasonably have been believed possible'. These working relationships were so successful that the War Department later recommended the award of decorations to Dan McKenna, the Irish Army Chief of Staff.[47]

David Gray became concerned when the OSS began to send positive reports on Irish counterintelligence operations back to the United States. He was not interested in being second fiddle when it came to being the information conduit to Washington, especially any information that contradicted his opinion of Irish actions, or at least his representations to Washington or the press about Irish actions. In July 1942 the Office of Strategic Services sent Ervin 'Spike' Marlin to Ireland to check on the stories of Nazi spies running rampant throughout the country. Posted under the cover of an economic adviser to the American legation, Marlin found nothing and reported so to Gray. In an oral history interview in 1978, Marlin said that Joseph Walshe had told him that there were over fifty thousand British supporters in Ireland who were 'straining at the leash' to report anything about German spies. Marlin said that he found no spies or spy centres, and that 'once they [the Irish government] realized it was in their interest to keep us informed, they were very good to us'. He told Gray that Irish security arrangements were satisfactory, and Gray asked for him to be recalled.[48]

Even though Gray knew the assumptions of the Note were false, he moved ahead to get British approval. The British Cabinet agreed to let Gray deliver the Note over the objections of MI5, the British security service. The official history reveals that the leaders of MI5 felt that 'there would be very little, if any, security advantage' by removing the legations. They argued that the efficiency of the cooperation between Britain and Ireland might be weakened because of the public pressure on de Valera and that, as the services had successfully comprised all Axis communications, the infusion of new covert agents might not be noticed for some time. Just six months earlier Maffey was telling the Irish that his government 'were very satisfied' with the situation in Ireland.[49]

After getting approval from the British, but with the State Department proviso that 'no publicity is contemplated at present', Gray delivered the Note to de Valera on 21 February. It began by mentioning de Valera's 14 December 1941 speech at Cork when he talked about Ireland being a 'friendly neutral'. It then proceeded to inform de Valera that Irish neutrality had in fact been operating and was continuing to operate in ways that aided the Axis. Agents from those governments had 'almost unrestricted opportunity for bringing military information' into Ireland and then on to Germany. While the Note offered no proof that this had occurred, it mentioned that Axis diplomats had used their covers for espionage 'over and over again'. With military preparations being conducted in Britain and Northern Ireland, the lives of 'thousands of United Nation soldiers' were at stake should Axis diplomats in Dublin disclose any information. The Note concluded with a request, as an 'absolute minimum', that the Axis diplomats be sent home, preferably with an Irish declaration of ending diplomatic relations with Germany and Japan.[50]

It would not have been difficult for Gray to imagine de Valera's response. De Valera's official biographers write that his immediate reaction was that the Note was an attempt to infringe on Irish sovereignty and that 'Irish independence of action had to be preserved despite outside pressures.' Gray reported to Washington that de Valera's first words after reading the Note were: 'Of course our answer will be no; as long as I am here it will be no.' He asked Gray if it were an ultimatum, to which Gray replied that as the Note contained no 'or else', that it was simply a request from a friendly state. When de Valera told Gray that the German minister had not acted improperly, Gray said that while he could not confirm any espionage in Dublin, but as it had happened in other neutral capitals the Allies could not take that risk.[51] Three days later, Walshe cabled Brennan in Washington:

> Taoiseach told Gray there is no question whatsoever of yielding to this pressure. It would be the first step to war and the end of democratic rule here. It is an act of aggression which would involve the loss of our independence if not resisted. There is no basis whatever for the allegations.[52]

De Valera turned to the Canadian High Commissioner in Ireland, John Kearney, to act as an intermediary between the parties and ask for a withdrawal of the Note. The Taoiseach turned to the Canadians because he believed they had a similar interest in establishing the principle of the independence of Dominions. The Canadian government waited until 10 September 1939, seven days after Britain had done so, before declaring war themselves. De Valera hoped that Ottawa would therefore be wary of seeing Ireland pressured into abandoning neutrality. De Valera also approached the Australians, but Australia never officially responded.[53]

Kearney met with Gray on 25 February and told him that the Canadian government felt an appropriate response would be to have all the governments mark the Note secret. Gray told Kearney that there was never any intention to inaugurate a propaganda campaign against de Valera, but that the American government could not agree to a limitation on its future actions with regard to publishing the Note. Failing to get approval, the Canadian government declined to continue to act as an intermediary, but did ask officially that both the British and American governments keep the Note secret.

Gray and the State Department, however, had no intention of keeping the Note secret because its whole rationale was to put de Valera on record as publicly refusing a request to assist in the war effort. This was especially important as the final preparations for a cross-channel invasion of France were being completed. John Hickerson from the State Department told Brennan:

> The principal sanction which may be expected if the Irish Government refuses our request will be the undying hatred on the part of mothers if they feel that military information was sent by the Axis representatives from Dublin that contributed to the German preparations to repel an allied attack.[54]

Gray also brought this possible scenario, which could only happen if the Note became public, to de Valera. Gray informed him that he heard that rumours about the Note were floating around Dublin, but that if the story became public it would not come from the Americans, nor he said he believed from the British. Gray went on: 'We have no desire to see you crucified by a press campaign ... but if you give it out and a storm breaks that is your affair. It is a matter of indifference to us.'[55]

In his formal reply of 7 March, de Valera confirmed his initial rejection of the Note. In a veiled reference to Gray's activities, de Valera wrote that Irish officials doubted that the US government had accurate information about the nature of Irish neutrality. (He deleted a section that mentioned how the United States did not enter the war until after it was attacked.) He then outlined the series of actions that helped the Allied cause, concluding with the argument that the Irish position on neutrality would not be developed out of fear of others' reactions. Coming as close as he could to make public how benevolent Ireland's neutrality was towards Allied interests, and conscious of the underlying ability of the Note to blame Ireland for any future Allied losses, de Valera made several points clear:

> Such a Note could [not] have been presented had the American Government been fully aware of the uniformly friendly character of Irish neutrality in relation to the United States and of the measures

which had been taken by the Irish Government, with the limits of their power, to safeguard American interests....

American officials have had the opportunity of seeing the measures which have been taken – they have, indeed, made favourable comments on their effectiveness – and it is satisfactory to observe that in the Note itself not a single instance of neglect is alleged and no proof of injury to American interests adduced. Should American lives be lost, it will not be through any indifference or neglect of its duty on the part of this State.[56]

It was not long before a firestorm of public debate began about the Note and the Irish response. The State Department began to get inquiries about the Note on 8 March; the full story broke in the press two days after that, and the State Department published the Note the next day.[57] The response was immediate, receiving banner headlines across the country. 'Call for St Patrick! The snakes are back in Ireland', declared a *Dallas Morning News* editorial. Repeating the standard inaccurate assessments of Irish counter-espionage, the *Atlanta Constitution* ran an article that stated Ireland was 'notoriously loose' in stopping Axis spying. The *New York Times* repeated the inaccurate reporting that the Axis missions could send secret reports out through their diplomatic pouches, although later editions did include the official Irish statement that neither mission had a diplomatic bag and that all cable traffic had to be routed through London. The front-page article also stated that 'the personality of David Gray evidently played a considerable part in the exchanges'.[58] In a follow-up article the next week, the *New York Times* discussed the 'highly efficient secret service' that the Irish military maintained. In a strange twist, however, the article also described independence as de Valera's 'ruling fetish' and that Itchi Hashi, the Japanese Consul in Dublin, was a 'ladies' man' who had recently been seen in a bar with 'an Irish girl' who was soon going to be working as a dietician at the Allied base in Foynes in Northern Ireland.[59] Perhaps the most understated assessment came from the BBC, which claimed: 'Eire as a Dominion of the British Commonwealth has an unquestionable legal right to do what she has done.'[60] As before, the Irish government worked hard to press its case in the United States. In early April 1944, Walshe conveyed to Brennan the suggestion of Frank Aiken that Irish-American newspapers publish editorials stating that there was 'resentment in Irish circles' in the United States that Ireland was being set up as a 'scapegoat for any postponement or failure' on a second front.[61]

Churchill took a public position that echoed the State Department's earlier warnings to Brennan. A week after the Irish reply, after mentioning that it was 'painful' to take such measures given the number of Irish in the British military, he told the House of Commons that 'if a catastrophe were to occur to the Allied armies which could be traced to the retention of the German and Japanese representatives in Dublin, a gulf would be opened between Great Britain on the one hand and Southern Ireland on the other which even generations would not bridge'. Churchill, of course, knew about the planning and schedule for what would become Operation Overlord, the cross-channel invasion of France. In the event of failure, the Irish refusal could have been used as a convenient scapegoat. Gray wrote to de Valera on 2 March: 'if American lives were lost in this way [from Axis espionage in Ireland] American mothers and the American press would most probably conduct just such a campaign of publicity against Eire as you would least desire'. Aware of the dangers, both for Allied soldiers and for Irish political fortunes, Walshe met with American officials in April 1944 and offered to have them send 'special man or men here during the critical period'.[62]

The overwhelming criticism of the Irish position was not reflected in the American Catholic press. Brennan passed to Dublin reports from *Commonweal* and the *Pittsburgh Catholic* as examples of a more nuanced argument against the Irish position and of support for Irish neutrality. *Commonweal*'s editorial of 24 March remarked: 'there can be no question ... as to the sincerity and conscientiousness with which the de Valera government in its neutrality has sought to prevent Axis espionage'. While agreeing that de Valera had a legal right to allow the missions to stay, the editorial also called for Ireland to 'sacrifice a certain measure of sovereignty' for the good of the world. In the *Pittsburgh Catholic* the editorial tried to counter the 'headlines, the editorials, the statements, the slurs and the insinuations that have appeared in the last few days'. It went on to discuss the Irish counter-espionage efforts, the number of Irish volunteers serving in the British armed forces, and how Ireland could not have affected the outcome of the war. Speculating on the real reason for the Note, it concluded: 'What part of the Allied military command's strategy is involved in raising this Irish issue at the present moment, the general public does not know – and neither do the "experts" who are doing the cause of national unity so much harm by their ignorant comments.'[63]

In an effort to convince the State Department that the Axis missions posed no security threat, on 18 March Walshe met with 'Spike' Marlin, whom he knew was an American intelligence officer. They were joined

4.2 *New York Times*, 11 March 1944

by Colonel Dan Bryan, the head of G2, the Irish security service. During the meeting Walshe showed Marlin the text of a 16 March *New York Herald Tribune* article which stated that 'for security reasons' the American Note did not contain all the evidence the American government had about the transmission of military intelligence from the Axis missions to Berlin and Tokyo. Walshe told Marlin, if 'any information we gave to him in confidence, as part of our secret arrangement for securing the safety of American interests in this country, were used for the purpose of trumping up a case against us, there would be a catastrophic breach' in American–Irish relations. Marlin agreed that the Irish anti-espionage activities were so 'completely successful' that there was no need for him to even be stationed in Ireland. Marlin suggested to de Valera that the State Department did not check Gray's reports of espionage with the Office of Strategic Services. Walshe told Brennan that all of the arrangements were done 'against wishes of David' (meaning Gray). Later, Gray was eager to back-pedal from the falsehoods in the Note, at least privately. In a 25 May 1944 letter to Colonel David Bruce, the OSS officer in London, Gray incredibly claimed that Spike Marlin was the source of the inaccurate information in the Note.[64]

American public opinion formed quickly once the news broke about the Note. A Gallup Poll conducted from 17 to 22 March 1944 found that 75 per cent of the respondents had heard about the request to force the Axis representatives to leave Ireland and 66 per cent of those felt the United States should 'do something further'. In another poll a few weeks later only 60 per cent of the respondents had 'heard or read about the United States request to Ireland that it expel Axis representatives'. Of those who said yes, 69 per cent favoured stopping all trade with Ireland if it continued to refuse to submit to American demands. All of this confirmed Brennan's fears and Gray's hopes about the Note's effect on American public opinion.[65]

Gray enjoyed the press attention aroused by the Note; indeed it had been the major, if not the only, intent of submitting it. He wrote to Washington requesting press clippings so he could judge the 'effectiveness' of his efforts. There is some uncertainty about who leaked the news of the Note, but Gray maintained that it must have been someone from Fine Gael who sat on the Irish Defence Conference. Walshe reported on 16 March that Gray was preoccupied with proving that he did not leak the news.[66] Gray also saw no need to follow up with any official actions, for 'the general condemnation of De Valera by our press will have its effect without our taking further official measures'. He argued that the best strategy at that point would be to have the United States government make some token release of extra supplies to Ireland to give 'this Legation a popular standing as a friend of the Irish people'. Appearing sorrowful and not angry about de Valera's decision was part of the plan to fight the Irish leader's efforts to appeal to the 'Irish-American front'.[67]

In late March Churchill and Roosevelt discussed delivering another note to de Valera stressing the need to remove the Axis legations, but on the advice of Gray and Maffey they choose not to do so. Gray felt that press reaction to the Irish refusal of the initial Note had already soured American public opinion on Ireland. Maffey contended that a second note would only antagonize de Valera to the point where he might terminate some of the covert aid the Irish were providing. In addition, the British did not want to have FDR push the Irish too far, out of fear that it might initiate some minor political problems for him among Irish Americans.[68]

After all of the publicity had broken, the American intelligence community pushed back against Gray's efforts to diminish or discount their work and the work of their Irish counterparts. Donovan sent FDR a memorandum on 30 March 1944 outlining the ways that the Irish cooperated with the Americans. He thought FDR might want to have the information 'in light of the present situation'. The heavily redacted document highlights how Gray initially supported the American–Irish liaison, but soon pushed Marlin out. In spite of this effort, Donovan listed the numerous types of information the Irish supplied:

> German agents in Ireland, their training, instructions, equipment (including radio equipment) and ciphers; radio activities, illicit radios, interception, and direction finding; the Irish Republican Army; complete lists of Axis nationals ... Axis diplomatic and Consular representatives and their known contacts; map of the Coast Watching System; ... Axis propaganda; submarine activity off the Irish coast to the extent known ... political groups in Ireland with Fascist leanings or ideologies.

He concludes by informing Roosevelt that 'the cooperation in intelligence matters offered and given by the Irish has been very full. It should be pointed out that we did not offer the Irish information in return and have given them little.'[69]

While Roosevelt and Churchill were soon preoccupied with the invasion of France, de Valera was left to salvage what he could from the public relations disaster in the United States following the news of the Note. In 1944 he published *Peace and War: Speeches by Mr de Valera on International Affairs* as evidence that from 1932 to 1938 Ireland had worked diligently through the League of Nations to preserve peace. The book was an effort to remove the sting of the allegation that Ireland and de Valera did not care about the morality of the international situation. The Taoiseach was determined to stress that he had led the calls for international cooperation and resolve during the 1930s, and it was actually the great powers that did not. The war, then, was the result of the inaction of the great powers. This argument fitted into one of the basic public arguments about the need for Irish neutrality: that once the war began, there was nothing little powers could do to influence the outcome. More important, de Valera was arguing that Ireland had done all it could before war broke out. Privately, Irish officials had discussed another line of argument that they knew would not work well publicly. In August 1944 Walshe wrote to Brennan a response to criticism of Irish neutrality, that 'it could be argued equally well that America's two years' delay in going into war must have caused deaths of thousands of Allied soldiers'.[70] That argument never saw the light of day.

In a behind-the-scenes effort to placate the American government, Walshe went to London in April 1944 to meet with US intelligence officers. He offered once again to allow the United States to station agents in Dublin to check directly on the status of Ireland's counter-espionage efforts and to conduct their own. Gray rejected the proposal out of fear that de Valera would gain favourable publicity for the measure after the war and that if the Axis mission did in fact learn of the European invasion plans, the presence of American agents would have exonerated the Irish government. By now, Walshe's frustrations with Gray had reached their maturation. He wrote that 'no other Government in the world would leave their affairs in the hands of a frustrated old man who has been so demonstrably hostile and foolish'.[71]

On 24 March 1944 Gray wrote a long personal letter to FDR on the Note, the responses to it, and his views of Irish policy in general. Writing, as he often did, to his 'Dear Boss', Gray called the Note a success because in the long term it would give de Valera little chance to make 'trouble' with the United States over partition. He complained that the only way to deal with de Valera and the Irish was to tell them 'go sit on a tack'. He then went on to explain how even so, it would be bad to have the Irish suffer from food shortages, but that any plan to aid them must be decided strictly on how well it would play politically in the United States. De Valera and his 'political racketeers' had captured the country and were not thinking straight. Gray wrote that he was glad there was so much resentment to the Note, because if you 'don't get into a fight in Ireland you never know anything about the Irish'. He closed by sending along his wife Maude's love.[72]

THE END OF THE WAR

Two incidents at the end of the war proved to be influential in subsequent British–Irish–American relations. The first was de Valera's visit to the German minister upon learning of Hitler's death and the public relations debacle that followed. The second was the public exchange of allegations and recriminations between Churchill and de Valera in the immediate aftermath of the war. Both of these developments had a long-lasting resonance in postwar British–American–Irish relations and a long-lasting effect on American and Irish-American public opinion.

After news of Hitler's death broke in Dublin, de Valera paid an official sympathy visit to Hempel on 2 May 1945. Fewer than six hours after the visit, Brennan sent Dublin the first reactions from the United States. 'Radio Commentator announced item in bitter and caustic tone'.[73] The *Washington Post* editorial of 5 May discussed the moral issues of the visit in light of the war and neutral countries. 'Can it be that the moral myopia they imposed upon themselves in the face of danger has now blinded them to all ethical values? Or is it that a pre-occupation with protocol has atrophied their emotions? In sober truth, there could be no real neutrality in this war.'[74] The *New York Times* declared that if de Valera claimed the visit was required as the obligation of protocol for a neutral nation, then 'there is obviously something wrong with the protocol, the neutrality, or Mr de Valera'.[75]

Many Irish Americans wrote directly to de Valera to express their dismay at his actions. Teresa Fitzpatrick, the circulation manager for the *Atlantic Monthly*, wrote that she knew in keeping Ireland neutral during the war that the Irish people were acting in the best interest of the country, but that she was dismayed that de Valera 'could have expressed regret at the death of a man who violated every code of decency'. Angela Walsh from New York wrote that she was 'horrified, ashamed, humiliated'. Referring to the news of death camps, she continued: 'Have you seen the living dead, de Valera?'[76]

In an attempt to help Brennan deflect some of the criticism, de Valera wrote to him and explained the visit:

> I could have had a diplomatic illness but, as you know, I would scorn that sort of thing ... So long as we retained our diplomatic relations with Germany, to have failed to call upon the German representative would have been an act of unpardonable discourtesy to the German nation and to Dr Hempel himself. During the whole of the war, Dr Hempel's conduct was irreproachable. He was always friendly and invariably correct – in marked contrast with Gray. I certainly was not going to add to his humiliation in the hour of defeat.[77]

It is important to note the personal nature of de Valera's defence, and that contrary to the many reports around the world, he did not visit the German legation, but Hempel's residence. The *Irish Press* report of 3 May stated that the Taoiseach 'called on Dr Hempel, the German minister, last evening, to express his condolences'. The *Irish Times* ran a similarly worded report, but under the inaccurate headline, 'Callers at German legation'.[78] The subtleties about the personal nature of the visit and its location naturally got lost in the wider implications of paying respects over the death of a man who had caused so much death and destruction.

Walshe and Brennan tried in vain to develop a public relations strategy to stem the criticism. Walshe immediately started looking for some international cover and telegraphed Irish missions around the world to send notice of what other governments had done. He was most concerned about Switzerland and was disheartened to learn that the Swiss had done nothing in regard to Hitler's death because they never received official notification of it.[79] Brennan's proposed response to the criticism was to call attention to the fact that the German representative in Washington attended Roosevelt's 1941 inauguration at the invitation of the Secretary of State, even after Germany had invaded Poland, Denmark, Norway, Luxembourg, Holland, Belgium and France.[80] Brennan realized, however, that this would not be very effective after the world's learning about Hitler's massacre of millions of European Jews and others. There was and is simply no effective way to defend de Valera's actions. Dermot Keogh's analysis is on the mark in describing de Valera as 'myopic and naïve', and that he visited Hempel 'without deep reflection on its wider implications'.[81]

De Valera fared much better in the second major development at the end of the war, his very public exchange with Churchill about the nature of Irish wartime neutrality. In his victory speech of 13 May 1945, recalling the dark days of the Battle of Britain, Churchill said:

> This was indeed a deadly moment in our life and if it had not been for the loyalty and friendship of Northern Ireland we should have been forced to come to close quarters with Mr de Valera or perish forever from the earth. However, with a restraint and poise to which, I say, history will find few parallels, His Majesty's Government never laid a violent hand upon them though at times it would have been quite easy and quite natural, and we left the Dublin Government to frolic with the Germans and later with the Japanese representatives to their hearts' content.[82]

Churchill later remarked to his son that 'perhaps I should not have made' the comments about Ireland, but that 'in the heat of the moment' he just could not tolerate the thought of a neutral Ireland gaining the advantages of freedom won by the defeat of the Nazis.[83]

De Valera waited three days before he responded in a national radio address.[84] After thanking God for sparing Ireland from the devastation of war, he told the country that he knew what he would have said twenty-five years earlier, but that the occasion and the development of British–Irish relations over the years demanded another response. He said that while Churchill could be excused for being taken up with the excitement of victory, he could not do the same. In an expression of Kantian philosophy, de Valera remarked:

> Mr Churchill makes it clear that, in certain circumstances, he

would have violated our neutrality and that he would justify his action by Britain's necessity. It seems strange to me that Mr Churchill does not see that this, if it be accepted, would mean that Britain's necessity would become a moral code ... It is quite true that other great powers believe in this same code – in their own regard – and have behaved in accordance with it. This is precisely why we have the disastrous succession of wars.

Then, in a masterful stroke, he commended Churchill:

It is, indeed, hard for the strong to be just to the weak. But acting justly always has its rewards. By resisting his temptation in this instance, Mr Churchill, instead of adding another horrid chapter to the already bloodstained record of the relations between England and this country, has advanced the cause of international morality an important step.

The response to the speech was tremendous and created a lasting positive impression of neutrality in Ireland. All of the Irish papers commended de Valera's philosophical and moral defence of Irish neutrality. The speech took a pragmatic policy that was a means to protect Ireland and a vehicle to promote an Irish identity, and infused it with an overriding sense that Ireland took the moral high ground during the world conflagration.

IRISH AMERICA AND THE CULTURE OF THE SECOND WORLD WAR

The war years, for a myriad of fairly obvious reasons, was a time of relative absence of Irish-American, or much other, ethnic cultural or political production. The vast majority of Americans of all races, classes and ethnicities were busy fighting the war or working to support the war effort. De Valera continued to count on Irish America to be a voice of caution against possible British action, and Gray began his effort to manipulate Americans' opinion of wartime Irish neutrality, but the vast majority of Irish Americans were simply not paying attention. This lack of specific Irish-American cultural or political activity is why major histories of Irish America almost completely omit the war years and why they have not been a major part of this chapter.[85]

What is important, however, within the story of the continuing effort of Irish America to find its place within America's cultural, social and political mainstream is how the Second World War subtly changed the predominant culture's view of ethnic identity. During and after World War One the rallying cry was '100 per cent Americanism'. There was no room for ethnic assertions. The federal government's efforts through the Committee on Public Information during the war and the raids by Attorney-General A. Mitchell Palmer after the war fuelled this resentment and fear. Many felt that any European ethnic group claiming some special status or asserting its cultural or social identity was a threat. The immigration restrictions of the early 1920s and the rise of the reinvigorated Ku Klux Klan and its fear of immigrants are potent symbols of this perception. None of those anti-ethnic actions repeated themselves after World War Two. Perhaps the cumulative effects of the economic ravishes of the Great Depression, which while affecting certain groups and classes more than others, still dealt crippling blows to so many, enabled a growing sense that concentrating on the differences between German Americans, Irish Americans and Anglo-Americans was a mere distraction. And certainly the Second World War itself, a fight perceived to be against the forces of racial superiority and the genocidal extensions of that ideology, influenced how the dominant culture saw European–American ethnics after the war. To be sure, however, the war did not affect the perceptions of most Americans of Japanese Americans or of the Japanese during the war, nor are there many signs that it affected the views of most Americans of African Americans at all. But for Irish Americans, at least, the homogenizing effects of the war, their active participation in it, and their strident anti-Communist stance after it allowed them to achieve a level of acceptance within the predominant culture that was simply not possible before.

The importance of the war, and of wartime culture, in shaping the nation's self-identity is clear. Gary Gerstle forcefully argues that the 'civic nationalism' that allowed Irish America greater acceptance existed alongside a 'racial nationalism' that excluded many. In World War Two, he contends, 'Euro-Americans achieved a unity and a sense of common Americanness greater than what they had previously known.'[86] The war itself, because many Americans saw it as a struggle against evil, helped to solidify the sense of common purpose. (Although from the start of the war until the attack on Pearl Harbor the majority wanted to stay out of the fighting.) Explicit government efforts to promote an inclusive and productive workforce also played a role. But perhaps the most important cultural force espousing the value of accepting white European ethnics and those of varying religions was Hollywood. Gerstle lists some of the films that had at their core a diverse ethnic and religious group of soldiers that come together from their varied backgrounds to work together as Americans in saving the world:

Guadalcanal Diary (1943), *Bataan* (1943), *Sahara* (1943), *Gung-Ho* (1943), *Action in the North Atlantic* (1943), *Air Force* (1943), *Destination Tokyo* (1943), *Purple Heart* (1944), *The Fighting Seabees* (1944) and *Objective Burma* (1945).[87] These films would often start with a ragtag group of men from different neighbourhoods engaging in activities that highlighted their diversity. Through a common struggle in battle, the men then fused into one cohesive unit that succeeded because their individual differences shrank away.

Lifeboat and *Going My Way*, two of the most important and popular movies of 1944, illustrate this shift in acceptance of white minorities in general and of Irish Americans in particular. John Steinbeck wrote the original story and Alfred Hitchcock directed *Lifeboat*, and both were nominated for Academy Awards. The movie centres on the tale of survivors of a luxury passenger liner that is attacked by a German submarine – the submarine is later sunk as well. The passengers on the lifeboat eventually allow a German survivor, whom they later discover was captain of the submarine, to join the boat. The central tension is whether the passenger ship survivors can overcome their class, racial and ethnic differences to meet the threat posed by their situation. The clear message is that only by accepting everyone as part of the effort can the menace be defeated. Lewis Erenberg and Susan Hirsch eloquently summarize the film's point and come to a wider conclusion about wartime culture: 'The terrible demands of total war required that former outsiders be included in a new pluralistic national self-definition.'[88] That African Americans were largely left out of that new national self-definition, certainly at least in practice after the war, lends credence to the argument that white ethnic groups had advantages that other outsiders did not.

Hitchcock and Steinbeck lost their respective categories of Best Director and Best Original Story to their counterparts who worked on *Going My Way*, which starred Bing Crosby as an Irish-American Catholic priest from East St Louis who becomes stationed in New York to help an Irish-born priest run a mostly Irish parish in Manhattan.[89] The plot centres on a series of efforts to save the parish finances, including Crosby's Father O'Malley selling a song and having the parish's choir go on a concert tour. Near the end, even with the misfortune of having the parish burn, all turns out well. The salient point, however, is how such a sentimental and positive portrait of Irish Catholics could prove so popular and win such critical acclaim a short twenty years after the Klan had marched openly in many places in the South and Midwest threatening Catholics in general and Irish

Catholics in particular. Film, and especially one film, cannot be the sole engine of social change, but the wide acceptance of *Going My Way* and other movies of the 1940s and early 1950s that portrayed Catholicism and Irish Catholics in a positive light deserve some recognition for the role they played in signalling and advancing a more accepting stance by the wider culture.

CONCLUSION

David Gray was the prime mover of events in British–Irish–American relations during the period of American involvement in World War Two. His motivation, however, was not the advancement of war aims, but a forestalling of the efforts of Irish Americans to play a role in post-war domestic politics and to discredit Irish neutrality and de Valera enough to prevent the Irish from interfering in postwar British–American relations. Eunan O'Halpin has summarized Gray's role accurately and succinctly: 'The problem was that he did not let his lack of knowledge of the workings of Irish–Allied security relations prevent him from pro-nouncing forthrightly on their inadequacy.'[90] It was not simply that, how-ever, as Gray did know of some of the arrangements. He simply wanted to bend the intelligence to suit his political agenda.

The seeds of Gray's distortions, aided without doubt by de Valera's unfortunate visit to Hempel at the close of the war, would bear fruit later. As a result, Irish Americans, along with most Americans, formed deeply held impressions of Irish actions during the war. Irish Americans disengaged further from Irish affairs until the violence in Northern Ireland in 1968. De Valera, ever eager to advance a sense of Irish identity, even at the risk of cementing partition, later turned again to the constitutional machinations he had set aside during the Emergency. He looked to Irish Americans for support, but they did not look back. They were starting to sense that there might be a real home for Irish Americans in the United States.

NOTES

1. 'Churchill to de Valera', 8 December 1941, Public Record Office (London), Records of the Prime Minister's Office, PREM 3/131/6 (hereafter cited as PRO, PREM and file number). In Churchill's *Second World War*, he quotes the message as: 'Now is your chance. Now or never! A nation once again! *I will meet you wherever you wish*'(my italics.) See Churchill, *Second World War*, vol. 3, *The Grand Alliance* (Boston: Houghton Mifflin, 1950), 606. Churchill

does not explain that it was not an offer to end partition.

2. Elizabeth Bowen, *Notes on Eire: Espionage Reports to Winston Churchill, 1940–42* (Aubane: Aubane Historical Society, 1999), 76.

3. Eunan O'Halpin, 'Irish Neutrality in the Second World War', in *European Neutrals and Non-Belligerents During the Second World War*, ed. Neville Wylie (Cambridge: Cambridge University Press, 2002), 182.

4. National Library of Ireland, MS 18,375, Frank Gallagher Papers (hereafter cited as NLI/file number/file name). See also Frank Pakenham Longford and Thomas P. O'Neill, *Eamon de Valera* (London: Arrow Books, 1974), 392.

5. 'Cranborne to Churchill', 8 December 1941, PREM 3/131/6.

6. Éamon de Valera, 'A Friendly Neutral', Cork, 14 December 1941, in Éamon de Valera, *Peace and War: Speeches by Mr de Valera on International Affairs* (Dublin: M.H. Gill & Son, 1944), 460–1. Brennan sent a copy of the speech to the State Department. See 'Irish Minister to the Secretary of State', 16 December 1941, in US Department of State, *Foreign Relations of the United States: Diplomatic Papers, 1941*, vol. 3, *The British Commonwealth, the Near East and Africa* (Washington, D.C.: US Government Printing Office, 1959), 250–1 (hereafter *Foreign Relations of the United States* citations will be cited as *FRUS*, year, vol. number: page); 'Frank Aiken's Speech', 9 December 1941, University College Dublin archives, Frank Aiken Papers, P104/3374 (hereafter manuscript collections from the Archives at University College, Dublin will be cited as UCD, collection name, file number).

7. 'Message of President Roosevelt to the Taoiseach', received 23 December 1941, National Archives of Ireland, Department of Foreign Affairs, P2 (hereafter as NAI/DFA/file number). The Department of External Affairs became the Department of Foreign Affairs in 1971.

8. See especially Senator George W. Norris, 'Ireland Will Respond', *The Nation*, 31 January 1942, 129.

9. William Shirer, 'Will Hitler Take Ireland?' *The Nation*, 31 January 1942, 133.

10. Maxwell Stewart, 'Ireland's Dilemma', *The Nation*, 31 January 1942, 137–40.

11. 'Irresponsible Neutrality', *The Nation*, 7 February 1942, 152.

12. There is some confusion about who broached the idea. In his version, Churchill writes that Roosevelt mentioned the plan and that he welcomed it. George Marshall's notes reflect that Roosevelt 'agreed with Churchill'on the importance of the troop substitution. See 'Prime Minister to War Cabinet and C.O.S. Committee', 23 December 1941, in Churchill, *Grand Alliance*, 664–5, and Forrest Pogue, *George C. Marshall: Ordeal and Hope, 1939–1942* (New York: Viking Press, 1965), 268. The most recent article on the deployment is Francis M. Carroll, 'United States Armed Forces in Northern Ireland During World War II', *New Hibernia Review* 12, no. 2 (summer 2008): 15–36.

13. 'Public Statement', 27 January 1942, in Éamon de Valera, *Speeches and Statements by Éamon de Valera, 1917–1973*, ed. Maurice Moynihan (New York: St Martin's Press, 1980), 465; *New York Times*, 28 January 1942; 'De Valera to Roosevelt', 20 April 1942, *FRUS*, 1942, 1: 761.

14. 'Gray to the Secretary of State', 30 January 1942, *FRUS*, 1942, 1: 753–4.

15. 'Gray to the Secretary of State', 21 March 1942, *FRUS*, 1942, 1: 759–60.

16. 'Gray to the Secretary of State', 14 February 1942, *FRUS*, 1942, 1: 758; 'Message from President Roosevelt to Mr de Valera', 26 February 1942, NAI/DFA/A53.

17. Available in University of Wyoming, American Heritage Center, David Gray Papers, boxes 34 and 35 (hereafter cited as UW/AHC, box number) and Irish Military Archives, Cathal Brugha Barracks, Director of Intelligence Files, G2/X/1092.

18. *Letter From America*, 8 January 1943; 15 January 1943; 4 December 1942; 20 April 1945.

19. 'Mr Brennan's Report on his Interview with President Roosevelt on 6th June 1942', UCD, De Valera Papers, P150/2604.

20. 'Secretary of State to the Ambassador in the United Kingdom', 15 August 1942, *FRUS*, 1942, 1: 764.

21. 'Secretary of State to Winant', 25 August 1942, *FRUS*, 1942, 1: 765; 'Gray to the Secretary of State', 26 August 1942, *FRUS*, 1942, 1: 766; Fisk, *In Time of War*, 325–6. One of the five spared was Joe Cahill, who later became a leader of the Provisional IRA in the late 1960s and early 1970s. See Tim Pat Coogan, *The IRA: A History*, 4th edn (New York: HarperCollins,

1995), 500.

22. 'Gray to McRory', 7 October 1942, FDR Library, PSF 40.

23. 'Pocket Guide to Northern Ireland', War and Navy Departments, pp. 10–11, Franklin Delano Roosevelt Library, Printed Materials Collection, box 618; 'Our Men in Ireland Warned to be Cautious', *New York Times*, 25 October 1942; Welles, 'Memorandum of Conversation', 29 October 1942, *FRUS*, 1942, 1: 768–9.

24. 'Aide-Mémoire', 16 November 1942, *FRUS*, 1942, 1: 771.

25. 'Godfrey Memoir', UCD, Bryan Papers, P71/138, pp. 193–6. John Godfrey was the chief of British Naval Intelligence during World War Two. He also reported that Gray 'considered that we had nothing to fear from the German legation'. See also John P. Duggan, *Neutral Ireland and the Third Reich* (Totowa, N.J.: Barnes & Noble, 1985), 160–7.

26. Office of War Information, Bureau of Intelligence, Report no. 40, 24 July 1942, National Archives of the United States.

27. 'Dublin to Nunan', 20 April 1942, NAI/DFA/2.

28. 'Gray to Roosevelt', 16 September 1942, FDR Library, President's Secretary's Files, box 40.

29. Welles, 'Memorandum of Conversation', 25 November 1942, *FRUS*, 1942, 1: 772.

30. 'Notes on Axis Activities in Ireland', UCD, De Valera Papers, P150/2589 and UW, AHC, box 20 (his emphasis); 'McCauley to Brennan', 4 November 1942, NAI/DFA/P10; *London Times*, 17 July 1940; 'German Legation Staff in Dublin Numbers Only 6', *New York Times*, 18 July 1940.

31. 'The Ireland That We Dreamed Of', 17 March 1943, *Speeches and Statements*, 466–9.

32. Sean Nunan, 'Notes', 20 August 1943 (on a 17 August 1943 meeting), NAI/DFA/2.

33. 'Memorandum by the Minister in Ireland on Recommendations for the Adoption of a Joint Anglo-American Economic Policy toward Eire Shaped With Reference to Political Considerations', 14 May 1943, *FRUS*, 1943, 3: 132–42.

34. Robert Brennan, 'The Case for Irish Neutrality', 4 April 1943, *New York Times*; Henry Steele Commager, 'A Challenge to Irish Neutrality', 7 March 1943, *New York Times*.

35. 12 May 1943, NAI/DFA/2.

36. Gray stayed in the White House during his time in Washington. Sean Nunan, 'Note on Meeting with Gray', 20 August 1943, NAI/DFA/2.

37. 'Harriman to the Author', 1 July 1971, in Seán Cronin, *Washington's Irish Policy, 1916–1986: Independence, Partition, Neutrality* (Dublin: Anvil Books, 1987), 170.

38. 'Secretary of State to President Roosevelt', 29 June 1943, *FRUS*, 1943, 3: 142–3; Cordell Hull, *The Memoirs of Cordell Hull* (New York: MacMillan, 1948), vol. 2, 1356–7.

39. Dwyer, *Strained Relations: Ireland at Peace and the USA at War, 1941–45* (New York: Barnes & Noble, 1988), 112–14.

40. 'Winant to Secretary of State', 19 September 1943 and 8 October 1943, *FRUS*, 1943, 3: 152–3, 158; 'Secretary of State to Gray', 5 October 1943, 9 November 1943, *FRUS*, 1943, 3: 155–6, 160.

41. 'Gray to Secretary of State', 28 September 1943 and 1 October 1943, *FRUS*, 1943, 3: 153–5. Gray's obsession was taking full hold by late fall 1943. He was also arguing that de Valera might incite an uprising similar to 1916 in order to have the British execute the 'ring leaders', thus generating American sympathy. See also 'Gray to Winant, Personal', 1 October 1943, FDR Library, David Gray Papers, box 7.

42. 'Gray to Secretary of State', 13 December 1943, *FRUS*, 1943, 3: 164. The official British rejection of the first draft came on 22 December 1943 through Winant; see 'Memorandum by the Secretary of State to President Roosevelt', 29 December 1943, *FRUS*, 1943, 3: 168. See also Hull, *Memoirs*, 1357. It is possible that Churchill gave Roosevelt the information at the Second Cairo Conference in early December 1943. See 'Editorial Note' for Tuesday, 7 December 1943, *FRUS, The Conferences at Cairo and Tehran, 1943*, 750. Winant went with Churchill to Cairo and they talked about the Irish bases en route; see 'Winant to the Secretary of State', 22 December 1943, *FRUS, The Conferences at Cairo and Tehran, 1943*, 853. Winant talked with Roosevelt in Cairo on 25 November, 26 November, and 3 December: 'The President's Log at Cairo, November 22–26, 1943', and 'The President's Log at Cairo, December 2–7, 1943', *FRUS, The Conferences at Cairo and Tehran, 1943*, 298–9, 656.

43. 'Gray to Winant', 20 January 1944, UW, AHC, box 23. Brian Girvin misses this motivation

for the Note in his very favourable analysis of Gray's actions. See Girvin, *The Emergency: Nuetral Ireland, 1939–45* (London: Macmillan, 2006), 302–16.

44. Robert Brennan, *Ireland Standing Firm: My Wartime Mission in Washington* (Dublin: University College Dublin Press, 2002), 75–6.

45. See Martin Quigley, 'Texts of OSS Reports', in his *A US Spy in Ireland* (Dublin: Marino Books, 1999), 115–205.

46. 'Gray to the Secretary of State', 30 January 1942, *FRUS*, 1942, 1: 753–4.

47. 'Gray to Secretary of State', 23 March 1942, UCD, Dan Bryan Papers, P71/120; Ronan Fanning, *Independent Ireland*, (Dublin: Helicon, 1983), 124.

48. Eunan O'Halpin, *Defending Ireland: The Irish State and its Enemies since 1922* (New York: Oxford University Press, 1999), 230. 'Oral Interview with the author', London, 14 March 1978, quoted in Fisk, *In Time of War*, 457. A 'confidential government source'told historian Carole Carter that part of Gray's impatience with Marlin was that many in Dublin, including Marlin, knew that Gray was being fed exaggerated reports of German intelligence activities by the few opposition members who opposed neutrality. Gray was particularly upset when Marlin called him 'gullible'. See Carter, 'America's Neutral Ally', *Eire-Ireland* 12, no. 2 (1977): 5–14, 11. Marlin's reports are in National Archives of the United States, Record Group 84 (Foreign Service Post Files), Dublin Legation Classified Records, 1943: 814–15 (hereafter NAUS/RG84/DLCR/file number). When Gray asked for him to be recalled, Marlin had already asked to be transferred to London because the situation in Dublin was under control; see Fisk, *In Time of War*, 531. Gray had a history of ignoring and misrepresenting intelligence information. See Michael Kennedy's discussion of Gray's actions on the treatment of downed Allied personnel, in *Guarding Neutral Ireland: The Coast Watching Service and Military Intelligence, 1939–1945* (Dublin: Four Courts Press, 2008), 213–18.

49. 'Note on the Work of the Irish Section of the Security Service, September 1939–1945', in Eunan O'Halpin, ed., *MI5 and Ireland, 1939–1945: The Official History* (Dublin: Irish Academic Press, 2003), 83: 'Walshe to de Valera', 12 September 1943, NAI/DFA/A2.

50. 'Hull to Winant', 3 February 1944, *FRUS*, 1944, 3: 217–18; 'Copies of American Note, British Note and Irish Reply', NAI, DFA/A53.

51. Longford and O'Neill, *De Valera*, 404–5; 'Gray to the Secretary of State', 21 February 1944, *FRUS*, 1944, 3: 221–2.

52. 'Dublin to Washington', 24 February 1944, NAI/DFA/A53.

53. For the entreaties to Canada, see Emma Cunningham, 'Ireland, Canada and the American Note', in *Ireland in World War Two: Neutrality and Survival*, ed. Dermot Keogh and Mervyn O'Driscoll (Cork: Mercier Press, 2004), 144–58. De Valera also had Dulanty, the Irish High Commissioner in London approach the Australians. See 'Bruce to Curtin', 29 February 1944, Cablegram 31[A], Australian Division of Foreign Affairs Archives, available at http://www.info.dfat.gov.au/info/historical/HistDocs.nsf/vVolume/.

54. 'Gray to the Secretary of State', 25 February 1944; 'Memorandum of Telephone Conversations', Hickerson, 28 February 1944; 'Winant to the Secretary of State', 28 February 1944, *FRUS*, 1944, 3: 225–30. It is possible that Gray got the idea of the public posturing after FDR went public with the sale of ships to Ireland in 1941. After that he wrote to FDR: 'You have invented the right technique for this situation.''Gray to FDR', 28 May 1941, FDR Library, David Gray Papers, box 6.

55. 'Gray to Secretary of State', 1 March 1944, *FRUS*, 1944, 3: 226–30.

56. 'Reply to American Note of the 21st February', 7 March 1944, NAI/DT/S13450A and NAI/DFA/A53.

57. 'United States Request for the Removal of Axis Diplomatic and Consular Representatives for Ireland', Department of State, *Bulletin* 10, no. 246 (11 March 1944): 235. Roosevelt approved the release; see margin note 'OK – F.D.R.'on 'Churchill to Roosevelt', 10 March 1944, FDR Library, President's Secretary's Files, box 40.

58. *New York Times*, 11 March 1944.

59. *New York Times*, 19 March 1944.

60. Quoted in Susan A. Brewer, *To Win the Peace: British Propaganda in the United States During World War II* (Ithaca, N.Y.: Cornell University Press, 1997), 136.

61. 'Dublin to Washington', 3 April 1944, NAI/DFA/A53. The Australian High Commissioner

speculated that was the case; see 'Bruce to Curtin', 29 February 1944, available at http://www.info.dfat.gov.au/historical.

62. *Commons Debates*, 14 March 1944, cols. 36–7. All debates in the House of Commons are available at http://www.hansard.millbanksystems.com/commons/C20. 'Gray to de Valera', 2 March 1944, UCD, De Valera Papers, P150/2658; 'Walshe to Brennan', 6 April 1944, NAI/DFA/A53.

63. *Commonweal*, 24 March 1944; *Pittsburgh Catholic*, 16 March 1944, NAI/DT/S13450A.

64. 'Most Secret', 18 March 1944, and 'Dublin to Washington', 27 March 1944, NAI/DFA/A53 and UCD, De Valera Papers, P150/2571; 'Gray to Bruce', 25 May 1944, UW, AHC, box 23.

65. George Gallup, *The Gallup Poll: Public Opinion, 1935–1971*, vol. 1, *1935–1948* (New York: Random House, 1972), 439, 442. The first poll was conduced 17–22 March 1944. The second poll was conducted 31 March–4 April 1944; 'Washington to Dublin', 23 February 1944, NAI/DFA/A53.

66. 'Gray to Secretary of State', 10 March 1944, UW, AHC, box 23; T. Ryle Dwyer, *Irish Neutrality and the USA, 1939–47* (Dublin: Rowman & Littlefield, 1977), 190. It is highly unlikely that an opposition member of the Defence Conference leaked the story because de Valera never brought the Note to them. See '84th Meeting of the Defence Conference', 22 March 1944, UCD, Aiken Papers, P104/3534. On 14 March de Valera seems to have believed Maffey's suggestion that the 'beans were spilled'in Dublin by a member of Fine Gael. Four days later, however, he was arguing vigorously with Maffey that he was 'nearly tired of hearing that argument'and that the British and American governments must have conspired to release it because the 'first positive'announcement came from the BBC at 6:00 p.m. on 10 March. See de Valera, 'Memorandum of Conversation', 14 March 1944; and 'Sir John Maffey-Sanctions', 18 March 1944, NAI/DFA/A53. The *New York Times* 10 March edition, however, had a 9 March by-line stating that 'reports circulated tonight'about a demand to remove the Axis missions and that Britain had approved the Note. In later years, de Valera tempered his suspicions and his official biographers write that he was 'unable to resolve whether the leakage was a deliberate attempt to increase the pressure on him or not'. Longford and O'Neil, *De Valera*, 407. It is probable that Gray had been pumping the primer for the story even earlier. In a 6 March story in the *New York Times*, 'Allies Fear Spies in Neutral States', James Reston wrote that 'Eire is in a particularly embarrassing situation'. For Walshe's report on his conversation with Gray, see 'Walshe to de Valera', 16 March 1944, NAI/DFA/A2. Gray wrote privately to Roosevelt that it was a Fine Gael leader who broke the news; see 'Gray to FDR', 24 March 1944, UW, AHC, box 23.

67. 'Gray to Secretary of State', 15 March 1944, *FRUS*, 1944, 3: 240–1.

68. See 'Halifax to Eden', 19 June 1944, 'Political Review of the United States for the First Quarter of 1944', in *Confidential Dispatches: Analyses of America by the British Ambassador, 1939–1945* (Evanston, Ill.: New University Press, 1974), 173.

69. 'Memorandum for the President', 30 March 1944, FDR Library, President's Secretary's Files – Safe Files, box 4.

70. De Valera, *Peace and War*. See especially 'Address from Geneva', 2 October 1932, and 'Speech at Special Session of the League of Nations Assembly', 2 July 1936; 'Dublin to Washington', 29 August 1944, NAI/DFA/A53.

71. The impetus for this overture probably came from de Valera, as he brought up that option in a meeting with Marlin on 18 March 1944; De Valera, 'Most Secret', NAI/DFA/A53. Hull knew about the offer; see Hull, *Memoirs*, 1359. For the Walshe quotation, see 'Walshe to Brennan', 6 April 1944, NAI/DFA/A53.

72. 24 March 1944, UW, AHC, box 23.

73. 'Washington to Dublin, 3 May 1945, 9:41 pm', NAI/DFA/P98. The State Department requested Gray to confirm the early news reports, which he did after calling Walshe; see 'Gray to Secretary of State', 4 May 1945, NAI/DFA/P98. News of the visit made the front page of the *New York Times*, right under 'Berlin Falls to the Russians; War in Italy Ends', 3 May 1945.

74. *Washington Post*, 5 May 1945.

75. *New York Times*, 4 May 1945.

76. 'Teresa S. Fitzpatrick to de Valera', 11 May 1945; 'Angela D. Walsh to de Valera', 3 May

1945, NAI/DFA/P98. There are eighty-four letters to de Valera on the topic in UCD, De Valera Papers, P150/2689.

77. Dermot Keogh, 'De Valera, Hitler and the Visit of Condolence: May 1945', *History Ireland* 5, no. 3 (1997): 59; UCD, De Valera Papers, P150/2676.

78. 'Interview with Eva Hempel', in Duggan, *Neutral Ireland and Third Reich*, 243. See also Dermot Keogh, 'Éamon de Valera and Hitler: An Analysis of International Reaction to the Visit to the German Minister, May 1945', *Irish Studies in International Affairs* 3, no. 1 (1989): 72. The mis-statement about the location of the visit will likely take some time to correct in the literature. For examples, see Carroll, *Ireland in the War Years*, 160, and Declan Kiberd, *Inventing Ireland: The Literature of the Modern Nation* (Cambridge, Mass.: Harvard University Press, 1996), 472.

79. 'Dublin to Cremins', and 'Cremins to Dublin', 4 May 1945, NAI/DFA P98.

80. 'Brennan to Dublin', 5 May 1945, NAI/DFA/P98.

81. Keogh, 'Visit of Condolence: May 1945', 59.

82. Churchill, 'Forward Till the Whole Task is Done', A World Broadcast, 13 May 1945, in *The War Speeches of the Rt Hon Winston S. Churchill* (London: Cassell & Co., 1952), 441.

83. *Irish Times*, 5 February 1979.

84. 'Taoiseach's Broadcast to the Nation', 16 May 1945, UCD, De Valera Papers, P150/2690; also printed in *Irish Press*, 17 May 1945.

85. For example, see Kevin Kenny, *The American Irish: A History* (New York: Longman, 2000), and Timothy J. Meagher, *The Columbia Guide to Irish American History* (New York: Columbia University Press, 2005). As there has not been many studies of the effects of the war on Irish America, the following section should simply be considered as some preliminary observations.

86. Gary Gerstle, *American Crucible: Race and Nation in the Twentieth Century* (Princeton, N.J.: Princeton University Press, 2001), 187.

87. Ibid., 204–5.

88. Lewis A. Erenberg and Susan E. Hirsch, 'Introduction', in *The War in American Culture: Society and Consciousness During World War II*, ed. Lewis A. Erenberg and Susan E. Hirsch (Chicago: University of Chicago Press, 1996), 4.

89. Lawrence J. McCaffrey, '*Going My Way* and Irish-American Catholicism: Myth and Reality', in *Screening Irish-America*, ed. Ruth Barton (Portland, Oreg.: Irish Academic Press, 2009), 181.

90. Eunan O'Halpin, 'Irish-Allied Security Relations and the "American Note" Crisis: New Evidence from British Records', *Irish Studies in International Affairs* 11 (2000): 74.

5

Postwar Consequences

> Mr De Valera ... maintained a neutrality which served only
> Hitler's objectives ... The Eire conception of neutrality permitted
> Axis missions to be maintained with their spy apparatus and secret
> wireless within the periphery of the allied defense. Throughout the
> war Dublin was a lighted city, serving as a beacon to guide German
> bombers proceeding north to attack Belfast. (David Gray, 1956)[1]

In the years following the Second World War, Irish Americans and the
Irish continued their quests to establish their unique identities. For
Irish Americans, removed from the economic and spiritual dislocations
of the Depression and renewed by a general prosperity after the war,
their quest would be significantly different than those of previous generations. No longer renewed by the influx of large numbers of immigrants, the number of first-generation and second-generation Irish
Americans decreased rapidly in the postwar years. The absence of these
new members would mean that Irish America would have to find
different means of crafting and maintaining its identity without the
rejuvenating influence of the experiences of those born in Ireland. For
the Irish government, its quest for an Irish identity at home and in the
eyes of the world was now hampered by the troublesome legacy of
wartime neutrality; a neutrality that became a core part of Irish identity
and which also left the nation's relations with the United States in
tatters. Wider and growing Cold War security concerns expressed by
American and British policy makers, however, soon opened the door
for Ireland's participation in the postwar international scene.

THE END OF GRAY'S TENURE

David Gray continued to serve as the American Minister in Ireland
until June 1947. Troy Davis, the only historian to complete a full

review of postwar American–Irish relations, argues that 'the continued presence of Gray himself' and Gray's 'personal antipathy for de Valera and his obsession with discrediting the Irish in the United States' were the major factors influencing the American–Irish relationship immediately after the war.[2] One of the clearest examples of Gray's attitude is his informal and personal postwar propaganda campaign among Irish Americans. In early January 1946 Gray began a letter campaign, unapproved by the State Department, to the newest American Catholic cardinals: Francis Spellman in New York, Edward Mooney in Detroit and Samuel Stritch in Chicago. He later sent copies of the letters and an accompanying memo, entitled 'The United States and Irish Partition', to John Hickerson at the State Department. He also noted that he planned to send the letter and memo to prominent Irish Americans, including Joseph P. Kennedy and Senator James Murray. Hickerson had to chastise Gray for his mixing of private and public matters.[3]

Considering his audience for these letters, Gray did not mention his concern that Irish Americans would attempt to obstruct the postwar British–American relationship in an effort to end partition. Nor did he elaborate on his belief that any Irish–American political activity on behalf of Ireland was antithetical to American interests. Instead he framed the letters and memo around a warning that any attempt by Irish Americans to lobby for Ireland would ultimately fail and bring about an anti-Catholic reaction in the United States. Specifically, he argued that should Irish-American Catholics raise the partition issue in the United States, Northern Ireland Protestants would also enter the debate. If the Protestants, appealing to the predominantly Protestant American public, successfully made a case that Catholics in Ireland and the United States were trying to force them into joining an implicitly Catholic nation, then the mission to end partition would not only fail, but it would foment an anti-Catholic backlash. Gray took a stern tone in his letter to Joseph Kennedy, writing: 'you Americans of Irish descent will have to learn' that Ireland is closer to Britain and that the Irish 'think and feel' more like the British than the Americans. In July 1946 he wrote to James Farley, who was a former Postmaster General and one of de Valera's friends, asking him to speak with de Valera to caution him to avoid an anti-partition campaign in the United States.[4]

The Irish government reacted to Gray's remaining in Dublin after the war with bitter complaints about his activities. Walshe commented to the Irish Minister in Washington Robert Brennan:

The general attitude of the Irish people towards David Gray is

one of complete astonishment that the representative of the democratic United States of America should pass at least four days out
of every seven with a group of effete nobles who are more vio-
lently anti-Irish than the worst John Bull in Britain.

He also wrote that the British representative in Dublin, Sir John
Maffey, had often declared 'in moments of excessive frankness' that
Gray did his (Maffey's) job better than himself.[5] Brennan brought up
Gray's appointment with President Truman at a Friendly Sons of St
Patrick dinner on 16 March 1946. Brennan discussed the harm Gray
had created in the American–Irish relationship, and in his report to
Dublin he quoted Truman as saying: 'let's bring him back right away'.
Later that same night, however, Truman said that it could not be
rushed, as there was a 'Roosevelt connection'.[6] Gray expected to be
replaced after the 1946 elections. He wrote to Joseph Kennedy: 'I shall
probably get thrown out soon to provide a place for some Democratic
casualty.'[7]

De Valera tried to work around Gray by returning to his practice,
suspended for some years during the war, of delivering St Patrick's Day
messages to the American people. In 1946 he began his address, in a
thinly veiled reference to Gray, by saying: 'there were those during
those years [1942–5] who would have us believe' that Irish neutrality
had 'alienated the sympathy of our American friends'. He argued that
real friends would not have expected the Irish to do what they themselves, under similar circumstances, would not have done. De Valera
continued:

> When a small nation engages in a modern war, it runs risks far
> beyond any incurred by a great power. Great powers, if they lose,
> may hope to somehow survive, but if a small state is on the losing
> side, it can be utterly annihilated. If, on the other hand, a small
> state is on the winning side, it has no means of insisting that the
> principles for which it fought and risked everything be put in
> effect.[8]

By 1947 the Irish government decided that there was nothing to be
lost by voicing officially its desire to have Gray removed. An informal
conversation at the end of 1946 between a member of the Irish legation in Washington and two Ireland specialists in the Department of
State paved the way for this decision. The State Department officers
talked about the unfortunate state of the American–Irish relationship
and placed the blame for it squarely on Gray. They expressed regret
that the American perception of Irish neutrality during the war had

been 'wrongly interpreted', again because of Gray. They said that Gray did not understand Irish nationalism and was unaware of Irish political realities. Finally, they mentioned Governor Maurice Tobin of Massachusetts as a possible successor. Brennan passed on the notes of the conversation with a cover letter stating that he was not able to determine if the conversation was 'inspired' by higher officials at the State Department.[9]

Sensing that it might reach a receptive audience, the next month Walshe instructed Brennan in Washington to meet with the State Department and to express regret over the state of the relationship. He was instructed to convey to the American government that the problem originated with David Gray, who 'has done more than any American in history to create misunderstanding and bad feeling' between the two countries. Informally, Brennan found out from a friend of Truman that it was Eleanor Roosevelt's continued influence that kept Gray in his post. Finally, maybe as a result of age, sensing the pressure, or thinking that his mission to discredit Ireland was a success, Gray resigned in April 1947, leaving Ireland two months later. Reports were that Gray asked to stay and introduce his replacement, George Garret, to some of his friends. The State Department replied that it would be better if Garret made his own friends.[10]

Gray, however, even in retirement in Florida, was not done trying to harm the perception of Ireland and of de Valera in the United States. Given a review of his writings, it is a distinct possibility that Gray was suffering from the early stages of dementia. In 1957 he wrote an introduction to a book on Ulster in which he argued that de Valera, 'even before the fall of France', felt that Germany would win the war, and in return for keeping the Allies out of the Treaty ports, Hitler would end partition. That would then allow de Valera to 'expel' the Protestant population and invite in an equal number of 'exiles'. Only when de Valera realized he had backed the loser, according to Gray, did the Irish leader build up the 'so-called "crime of partition" as a grievance and an excuse'. The Irish Department of External Affairs felt compelled to respond publicly that Gray's account was so distorted that it shed light 'not on events, but on the character of the man who was America's envoy to Ireland at that critical period'.[11]

Gray's unpublished manuscript, 'Behind the Green Curtain', exhibits the same type of intense criticism of Irish neutrality mixed with an almost fantastical sense of what actually happened during the war. Gray begins by claiming that Irish unification was a reasonable hope before de Valera, but that the Irish leader's 'stupidities' made his entire tenure a 'complete failure' and foreclosed any possibility of ending partition. Gray wrote that de Valera had a pact with Berlin, but that was natural because 'the same psychotic forces of revolution which produced Hitler also produced de Valera', although the two men differed in 'personal characteristics'. In discussing the ports, Gray argued that de Valera's 'undertaking to destroy England by withholding the Irish Treaty ports ... [contributed] to the murder of not one, but six million Jews'. Gray recounted all of the ways he believed that Hitler and de Valera were alike, then chillingly wrote: 'Reality caught up with Hitler in the "Bunker", as the Allies entered Berlin. The hounds of truth are now on de Valera's trail, relentless, inexorable.' By the time of this writing, somewhere between October 1961 and November 1963, Gray had become unhinged.[12]

IRELAND, THE UNITED NATIONS AND THE MARSHALL PLAN

In the first year or so after the war, American policy makers were largely unconcerned about Ireland. When they did deal with Ireland, they focused their efforts on retaliating for Irish neutrality during the war. Such was the case when it came time to decide whom to invite as charter members of the United Nations. Ireland did not receive an initial invitation, as the United States government felt that Ireland's wartime neutrality did not warrant it a seat. By the end of 1945, however, as the growing Soviet–American split was taken into account, US policy makers began to change their attitudes towards Irish admission.[13] Such would be the pattern for American policy makers as they attempted to find a place for Ireland in the new postwar security arrangement that was starting to be defined by the antagonism between the United States and the Soviet Union. By May 1946 the War Department's intelligence review focused on the importance of all western European countries in the confrontation with the Soviet Union. By April 1949 a Central Intelligence report concluded that Ireland was 'potentially a valuable ally' and that 'the denial of Ireland to an enemy is an unavoidable principle of United States security'.[14]

After being denied a charter invitation, de Valera was reluctant to have Ireland apply for membership in the United Nations until he was sure that Britain and the United States would support its efforts. In March 1946 the US State Department completed a review of membership for neutral nations that reinforced the commitment of the Potsdam agreements to include former neutrals in the organization.[15] Prompted in part by a desire to admit pro-western nations to counter the anticipated applications of pro-Soviet nations (Albania had recently applied), the American and British governments approached de Valera in July 1946. The month before, de Valera delivered a long speech in the Dáil about possible Irish membership in the United Nations. In a debate over the final Irish payments due to the League of Nations, de Valera called that body 'one of the, or perhaps greatest, experiment in international cooperation the world has ever known'. The failure of the League, according to de Valera, was that the members 'were not willing to face war and to wage war in order to prevent war'. He then argued that the new organization did not seem to protect the rights of smaller states as well as the League had been designed to do, but that smaller states would benefit under the new organization if larger states had learned the lessons from the recent war.[16]

Soon after getting the official invitation from the British, de Valera started the process of bringing the application before the Dáil.[17] He stressed that membership in the UN meant that Ireland accepted the responsibility to fight when called upon. Neutrality, by itself and apart from participation in an effective world body, was only an option if the larger powers allowed it to be one. Referring to the recent war, de Valera said that Irish neutrality rested on 'the concurrence of wills of perhaps two people', Churchill and Roosevelt.[18] While not perfect, de Valera argued that the UN represented the best hope of maintaining Ireland's neutrality and that agreeing to participate in wars to defend the goals of the UN charter would be Ireland's best hope to maintain its identity.

Ireland's application to the United Nations was eventually a casualty in the growing Soviet–American split. When Ireland did forward its formal application in 1946, the Soviet Union vetoed it, along with the applications of Portugal, Austria, Finland, Jordan and Ceylon. Soviet Foreign Minister Andre Gromyko publicly argued that the veto was justified because Ireland 'brought no assistance to the United Nations' in the war. In reality the Soviets were using the applications of Ireland and the other nations as bargaining chips to admit Bulgaria, Hungary and other pro-Soviet states. Ireland did not gain entry into the United Nations until 1955, and it did so only then as part of a package deal between Washington and Moscow.[19]

The other major issue in the American–Irish relationship in the postwar years concerned Ireland's participation in the Marshall Plan. Gray and Brennan were no longer serving in Dublin and Washington when the Irish and American governments discussed Marshall Plan aid. Brennan left the Irish diplomatic corps in March 1947 to become

Ireland's Director of Broadcasting. Seán Nunan, the long-time Irish Consul General in Washington and New York, took his place. In Dublin, George Angus Garrett replaced Gray in July 1947. Garrett was an investment banker from Wisconsin and was friends with an earlier American representative in Dublin, Frederick Sterling.[20] Both of the new envoys worked to repair the damaged American–Irish relationship.

From the perspective of the American government, there was a tension in postwar strategies concerning Ireland. On the one hand, as evidenced by the reluctance to include Ireland in the initial organization of the United Nations, there was a desire to punish Ireland for its wartime neutrality. During the late 1940s, however, that desire had to be balanced against the need to formally include Ireland in the West as fears over the Cold War began to take hold. Given the unstable postwar economic situation in Ireland, one that Garrett felt might lead to communist activity, as well as the desire to have a financially secure Ireland serve as a trading partner and food supplier to Britain, American policy makers decided to include Ireland in the European Recovery Program (ERP), better known as the Marshall Plan. For the Irish government, the invitation to participate in the ERP was an opportunity to regain some international standing, badly wounded because of the public face of neutrality, and to gain some badly needed economic assistance without having to turn to already economically ravaged Britain.

There are several specific reasons why the United States decided to include Ireland in the ERP, in spite of the legacy of the wartime relationship. First, in a bid to isolate the Soviet Union and make it responsible for the division of Europe, George Kennan in the State Department had been urging that the programme include a wide spectrum of countries, including neutrals. Once the Soviet Union rejected Ireland's participation in the UN, it would have been awkward at best not to include Ireland in a programme of western European democracies. In addition, Ireland's strategic position, highlighted by a May 1946 War Department memorandum, argued for Ireland's participation. Finally, American policy makers took seriously the desire of British leaders to include Ireland out of fear that denying aid might strengthen any potential anti-partition campaign and a recognition of the interdependence of the British and Irish economies.[21]

Some of the same fears of postwar instability and possible Soviet aggression that motivated the Marshall Plan came into play with the creation of the North American Treaty Organization. Fine Gael leaders, in power by then as part of the power-sharing government that succeeded de Valera in 1948, were much more likely than he was to pursue membership in such a western military alliance. The staunch anti-communism of the Irish people and of the Irish Catholic hierarchy would also be likely forces in favour of joining the coalition. Hoping that all this would bring the Irish government on board, in April 1948 the NATO governments made an informal inquiry to Ireland's representative to Canada.[22] At first the Irish government made no official or informal response. But by July it began to make it clear that the ending of partition was the price of its participation.[23] If the Irish government truly believed it could end partition by withholding Irish participation in NATO, its ministers were clearly not able to read the international situation. What is more likely, given the now long-standing resilience of Irish neutrality, is that it was so clearly a part of Irish identity after the war that no government could abandon it, even for an effort that had the support of so many of its people. As a consequence, Ireland did not have a relationship with NATO until it joined NATO's Partnership for Peace initiative on 1 December 1999.[24]

IRELAND AND POSTWAR AMERICA

Irish America was a topic of some concern in domestic Irish politics following the war. One of the newest postwar Irish political parties, born from the economic drift of the postwar years, was Clann na Poblachta (Family of the Republic). Seán MacBride, the former IRA Chief of Staff, quickly became the standard-bearer of the new party. Tim Coogan has described the creation of Clann na Poblachta in 1946 as the 'most important break in "physical force" Republicanism since the creation of Fianna Fáil' twenty years earlier'.[25] In many ways, Clann na Poblachta was more Fianna Fáil than Fianna Fáil. MacBride was able to put forth more recent republican credentials than de Valera, and the party embraced a radical social programme grounded in Catholic social teaching. The latter enabled the party to appeal to a dissatisfied electorate concerned about economic conditions, while the former allowed those impatient with the continuation of partition to register their complaint. Bernadette Whelan has succinctly summarized Ireland's postwar economic situation: 'By 1947 the continuation of war-time dislocation was manifested in rationing, rising inflation, falling living standards, frequent strikes, unemployment and emigration.'[26] Fearful of the growing support for Clann na Poblachta in by-elections in 1946 and 1947, de Valera called for general elections in February 1948.

Fine Gael leader James Dillon and de Valera debated the issue of

Irish Americans and partition in 1947 during election season. Fine Gael did not want to run against de Valera in an election based on each party's republican credentials. Urging de Valera not to stir up Irish-American passions, Dillon told de Valera to 'give up living in his salad days' because 'the world has changed greatly since he was careering [careening] about the American Continent 25 years ago'. True and patriotic Irish Americans, Dillon argued, saw that it was the 'Bolsheviks' who were trying to disrupt the Anglo–American alliance and that any effort by the Irish to do the same thing, even for a differ-ent purpose, would be tainted by the same brush.[27] Dillon then went on to highlight the difference between the amount of energy Fianna Fáil put into an anti-partition campaign compared to the level of rhetoric it used to describe the campaign:

MR DILLON: The ... Minister for Posts and Telegraphs ... announced here that a short-wave radio station was to be established for which the ex-ambassador in Washington had been brought home as director, and it was to be largely employed for the purpose of communicating to the people in America the facts about Partition.

THE TAOISEACH: That was never stated.

MR DILLON: Now, you cannot have it both ways. Do not go bleating to our people in this country that you are going to bust everything about Partition wide open with your propaganda, and then start trying to persuade those in a position to know what you are up to that you have no intention of that kind. You cannot have it both ways; you cannot go on living a lie.

THE TAOISEACH: That is stupid – you are stupid, and worse.[28]

When it was his turn to take the floor, after a long debate where Dillon and others called many Irish-American activists communists, de Valera seemed resigned to abandon any active role for Irish-American groups in any immediate anti-partition campaign. He said that for partition to end, there needed to be 'a concurrence of wills' between the people of Ireland, the people of Northern Ireland and the members of the British Parliament.[29]

Fianna Fáil won only 41 per cent of the vote in the February 1948 elections and lost its majority in the Dáil. The opposition parties then banded together, united only by their opposition to de Valera's rule, to form the nation's first inter-party government. After his electoral defeat, de Valera went to the United States once again, in another of his career-long efforts to bring Irish America into service in support of his sense of Irish interests, sovereignty and identity. The trip was part of a larger post-election effort on the part of Fianna Fáil and the new governing coalition to weaken each other by taking on the mantle of Irish republicanism. The issue at hand was partition, but perhaps as a result of being out of power, de Valera did not mount a particularly vigorous campaign and consciously avoided offending the Irish government or linking partition to Irish participation in the Marshall Plan. He did pay a courtesy visit to President Truman, bringing Aiken along for another visit to the White House, but there were no fireworks this time. De Valera's American tour did little, however, to line up significant Irish-American opposition to the British–American relationship. Troy Davis argues that one of the two main reasons for this lack of support was Irish Americans' acceptance of the Cold War consensus view that the United States needed to act in the world with Great Britain as its main ally. The long history of Catholic anti-communism played its role in this development. The second reason grew out of the entire World War Two experience that led to changes in the Irish-American community's sense of identity, a 'political assimilation'.[30]

THE IRISH REPUBLIC

In September 1948, in a surprising move during an official visit to Canada, the new Taoiseach, John Costello, announced his government's intention to repeal the External Relations Act, the last link with the Crown and the Commonwealth, and to establish an Irish Republic. There is some indication that the governing parties discussed this move, rejected by de Valera when fashioning the new constitution in 1937, but by most accounts Costello's announcement came as a surprise even to MacBride.[31] The move to become a republic was mostly symbolic. In any real sense, short of simply upsetting the British for no cause and even further retarding the possibility of a reconciliation and 'concurrence of the wills' with the people of Northern Ireland, the announcement of the Republic served no purpose. De Valera had effectively created a republic, although with links to the British monarch, with the 1937 constitution.[32] The government introduced the Republic of Ireland Act in the Dáil on 8 November 1948. The Act repealed the External Relations Act of 1936, and, although it did not change the official name of the state, it declared 'the *description* of the State shall be the Republic of Ireland'. It became law on Easter Monday 1949, on the thirty-third anniversary of the Easter Rebellion.[33]

British reaction to the creation of the Irish Republic, thereby officially taking Ireland out of the Commonwealth, was swift. Prime Minister Clement Atlee gave the Northern Ireland government assurances that partition would not end without formal approval from the Parliament in Belfast. The British Parliament within two months passed the Ireland Act of 1949, which declared that Ireland ceased to be part of the crown's dominions and that 'in no event will Northern Ireland or any part thereof cease to be a part of His Majesty's dominions and of the United Kingdom without the consent of the Parliament of Northern Ireland'.[34]

POSTWAR IRISH-AMERICAN IDENTITY

The economic boom following the Second World War allowed many Irish Americans, along with many other Americans, to move out of urban ethnic neighbourhoods and into the burgeoning suburbs. The G.I. Bill, mortgage financing and highway construction fuelled this exodus. Irish Americans, however, did not leave the cities at the same rate as other Americans. There was still a sizeable percentage of Irish Americans living in the major cities of the north-east through 1980.[35] Part of the explanation for this decreased mobility may be related to the fact that Irish Americans in 1950 remained at the bottom of the economic ladder compared to other pre-1890 immigrant groups. Both first-generation and second-generation Irish Americans advanced at a slower rate than other groups. In some urban areas it was even worse. In Boston, for example, in the 1950s and 1960s Irish Americans lagged behind all other white groups in many economic categories.[36]

One Irish-American group capitalized on the postwar political and economic developments to strengthen its position within the Irish-American community and on the national scene. The Ancient Order of Hibernians (AOH) was almost defunct right before the war. The cumulative effect of declining economic fortunes of members and potential members, combined with the New Deal's social safety net efforts that rendered the AOH mutual aid programmes expendable, meant that a once thriving agent of community identity was on the brink of extinction before World War Two. While the general postwar flight to the suburbs ruptured many of the Irish-American bonds of parish and neighbourhood, at least in the north-east and in some Midwest urban areas the Irish-American community did enjoy a general and national

upsurge in acceptance of ethnic identification. It is possible this acceptance grew out of a desire by Americans to differentiate themselves
from the racial superiority ideology of Nazi Germany; moreover, it certainly only extended to white ethnics, not African Americans.
Whatever the cause, Irish Americans found themselves championed as
national heroes for their military sacrifices during the war and highlighted in textbooks as 'archetypal patriotic immigrants'. The AOH
recognized these developments and started an effort to rebrand itself as
a leading civic organization in the new Cold War struggle against com-
munism both at home and abroad. The 1948 membership manual, in
a rebuke to wartime Irish neutrality, claimed that the clash with com-
munism was a clash between the forces of Christ and Anti-Christ and
that 'there can be no neutrality'. Irish Americans joining the postwar
AOH were joining an organization where they were proclaiming their
American sense of self and political mission more than they were proclaiming their Irish-American sense of identity.[37]

The steady influx of Irish immigrants that had always rejuvenated
and energized the Irish-American community began to diminish even
before the war. The Great Depression made Britain the preferred destination of Irish emigrants in the 1930s. By 1950 there were more
Irish-born people in Britain than the United States. There were almost
500,000 first-generation or second-generation Irish in New York City
in 1940; by 1960 there were just over 300,000. For most of the 1950s
the Irish did not even fill 50 per cent of their yearly quota of visas to
come to the United States.[38] The consequence was that Irish-American
writers began to look even more deeply into the uniquely American
aspects of the Irish-American experience.

One postwar Irish-American novel in particular bridges the literary
gap between expressions of Irish ethnicity and the pulls of assimilation.
Edward McSorley's *Our Own Kind* (1946) explores the tensions within
Irish America as the economic opportunities of the postwar boom and
the growing sense of acceptance of Irish Americans into the cultural
and social mainstream clashed with the persistent tug of feelings of
alienation. The main character, Willie McDermott, explores the Irish-
American neighbourhoods of Providence, Rhode Island, through visits
to his extended family. These trips take the reader from churches to
bars, racetracks to large family meals. Willie's grandparents raise him
after the death of his parents, sending him to Catholic schools and
teaching him their own oral traditions of Irish nationalism. When
Willie's grandfather senses that the influences of the Irish-American
neighbourhood itself might be holding Willie down, they move out,

but only to a new parish in South Providence. Eventually, after his grandfather's death, Willie has to quit school and work to help support the family. Willie's dream, and McSorley's vision, of a valiant effort to move away from and out of an insular community to a wider success is only partially realized.[39]

Charles Fanning has characterized the Irish-American authors who wrote autobiographical novels in the 1940s as 'regional realists'. Much of their work focused on recreating in fiction the Irish-American neighbourhoods, families and social structures that surrounded them and was about to be lost. In spite of the economic rise of Irish America, the recurring themes of alcoholism, domestic violence, economic hardship and what Fanning describes as 'working-class-Irish emotional inarticulateness' form the backbone of these works. Many of these postwar authors drew their influence from the earlier works of O'Hara and Farrell. Pete Hamill, the author of several Irish-American novels set in the 1950s, claimed that Farrell taught him 'to look with pity and terror and compassion at the people we knew and at ourselves ... to speak in some way for those who have no voices'.[40] It was this sense of having no voice that led Irish Americans to be receptive to Ireland's call before the war, and until 1968 and the Troubles in Northern Ireland, Irish Americans would face their continuing struggle for identity without looking across the Atlantic to their Irish cousins.

NOTES

1. David Gray, introduction to *Ulster and the Irish Republic* by William A. Carson (Belfast: William W. Cleland, 1957), ii.
2. The research for this chapter owes much to Troy Davis's *Dublin's American Policy: Irish American Diplomatic Relations, 1945–1952* (Washington, D.C.: Catholic University Press, 1998). For the quotations, see p. 29.
3. 'Hickerson to Gray', 11 February 1946, US Department of State, *Foreign Relations of the United States: Diplomatic Papers, 1946*, vol. 5, *The British Commonwealth; Western and Central Europe* (Washington, D.C.: US Government Printing Office, 1969), 113–14 (hereafter citations will be in the form *FRUS*, year, vol. number: page). See also Davis, *Dublin's American Policy*, 36–9.
4. Davis, *Dublin's American Policy*, 39.
5. 'Walshe to Brennan', 11 June 1945, National Archives of Ireland, Department of Foreign Affairs, P48 (hereafter cited as NAI/DFA/file number). The Department of External Affairs became the Department of Foreign Affairs in 1971.
6. 'Brennan to Walshe', 18 March 1946, NAI/DFA/P48.
7. 'Gray to Kennedy', 12 November 1946, FDR Library, David Gray Papers, box 4.
8. 'Broadcast by An Taoiseach – St Patrick's Day, 1946', NAI/DFA/2.
9. 'Brennan to Walshe', 31 December 1946, NAI/DFA/P48.
10. 'Walshe to Brennan', 25 January 1947, 'Brennan to Walshe', 19 February 1947, and 'Nunan to Walshe', 25 June 1947, NAI/DFA/P48. Rep. John McCormack of Massachusetts also confirmed the importance of the Roosevelt connection in the retention of Gray; see 'Brennan to Walshe', 15 March 1947, NAI/DFA/P48A.

11. 'Weekly Bulletin of the Department of External Affairs', 9 November 1957, University College Dublin archives, Éamon de Valera Papers, P150/2709 (hereafter manuscript collections from the Archives at University College, Dublin will be cited as UCD, collection name, file number).

12. David Gray, 'Behind the Green Curtain', unpublished manuscript, pp. 1, 24, 28, 31, 66, and 67, in University of Wyoming, American Heritage Center, David Gray Papers, box 1 (hereafter cited as UW/AHC, box number).

13. This section on Ireland the United Nations is deeply indebted to Davis, *Dublin's American Policy*, 39–57.

14. Quoted in Bernadette Whelan, 'Integration or Isolation? Ireland and the Invitation to Join the Marshall Plan', in *Irish Foreign Policy, 1919–66: From Independence to Internationalism*, ed. Michael Kennedy and Joseph Morrison Skelly (Dublin: Four Courts Press, 2000), 204; Seán Cronin, *Washington's Irish Policy, 1916–1986: Independence, Partition, Neutrality* (Dublin: Anvil Books, 1987), 250–81.

15. 'United States Attitude Toward membership Questions During Coming Security Council Meetings', 15 March 1946, *FRUS*, 1946, 5: 363–4. For the Potsdam agreement, see 'Protocol of Proceedings, by the Heads of Government of the United States, United Kingdom, and Soviet Union, August 1, 1945', in *In Quest of Peace and Security: Selected Documents on American Foreign Policy, 1941–1951* (Washington, D.C.: US Government Printing Office, 1951), 25–38.

16. *Dáil Debates*, 26 June 1946, cols. 2430–2.

17. 'Boland to Moynihan', 10 July 1946, NAI/DT/S13750A. The Cabinet discussed the application on 12, 16 and 19 July. See 'Cabinet Minutes', NAI/DT/S13750A.

18. *Dáil Debates*, 25 July 1946, col. 1467.

19. Dermot Keogh, *Ireland and Europe, 1919–1948* (Dublin: Gill & Macmillan, 1988), 202–5; Joseph Morrison Skelly, *Irish Diplomacy at the United Nations, 1945–1965: National Interests and the International Order* (Dublin: Irish Academic Press, 1997), 15–29.

20. Davis, *Dublin's American Policy*, 95–7; Bernadette Whelan, *Ireland and the Marshall Plan, 1947–57* (Dublin: Four Courts Press, 2000), 397.

21. See Bernadette Whelan, 'Ireland, the Marshall Plan, and US Cold Concerns', *Journal of Cold War Studies* 8, no. 1 (winter 2006): 68–94.

22. 'Hearne to Boland', 15 April 1948, NAI/DT/S14291/A1.

23. See the remarks of Minister of External Affairs Seán MacBride in *Dáil Debates*, 20 July 1948, cols. 903–11.

24. Róisín Doherty, *Ireland, Neutrality and European Security Integration* (Burlington, Vt.: Ashgate Publishing, 2002), 21.

25. Tim Pat Coogan, *The IRA: A History*, 4th edn (New York: HarperCollins, 1995), 127; Maurice Manning, *Irish Political Parties* (Dublin: Gill & Macmillan, 1972), 110–14.

26. Whelan, *Ireland and the Marshall Plan*, 50.

27. *Dáil Debates*, 20 June 1947, col. 2336. All Dáil debates are available at http://www.historical-debates.oireachtas.ie/.

28. Ibid.

29. *Dáil Debates*, 24 June 1947, col. 79. See also Davis, *Dublin's American Policy*, 66–8.

30. Troy Davis, '"The Irish Movement in this Country is Now Moribund": The Anti-Partition Campaign of 1948–51 in the United States', in *After the Flood: Irish America, 1945–1960*, ed. James Silas Rogers and Matthew J. O'Brien (Dublin: Irish Academic Press, 2009), 51; Davis, *Dublin's American Policy*, 69–72; Tim Pat Coogan, *Eamon De Valera: The Man Who Was Ireland* (New York: HarperCollins, 1995), 638. There were a series of votes in state legislatures and in Congress about partition, but for the most part these were merely symbolic gestures for local constituents. See Davis, *Dublin's American Policy*, 74–94.

31. There has been much debate about what prompted Costello to make the announcement. There had been several snubs to Irish independence during this visit, including several toasts to the King and the heads of state of sovereign nations, but not Ireland, and the placing on Costello's table at a formal dinner a replica of the cannon used by Protestants during the siege of Derry in 1689. Costello described the cannon as 'one of the guns used against our people'. For a review, see Ian McCabe, *A Diplomatic History of Ireland, 1948–49: The Republic, the Commonwealth, and NATO* (Dublin: Irish Academic Press, 1991), 40–4.

32. In January 1948 de Valera drafted a revision to the External Relations Act that would have removed the British monarch from the diplomatic activities of Ireland. His draft also referred to the country as the 'Republic'. See 'The Presidential (International Powers and Functions)

Act, 1948', UCD, Cearbhall Ó Dálaigh Papers, P51/2.

33. 'The Republic of Ireland Act, 1948', my italics. All Irish legislation is available at http://www.irishstatutebook.ie/.
34. 'The Ireland Act, 1949'available at http://www.opsi.gov.uk/RevisedStatutes/ Acts/ukpga/1949/ cukpga_19490041_en_1.
35. Morton Winsberg, 'The Suburbanization of the Irish in Boston, Chicago and New York', *Eire-Ireland* 21 (fall 1986): 92.
36. Kevin Kenny, *The American Irish: A History* (New York: Longman, 2000), 227–8.
37. Matthew J. O'Brien, '"Hibernians on the March": Irish-American Ethnicity and the Cold War', in *After the Flood*, 57–70.
38. Mary E. Daly, 'Nationalism, Sentiment, and Economics: Relations Between Ireland and Irish America in the Postwar Years', *Eire-Ireland* 37 (spring/summer 2002): 76; Kenny, *American Irish*, 226.
39. Edward McSorley, *Our Own Kind* (New York: Harper & Bros, 1946); Christopher Shannon, 'Beyond St Malachi's, There is Nothing: Edward McSorley and the Persistence of Tradition', in *After the Flood*, 174–88.
40. Charles Fanning, *The Irish Voice in America: 250 Years of Irish-American Fiction*, 2nd edn (Lexington: University Press of Kentucky, 2000), 292–311. See also Shaun O'Connell, 'That Much Credit: Irish-American Identity and Writing', *Massachusetts Review* 44 (2003): 251–67.

Conclusion

Three issues – the assertion of its identity, the recognition of that identity by others, and the promotion and development of exchanges with other nations – are basic aspects of any country's relations with the world ... As a people we have certain fairly clear concepts of right and wrong in human relations ... We owe these moral values largely to basic religious beliefs which permeate our culture. But we also have certain distinctive attitudes and sympathies which are shaped by our view of our own history – among them a strong fellow-feeling for any people who struggle to maintain their identity against greater force. (Irish Minister for Foreign Affairs, Patrick Hillery, 18 April 1972)[1]

The awareness of being Irish came to us as small children, through plaintive song and heroic story ... As children, we drew in a burning hatred of British rule with our mother's milk. (Elizabeth Gurley Flynn)[2]

The past, and our understanding of its meaning through our histories, have a central role in the identities of the Irish and of Irish Americans. As Hillery and Flynn suggest, the history and memory of the past serve as the backdrop against which identity is created, and they sustain that identity across generations. Historical understanding becomes, then, a vehicle to infuse group memories with the core elements of 'peoplehood'. For Éamon de Valera, the mission to create a rural, Gaelic and independent Irish identity permeated much of his public life. He wanted to forge a new Irish identity that allowed the relatively new nation to find a place in the world apart from Britain and apart from the legacy of British domination. In doing so, he often turned to Irish America for support. In turn, Irish Americans brought with them across the Atlantic their understanding of Irish history, and saw themselves as exiles because of British misrule of Ireland. That sense of displacement led them to be deeply concerned about Irish political affairs in the first part of the twentieth century. They passed that passion, as a part of their identity, on to later generations. After Ireland's independence, however, Irish Americans became less concerned with the nationalism that was still very much a part of de Valera's world, even though they never felt entirely at ease with their place in American society. After World War Two the interrelated struggles for identity, which involved both the Irish at home and the Irish in America looking for support from each other, began to untangle.

It is no easy task to develop insights into the creation and development of Irish-American identity, in part because of the somewhat amorphous nature of ethnic identity in general. Even so, what historian Mathew Jacobson has described as the 'diasporic imagination' and the 'shared cultural imagery' of Irish Americans offers a window into what Irish Americans felt about themselves, their relationship to Ireland and their place in American society. How Irish Americans represented themselves in novels and comics and how the larger society represented them in films and songs and plays compose the elements that defined the public aspect of their ethnic identity. That identity then became an 'inner geography' for Irish Americans as family, social groups and educational institutions reinforced it.[3]

Irish-American identity, however, never became fully enmeshed with wider American society's values; Irish America never fully assimilated. Even after Irish Americans began to move up the economic ladder and to encounter fewer instances of overt hostility for their race or religion, as a group they never felt completely at home, culturally, in the United States. The loud and public displays of patriotism, at first efforts to prove their worth as Americans, did become real reflections of Irish Americans' love for their country. Even so, their ambivalence about their place in the nation's life became a constant theme of their novelists and cartoonists in the 1930s and 1940s, and continues today, in the works of Alice McDermot and others.[4] Irish America is still defining itself. The circumstances are different, but the search is still influenced by the past and their community's (or imagined community's) struggle against those who would define them.

For the Irish at home, the early years of the twentieth century were a time of searching for a cultural identity. The efforts of Irish nationalists to strengthen the Irish language and Irish sports were part of a wider effort to establish the justification for Irish independence. If there were a uniquely Irish identity that the world could recognize, the leaders hoped, then perhaps the Irish people and the nations of the world would force the British to give Ireland its independence. During World War One those committed Irish nationalists forced the issue during the Easter Rising of 1916.

After independence and civil war, de Valera led the Irish on a path to find a political identity for Ireland in the world, one that would encompass that earlier effort to define an Irish cultural identity. Throughout the 1930s he worked to separate Ireland from Britain economically, diplomatically, culturally and territorially. When the Second World War broke out, de Valera felt that given the nature of the Irish strategic position, the continuation of the partition of the island and the relatively recent and unfinished efforts to create an Irish identity in the world, neutrality was the only viable option. That neutrality became a target for British and American officials wishing to either bring Ireland into the war or at least allow its territory to be used by the Allied armed forces. Those efforts, especially by Churchill and Gray, clashed with de Valera's spirited defence of Irish neutrality. De Valera developed a practical policy on a par with a moral imperative for small countries that helped make neutrality itself an integral part of Irish identity for the rest of the twentieth century and into the twenty-first.

The homogenizing effects of World War Two in part explain the sporadic and obviously ineffectual Irish-American action on the issue of Irish partition in the immediate postwar years. While Gray may have liked to take credit for the weakness of that effort, it is impossible to judge just how much damage he did to Ireland's reputation in the United States during the war. The fact is that his machinations to limit the ability of Irish Americans to influence American policy were based on falsehoods and premised on the idea that some Americans did not merit the right to bring their concerns about American policy to the attention of the wider public and the American government. When government decides that citizens either do not deserve to learn the truth or that some citizens do not deserve the right to shape government policy, democracy cannot thrive.

Irish Americans embraced the postwar Cold War consensus and continued their search for identity in a climate that was by then much more accepting than the one encountered by their parents and grandparents. The decline of Irish-America's participation in Irish affairs that began after 1920 merely continued after 1945, only to be rekindled when the events of the late 1960s in Northern Ireland again put the spotlight on Ireland's, and Northern Ireland's, relationship with the Irish diaspora. That relationship, in turn, was defined by its own past, a past which included the relationship between Ireland and Irish Americans between 1932 and 1945.

Irish wartime neutrality was a concerted effort to establish identity in addition to being a practical policy for survival. That it survived at all was a function of Irish public diplomacy efforts in the United States and the receptivity to those efforts by Irish Americans who were struggling with their own sense of identity as Americans. British and American policy makers took that public diplomacy, and their perceptions about the power of American and Irish American public opinion, into account in many of the decisions concerning the British–American security relationship. In the end, many in Great Britain and the United States saw Irish neutrality as a retreat in the face of a moral imperative. Concerned primarily with their own strategic situations during and after the war, buoyed by victory and deluded by false reports, they failed to comprehend the true nature of Irish neutrality and the reason for its existence.

NOTES

1. *Dáil Debates*, 18 April 1972, cols. 384 and 389.
2. Elizabeth Gurley Flynn, *I Speak My Own Piece* (New York: Masses and Mainstream, 1955), 13.
3. Matthew Frye Jacobson, *Special Sorrows: The Diasporic Imagination of Irish, Polish, and Jewish Immigrants in the United States* (Cambridge, Mass.: Harvard University Press, 1995), 7.
4. See Shaun O'Connell, 'That Much Credit: Irish-American Identity and Writing', *Massachusetts Review* 44 (2003): 251–67.

Select Bibliography

PRIMARY SOURCES

Ireland

Dáil Éireann
Parliamentary Debates. Official Reports
Irish Military Archives, Cathal Brugha Barracks, Dublin
Department of Defence Files
Director of Intelligence Files
National Archives, Dublin
Department of Foreign Affairs, 'DFA' Files
Department of the Taoiseach, Private Office Files
Department of the Taoiseach, Secretariat 'S' Files
National Library, Dublin
    Frank Gallagher Papers
    Joseph McGarrity Papers
University College, Dublin, Department of Archives
    Frank Aiken Papers
    Dan Bryan Papers
    Éamon de Valera Papers
    Richard Mulcahy Papers
    Cearbhall Ó Dálaigh Papers

United Kingdom

Public Record Office (via microfilm)
    Cabinet Papers
Office of the Prime Minister Records

United States

Franklin Delano Roosevelt Library, Hyde Park, New York
    David Gray Papers

President's Personal Files
President's Secretary's Files – Safe File

Printed Materials:
National Archives, Suitland, Maryland
    Dublin Legation Classified Records (Record Group 84)
    General Records of the Department of State (Record Group 59)
University of Wyoming, American Heritage Center
    David Gray Papers

Newspapers and Periodicals

Irish Press (Dublin)
Irish Times (Dublin)
Irish World (New York)
Nation
New York Times

Published Official Documents

Crowe, Catriona, Ronan Fanning, Michael Kennedy, Dermot Keogh and Eunan O'Halpin, eds. *Documents on Irish Foreign Policy*, 6 vols. Dublin: Royal Irish Academy, 1998–2006.

De Valera, Éamon and Irish Free State. Oireachtas. Seanad. *The Unity of Ireland: Partition Debated in Seanad Éireann (the Irish Senate): Mr De Valera's Speech (from Seanad Éireann Official Reports)*. Dublin: Stationery Office, 1939.

Documents on German Foreign Policy, Series D, *1937–1945*. 13 vols. Washington, DC: US Government Printing Office, 1949–64.

Great Britain. Embassy (United States). *Confidential Dispatches: Analyses of America by the British Ambassador, 1939–1945*. Edited by Thomas E. Hachey and Edward Frederick Lindley Wood Halifax. Evanston, Ill.: New University Press, 1974.

Mansergh, Nicholas, ed. *Documents and Speeches on British Commonwealth Affairs, 1931–1952*. 2 vols. Oxford: Oxford University Press, 1952–3.

Mitchell, Arthur and Pádraig Ó Snodaigh, eds. *Irish Political Documents, 1916–1949*. Dublin: Irish Academic Press, 1985.

O'Day, Alan and John Stevenson, eds. *Irish Historical Documents Since 1800*. Savage, Md.: Barnes & Noble, 1992.

O'Halpin, Eunan, ed. *MI5 and Ireland, 1939–1945: The Official History*. Dublin: Irish Academic Press, 2003.

US Department of State. *A Decade of American Foreign Policy: Basic Documents 1941–1949*. Washington, DC: US Government Printing Office, 1985.

— *Foreign Relations of the United States: Diplomatic Papers*. Washington, DC: US Government Printing Office, 1949–69.

— *Letter from America*. Dublin: US Legation, 1942–45.

— Office of Public Affairs. *In Quest of Peace and Security: Selected Documents on American Foreign Policy, 1941–1951*. Washington, DC: US Government Printing Office, 1951.

Additional Published Primary Sources

Bowen, Elizabeth. *Notes on Eire: Espionage Reports to Winston Churchill, 1940–42*. Aubane, Ireland: Aubane Historical Society, 1999.

Brennan, Robert. *Ireland Standing Firm: My Wartime Mission in Washington*. Dublin: University College Dublin Press, 2002.

— *Allegiance*. Dublin: Browne & Nolan, 1950.

Carson, William Arthur. *Ulster and the Irish Republic*. Introduction by David Gray. Belfast: William W. Cleland, 1957.

Churchill, Winston. *The Aftermath*. New York: Charles Scribner's Sons, 1929.

— *The Second World War*. 6 vols. Boston: Houghton Mifflin, 1948–53.

— *The War Speeches of the Rt Hon Winston S. Churchill*. Compiled by Charles Eade. Vol. 3. London: Cassell & Co., 1952.

— *Winston S. Churchill: Companion*. Vol. 5, *1922–1939*. Edited by Martin Gilbert. Boston: Houghton Mifflin, 1978.

Cudahy, John. *The Armies March: A Personal Report*. New York: Charles Scribner's Sons, 1941.

Cronin, Seán, ed. *The McGarrity Papers: Revelations of the Irish Revolutionary Movement in Ireland and America, 1900–1940*. Tralee, Ireland: Anvil, 1972.

De Valera, Éamon. *Ireland's Stand: Being a Selection of Speeches of Éamon de Valera During the War*. Dublin: Stationery Office, 1946.

— *Peace and War: Speeches by Mr de Valera on International Affairs*. Dublin: M.H. Gill & Son, 1944.

— *Speeches and Statements by Éamon de Valera, 1917–1973*. Edited by Maurice Moynihan. New York: St Martin's Press, 1980.

Farrell, James T. *Studs Lonigan: A Trilogy Comprising Young Lonigan, the Young Manhood of Studs Lonigan, and Judgment Day*. Urbana: University of Illinois Press, 1993.

— *The League of Frightened Philistines and Other Papers*. New York: Vanguard Press, 1945.

Flynn, Elizabeth Gurley. *I Speak My Own Piece*. New York: Masses and Mainstream, 1955.

Gallup, George. *The Gallup Poll: Public Opinion, 1935–1971*. Vol. 1, *1935–1948*. New York: Random House, 1972.

Hull, Cordell. *The Memoirs of Cordell Hull*. 2 vols. New York: MacMillan, 1948.

Joyce, James. *Ulysses*. Paris: Shakespeare & Co., 1922.

Kimball, Warren F., ed. *Churchill and Roosevelt: The Complete Correspondence*. 3 vols. Princeton, N.J.: Princeton University Press, 1984.

Lindbergh, Charles. *The Wartime Journals of Charles A. Lindbergh*. New York: Harcourt Brace Jovanovich, 1970.

MacDonald, Malcolm. *Titans & Others*. London: Collins, 1972.

MacNeice, Louis. *Collected Poems, 1925–1948*. London: Faber & Faber, 1949.

McDermott, Alice. *Charming Billy*. New York: Dell, 1998.

McManus, George. *Jiggs is Back*. Berkeley, Calif.: Celtic Book Co., 1986.

McSorley, Edward. *Our Own Kind*. New York: Harper & Bros, 1946.

O'Brien, William and Desmond Ryan, eds. *Devoy's Post Bag, 1871–1928*. Dublin: C.J. Fallon, 1948.

O'Hara, John. *Butterfield 8*. New York: Harcourt, Brace & Co., 1935.

Quigley, Martin. *A US Spy in Ireland*. Dublin: Marino Books, 1999.

Wills, Gary. *Bare Ruined Choirs: Doubt, Prophecy, and Radical Religion*. First edition. Garden City, N.Y.: Doubleday, 1972.

Secondary Sources

Anderson, Benedict. *Imagined Communities: Reflections on the Origin and Spread of Nationalism*. Revised edition. New York: Verso, 1991.

Appel, John J. and Selma Appel. *Pat-Riots to Patriots: American Irish in Caricature and Comic Art*. East Lansing: Michigan State University Museum, 1990.

Bayor, Ronald H. *Neighbors in Conflict: The Irish, Germans, Jews, and Italians of New York City, 1929–1941*. Baltimore, Md.: Johns Hopkins University Press, 1978.

Bayor, Ronald H. and Timothy J. Meagher, eds. *The New York Irish*. Baltimore, Md.: Johns Hopkins University Press, 1996.

Bell, J. Bowyer. *The Secret Army: The IRA, 1916–1979*. Cambridge, Mass.: MIT Press, 1983.

Blessing, Patrick J. 'Irish Emigration to the United States, 1800–1920: An Overview'. In *The Irish in America: Emigration, Assimilation, and Impact*, edited by P.J. Drudy, 11–37. New York: Cambridge University Press, 1985.

Bowman, John. *De Valera and the Ulster Question, 1917–1973*. New York: Oxford University Press, 1982.

Boyce, George. *The Irish Question and British Politics, 1868–1996*. Second edition. New York: Macmillan, 1996.

— 'From War to Neutrality: Anglo-Irish Relations, 1921–1950'. *British Journal of International Studies* 5, no. 1 (1979): 15–36.

Branch, Edgar M. *Studs Lonigan's Neighborhood and the Making of James T. Farrell*. Newton, Mass.: Arts Ends Books, 1996.

Brewer, Susan A. *To Win the Peace: British Propaganda in the United States During World War II*. Ithaca, N.Y.: Cornell University Press, 1997.

Brown, Richard Danson. 'Neutrality and Commitment: MacNeice, Yeats, Ireland and the Second World War'. *Journal of Modern Literature* 28, no. 3 (2005): 109–29.

Brown, Terence. *Ireland: A Social and Cultural History: 1922 to the Present*. Ithaca, N.Y.: Cornell University Press, 1985.

Brown, Thomas N. *Irish-American Nationalism, 1870–1890*. Philadelphia: J.B. Lippincott, 1966.

Buckley, John Patrick. *The New York Irish: Their View of American Foreign Policy, 1914–1921*. New York: Arno Press, 1976.

Byron, Reginald. *Irish America*. New York: Oxford University Press, 1999.

Canning, Paul. *British Policy Towards Ireland, 1921–1941*. New York: Oxford University Press, 1985.

Carroll, Francis M. *American Opinion and the Irish Question: 1910–1923*. New York: St Martin's Press, 1978.

— 'United States Armed Forces in Northern Ireland During World War II'. *New Hibernia Review* 12, no. 2 (summer 2008): 15–36.

Carroll, Joseph T. *Ireland in the War Years, 1939–1945*. San Francisco, Calif.: International Scholars Publications, 1998.

Carter, Carole. 'America's Neutral Ally'. *Eire-Ireland* 12, no. 2 (1977): 5–14.

Clark, Dennis. *Erin's Heirs: Irish Bonds of Community*. Lexington: University Press of Kentucky, 1991.

Cole, Robert. *Propaganda, Censorship and Irish Neutrality in the Second World War*. Edinburgh: Edinburgh University Press, 2006.

Conzen, Kathleen, David A. Gerber, Ewa Morawska, George E. Pozzetta and Rudolph J. Vecoli. 'The Invention of Ethnicity'. *Journal of American Ethnic History* 12 (1992): 3–41

Coogan, Tim Pat. *Éamon De Valera: The Man Who Was Ireland*. New York: HarperCollins, 1995.

— *The IRA: A History*. Fourth edition. New York: HarperCollins, 1995.

Cronin, Mike. *The Blueshirts and Irish Politics*. Dublin: Four Courts Press, 1997.

— *Sport and Nationalism in Ireland: Gaelic Games, Soccer and Irish Identity since 1884*. Dublin: Four Courts Press, 1999.

Cronin, Mike and Daryl Adair. *The Wearing of the Green: A History of St Patrick's Day*. New York: Routledge, 2002.

Cronin, Seán. *Washington's Irish Policy, 1916–1986: Independence, Partition, Neutrality*. Dublin: Anvil Books, 1987.

Cuddy, Joseph Edward. *Irish-America and National Isolationism, 1914–1920*. New York: Arno Press, 1976.

Cunningham, Emma. 'Ireland, Canada, and the American Note'. In *Ireland in World War Two: Neutrality and Survival*, edited by Dermot Keogh and Mervyn O'Driscoll, 144–58. Cork: Mercier Press, 2004.

Curran, Joseph M. *Hibernian Green on the Silver Screen: The Irish and American Movies*. New York: Greenwood Press, 1989.

Daly, Mary E. 'Nationalism, Sentiment, and Economics: Relations Between Ireland and Irish America in the Postwar Years'. *Eire-Ireland* 37 (spring/summer 2002): 71–94.

Davis, Troy D. 'Diplomacy as Propaganda: The Appointment of T.A. Smiddy as Irish Free State Minister to the United States'. *Eire-Ireland* 31, nos. 3–4 (1996): 117–29.

— *Dublin's American Policy: Irish-American Diplomatic Relations, 1945–1952*. Washington, D.C.: Catholic University of America Press, 1998.

— 'Éamon de Valéra's Political Education: The American Tour of 1919–20'. *New Hibernia Review/Irish Éireanach Nua* 10, no. 1 (spring 2006): 65–78.

DeConde, Alexander. *Ethnicity, Race, and American Foreign Policy: A History*. Boston, Mass.: Northeastern University Press, 1992.

Diner, Hasia R. *Erin's Daughters in America: Irish Immigrant Women in the Nineteenth Century*. Baltimore, Md.: Johns Hopkins University Press, 1983.

Doherty, Richard. *Irish Men and Women in the Second World War*. Dublin: Four Courts Press, 1999.

Doherty, Róisín. *Ireland, Neutrality and European Security Integration.* Burlington, Vt.: Ashgate Publishing, 2002.

Donnelly, James Jr. *The Great Irish Potato Famine.* Charleston, S.C.: History Press, 2008.

Doorley, Michael. *Irish-American Diaspora Nationalism: The Friends of Irish Freedom, 1916–1935.* Portland, Oreg.: Four Courts Press, 2005.

Duggan, John P. 'Germany and Ireland in World War II'. *Irish Sword* 75–6 (1993): 93–8.

— *Herr Hempel at the German Legation in Dublin, 1937–1945.* Dublin: Irish Academic Press, 2003.

— *Neutral Ireland and the Third Reich.* Totowa, N.J.: Barnes & Noble, 1985.

Dwyer, T. Ryle. *De Valera: The Man & The Myths.* Dublin: Poolbeg, 1991.

— *Guests of the State: The Story of Allied and Axis Servicemen Interned in Ireland During World War II.* Dingle, Co. Kerry: Brandon, 1994.

— *Irish Neutrality and the USA, 1939–47.* Dublin: Rowman & Littlefield, 1977.

— *Strained Relations: Ireland at Peace and the USA at War, 1941–45.* New York: Barnes & Noble, 1988.

Emmons, David M. *The Butte Irish: Class and Ethnicity in an American Mining Town, 1875–1925.* Urbana: University of Illinois Press, 1990.

Erenberg, Lewis A. and Susan E. Hirsch, eds. *The War in American Culture: Society and Consciousness During World War II.* Chicago, Ill.: University of Chicago Press, 1996.

Evans, William B. 'Senator James E. Murray: A Voice of the People in Foreign Affairs'. *Montana: The Magazine of Western History* 32, no. 1 (winter 1982): 24–35.

Fallon, Brian. *An Age of Innocence: Irish Culture 1930–1960.* New York: St Martin's Press, 1999.

Fallows, Marjorie R. *Irish Americans: Identity and Assimilation.* Englewood Cliffs, N.J.: Prentice-Hall, 1979.

Fanning, Charles. *The Irish Voice in America: 250 Years of Irish-American Fiction.* Second edition. Lexington: University Press of Kentucky, 2000.

Fanning, Charles, ed., *New Perspectives on the Irish Diaspora.* Carbondale, Ill.: Southern Illinois University Press, 2000.

Fanning, Ronan. 'The Anglo-American Alliance and the Irish Application for Membership of the United Nations'. *Irish Studies in International Affairs* 2, no. 2 (1985): 35–61.

— *Independent Ireland*. Dublin: Helicon, 1983.

— 'Irish Neutrality: An Historical Overview'. *Irish Studies in International Affairs* 1 (1982): 27–38.

— *'Raison d'État* and the Evolution of Irish Foreign Policy'. In *Irish Foreign Policy, 1919–66: From Independence to Internationalism*, edited by Michael Kennedy and Joseph Morrison Skelly, 308–26. Dublin: Four Courts Press, 2000.

Fisk, Robert. *In Time of War: Ireland, Ulster, and the Price of Neutrality, 1939–45*. Brandon, Ireland: A. Deutsch, 1983.

Fitzgerald, Maurice. 'Irish-American Diplomatic Relations, 1948–1963'. Ph.D. dissertation, University College, Cork, 1997.

Foster, R.F. *Modern Ireland 1600–1972*. London: Allen Lane, 1988.

Gerstle, Gary. *American Crucible: Race and Nation in the Twentieth Century*. Princeton, N.J.: Princeton University Press, 2001.

Girvin, Brian. *Between Two Worlds: Politics and Economy in Independent Ireland*. New York: Gill & Macmillan, 1989.

— *The Emergency: Neutral Ireland, 1939–45*. London: Macmillan, 2006.

Girvin, Brian and Geoffrey Roberts. 'The Forgotten Volunteers of World War II'. *History Ireland* 6, no. 1 (1998): 46–51.

Girvin, Brian and Geoffrey Roberts, ed. *Ireland and the Second World War: Politics, Society and Remembrance*. Dublin: Four Courts Press, 2000.

Glazer, Nathan and Daniel Patrick Moynihan. *Beyond the Melting Pot: The Negroes, Puerto Ricans, Jews, Italians, and Irish of New York City*. Cambridge, Mass.: Harvard University Press, 1963.

Golway, Terry. *Irish Rebel: John Devoy and America's Fight for Ireland's Freedom*. New York: St Martin's Griffin, 1999.

Gordon, Milton M. *Assimilation in American Life: The Role of Race, Religion, and National Origins*. New York: Oxford University Press, 1964.

Griffin, William D. *The Irish Americans*. New York: Hugh Lauter Levin Associates, 1998.

Handlin, Oscar. *Boston's Immigrants, 1790–1880: A Study in Acculturation*. Cambridge, Mass.: Harvard University Press, 1959.

Harkness, D.W. *The Restless Dominion: The Irish Free State and the British Commonwealth of Nations, 1921–31*. New York: New York University Press, 1970.

Hartley, Stephen. *The Irish Question as a Problem in British Foreign Policy, 1914–18*. New York: St Martin's Press, 1987.

Hogan, Michael J. *The Marshall Plan: America, Britain, and the*

Reconstruction of Western Europe, 1947–52. New York: Cambridge University Press, 1987.

Hull, Mark. *Irish Secrets: German Espionage in Wartime Ireland, 1939–1945*. Dublin: Irish Academic Press, 2003.

Hutchinson, John. *The Dynamics of Cultural Nationalism: The Gaelic Revival and the Creation of the Irish Nation State*. Boston, Mass.: Allen & Unwin, 1987.

Ibson, John Duffy. *Will the World Break Your Heart?: Dimensions and Consequences of Irish–American Assimilation*. New York: Garland, 1990.

Ignatiev, Noel. *How the Irish Became White*. New York: Routledge, 1995.

Jacobson, Matthew Frye. *Special Sorrows: The Diasporic Imagination of Irish, Polish, and Jewish Immigrants in the United States*. Cambridge, Mass.: Harvard University Press, 1995.

Kazal, Russell A. 'Revisiting Assimilation: The Rise, Fall, and Reappraisal of a Concept in American Ethnic History'. *American Historical Review* 100, no. 2 (April 1995): 437–71.

Kennedy, Michael. *Ireland and the League of Nations, 1919–1946: International Relations, Diplomacy, and Politics*. Dublin: Irish Academic Press, 1996.

— *Guarding Neutral Ireland: The Coast Watching Service and Military Intelligence, 1939–1945*. Dublin: Four Courts Press, 2008.

Kennedy, Michael and Joseph Morrison Skelly, eds. *Irish Foreign Policy, 1919–66: From Independence to Internationalism*. Dublin: Four Courts Press, 2000.

Kenny, Kevin. *The American Irish: A History*. New York: Longman, 2000.

Keogh, Dermot. 'De Valera, Hitler and the Visit of Condolence: May 1945'. *History Ireland* 5, no. 3 (1997): 58–61.

— 'Éamon de Valera and Hitler: An Analysis of International Reaction to the Visit to the German Minister, May 1945'. *Irish Studies in International Affairs* 3, no. 1 (1989): 69–92.

— *Ireland and Europe, 1919–1948*. Dublin: Gill & Macmillan, 1988.

— *Ireland and the Vatican: The Politics and Diplomacy of Church–State Relations, 1922–1960*. Cork: Cork University Press, 1995.

— *Twentieth-Century Ireland: Nation and State*. New York: St Martin's Press, 1995.

Kiberd, Declan. *Inventing Ireland: The Literature of the Modern Nation*. Cambridge, Mass.: Harvard University Press, 1996.

Krenn, Michael L. *Black Diplomacy: African Americans and the State Department, 1945–1969*. Armonk, N.Y.: M.E. Sharpe, 1999.

Longford, Frank Pakenham and Thomas P. O'Neill. *Éamon De Valera*. London: Arrow Books, 1974

MacCarron, Donal. *Step Together!: The Story of Ireland's Emergency Army as told by its Veterans*. Dublin: Irish Academic Press, 1999.

MacDermott, Eithne. *Clann na Poblachta*. Cork: Cork University Press, 1998.

MacShane, Frank. *The Life of John O'Hara*. New York: Dutton, 1980.

Manning, Maurice. *Irish Political Parties: An Introduction*. Dublin: Gill & Macmillan, 1972.

Marcuson, Lewis R. *The Stage Immigrant: The Irish, Italians, and Jews in American Drama, 1920–1960*. New York: Garland, 1990.

McBride, Lawrence W., ed. *Images, Icons and the Irish Nationalist Imagination*. Dublin: Four Courts Press, 1999.

McCabe, Ian. *A Diplomatic History of Ireland, 1948–49: The Republic, The Commonwealth and NATO*. Dublin: Irish Academic Press, 1991.

McCaffrey, Lawrence J. 'Going My Way and Irish-American Catholicism: Myth and Reality'. In *Screening Irish-America*, edited by Ruth Barton, 180–90. Portland, Oreg.: Irish Academic Press, 2009.

McMahon, Deirdre. *Republicans and Imperialists: Anglo–Irish Relations in the 1930s*. New Haven, Conn.: Yale University Press, 1984.

McMahon, Eileen M. *What Parish Are You From? A Chicago Irish Community and Race Relations*. Lexington: University Press of Kentucky, 1995.

Meagher, Timothy J. *The Columbia Guide to Irish American History*. New York: Columbia University Press, 2005.

— *Inventing Irish America: Generation, Class, and Ethnic Identity in a New England City, 1880–1928*. Notre Dame, Ind.: University of Notre Dame Press, 2001.

Meagher, Timothy, ed., *From Paddy to Studs: Irish-American Communities in the Turn of the Century Era, 1880 to 1920*. Westport, Conn.: Greenwood Press, 1986.

Miller, Kerby A. *Emigrants and Exiles: Ireland and the Irish Exodus to North America*. New York: Oxford University Press, 1985.

— *Ireland and Irish America: Culture, Class, and Transatlantic Migration*. Dublin: Field Day, 2008.

— '"Scotch-Irish" Myths and "Irish" Identities in Eighteenth- and Nineteenth-Century America'. In *New Perspectives on the Irish Diaspora*, edited by Charles Fanning, 75–92. Carbondale: Southern Illinois University Press, 2000.

Murray, Williamson, and Allan R. Millett. *A War to be Won: Fighting the Second World War*. Cambridge, Mass.: Belknap Press/Harvard University Press, 2000.

Noer, Thomas J. 'The American Government and the Irish Question During World War I'. *South Atlantic Quarterly* 72, no. 1 (1973): 95–114.

Nolan, Janet A. *Ourselves Alone: Women's Emigration from Ireland, 1885–1920*. Lexington: University Press of Kentucky, 1989.

Nowlan, Kevin B. and Thomas Desmond Williams, ed. *Ireland in the War Years and After, 1939–51*. Notre Dame, Ind.: University of Notre Dame Press, 1970.

O'Connell, Shaun. 'That Much Credit: Irish-American Identity and Writing'. *Massachusetts Review* 44 (2003): 251–67.

O'Donnell, L.A. *Irish Voice and Organized Labor in America: A Biographical Study*. Westport, Conn.: Greenwood Press, 1997.

O'Donoghue, David. *Hitler's Irish Voices: The Story of German Radio's Wartime Irish Service*. Belfast: Beyond the Pale Publications, 1998.

O'Driscoll, Mervyn. *Irish–German Relations, 1919–1939*. Dublin: Four Courts Press, 2000.

O'Grady, Joseph P. *How the Irish Became Americans*. New York: Twayne, 1973.

O'Halpin, Eunan. *Defending Ireland: The Irish State and its Enemies since 1922*. New York: Oxford University Press, 1999.

— 'Intelligence and Security in Ireland, 1922–45'. *Intelligence and National Security* 5, no. 1 (1990): 50–83.

— 'Irish-Allied Security Relations and the "American Note" Crisis: New Evidence from British Records'. *Irish Studies in International Affairs* 11 (2000): 71–83.

— 'Irish Neutrality in the Second World War'. In *European Neutrals and Non-Belligerents During the Second World War*, edited by Neville Wylie, 283–303. Cambridge: Cambridge University Press, 2002.

— *Spying on Ireland: British Intelligence and Irish Neutrality During the Second World War*. New York: Oxford University Press, 2008.

O'Mahony, Patrick and Gerard Delanty. *Rethinking Irish History: Nationalism, Identity and Ideology*. New York: St Martin's Press, 1998.

O'Rourke, Kevin. 'Burn Everything British but their Coal: The Anglo-Irish Economic War of the 1930s'. *Journal of Economic History* 51, no. 2 (1991): 357–66.

Plummer, Brenda Gayle. *Rising Wind: Black Americans and US Foreign*

Affairs, 1935–1960. Chapel Hill: University of North Carolina Press, 1996.

Pogue, Forrest. *George C. Marshall: Ordeal and Hope, 1939–1942*. New York: Viking Press, 1965.

Potter, George W. *To the Golden Door: The Story of the Irish in Ireland and America*. Westport, Conn.: Greenwood Press, 1973.

Raymond, James. 'David Gray, the Aiken Mission and Irish Neutrality, 1940–41'. *Diplomatic History* 9, no. 1 (1985): 55–71.

Reynolds, Moira Davison. *Comic Strip Artists in American Newspapers: 1945–1980*. Jefferson, N.C.: McFarland & Co., 2003.

Roediger, David R. *How Race Survived US History: From Settlement and Slavery to the Obama Phenomenon*. New York: Verso, 2008.

— *Working Toward Whiteness – How America's Immigrants Became White: The Strange Journey from Ellis Island to the Suburbs*. New York: Basic Books, 2005.

Rogers, James Silas and Matthew J. O'Brien, eds. *After the Flood: Irish America, 1945–1960*. Dublin: Irish Academic Press, 2009.

Rowland, Thomas. 'Irish-American Catholics and the Quest of Respectability in the Coming of the Great War'. *Journal of American Ethnic History* 15 (winter 1996): 6–18.

Salmon, Trevor. *Unneutral Ireland: An Ambivalent and Unique Security Policy*. New York: Oxford University Press, 1989.

Sarbaugh, Timothy. 'British War Policies in Ireland, 1914–1948: The California Irish-American Reaction'. *San Jose Studies* 9, no. 1 (1983): 107–16.

Townshend, Charles. *Ireland: The Twentieth Century*. New York: Oxford University Press, 1998.

Von Eschen, Penny M. *Race Against Empire: Black Americans and Anticolonialism, 1937–1957*. Ithaca, N.Y.: Cornell University Press, 1997.

Ward, Alan J. *Ireland and Anglo-American Relations, 1899–1921*. Toronto: University of Toronto Press, 1969.

— 'America and the Irish Problem, 1899–1921'. *Irish Historical Studies* 16, no. 61 (1968): 64–90.

Waters, Mary C. *Ethnic Options: Choosing Identities in America*. Berkeley: University of California Press, 1990.

Whelan, Bernadette. *Ireland and the Marshall Plan: 1947–1957*. Dublin: Four Courts Press, 2000.

— 'Integration or Isolation? Ireland and the Invitation to Join the Marshall Plan'. In *Irish Foreign Policy, 1919–66: From Independence to Internationalism*, ed. Michael Kennedy and Joseph

Morrison Skelly. Dublin: Four Courts Press, 2000.

— 'Ireland and the Marshall Plan'. *Irish Economic and Social History* 19 (1992): 49–70.

Whelan, Kevin. *The Tree of Liberty: Radicalism, Catholicism and the Construction of Irish Identity, 1760–1830.* Notre Dame, Ind.: University of Notre Dame Press, 1996.

Williams, Richard. *Hierarchical Structures and Social Value: The Creation of Black and Irish Identities in the United States.* New York: Cambridge University Press, 1990.

Williams, William H.A. *'Twas Only an Irishman's Dream: The Image of Ireland and the Irish in American Popular Song Lyrics, 1800–1920.* Urbana: University of Illinois Press, 1996.

Wills, Clair. *That Neutral Island: A Cultural History of Ireland During the Second World War.* London: Faber & Faber, 2007.

Winsberg, Morton. 'The Suburbanization of the Irish in Boston, Chicago and New York'. *Éire-Ireland* 21 (fall 1986): 90–106.

Wolff, Geoffrey. *The Art of Burning Bridges: A Life of John O'Hara.* New York: Alfred A. Knopf, 2003.

Index